Spiritual Wisdom of the Native Americans

By John Heinerman, Ph.D.

Cassandra Press
San Rafael, Ca.

Cassandra Press
P.O. Box 868
San Rafael, Ca. 94915

Printed in the United States of America.

ISBN 0-945946-05-8

Library of Congress 89-62273

The use of the material described in this text is not meant to replace the services of a physician who should always be consulted for any condition requiring his or her aid.

Front cover art designed by Susan St. Thomas.

TABLE OF CONTENTS

TABLE OF CONTENTS

To

Samuel the Lamanite
the best Native American I ever knew.
And To
Matthew and Jason Fountaine,
Who someday may know him as well as I do.

****

"I believe that no white man can ever penetrate the mystery of their mind or explain the reason for their acts."

Frederic Remington (Artist)

INTRODUCTION

This book is about Native American principles and practices, both ancient and modern. Many different tribes and civilizations are represented herein, from the mighty Sioux and Seneca nations of North America to the ancient Maya empire in Central America.

Additionally, this book contains frequent historical references and incidences taken from the annals of America's *only* Christian denomination which has always held a deep respect and reverence for the Native American culture—this being The Church of Jesus Christ of Latter-Day Saints ("The Mormons"), of which I am an active and devout member.

The business of anthropology demands that one try to keep an open mind to new and different things that may not necessarily fit within the convenient norms established by science or our regularly accepted ways of thinking and acting. As a professional scientist, therefore, I have tried over the years always to maintain an open mind and an almost childlike belief for anything in the realm of the unusual and impossible.

One cannot help but be influenced in a positive way by much of what our Native American neighbors have had to offer us. With the single exception of the Mormons, most other Christian sects have tried to shove Bible truths and teachings down the throats of early Native Americans in a clumsy effort to supposedly "Christianize" them. But for the most part, such efforts met with strong and determined resistance from a people who knew better.

One of life's little-known ironies is this: the white man's priests and "born-again" preachers thought they were teaching the Red Man truth and honesty, when in effect, they were only showing how corrupt their own systems of religion really were. It is a *historical fact* that until Christians came from Europe, most Native Americans never stole from one another, nor ever lied. It was only after these high and mighty religionists with their black garb, white collars, and big black leather Bibles had arrived that Native Americans found it necessary to begin putting locks on their doors when they left home.

The wealth of information contained within these pages has been drawn from a wide variety of sources. They include a number of important anthropological, ethnological, social, and archaeological books devoted to the Native American cultures scattered throughout the Western Hemisphere. Additionally, the *Book of Mormon* has occasionally been referred to, since it represents a true account of the ancient civilizations which resided in the Americas at one time and from whom all Native Americans themselves eventually descended.

It is hoped that the reader may enjoy what has been presented, and find truth and things of beauty and strength contained herein. Every effort has been made to present that data which is *authentic* Native American wisdom and spiritual power and to omit that which never had a place in its culture or religion, such as reincarnation.

First as a trained anthropologist, and secondly as a deep admirer of all that is lovely, praiseworthy and of good report within Native American cultures, I have endeavored to extract only those things which will ultimately build the human soul by instilling in each reader a faith, humility, reverence, kindness, and compassion not found on earth but only in Heaven. And who better are qualified to teach us these things than they whom we have robbed, persecuted, and ignored. For only in them, through them, and by them can we ever hope to regain our self-respect and decency again. We are the children and the Native Americans are *our* teachers! It's just as simple as that!

John Heinerman, Ph.D.

CHAPTER ONE

HIDDEN CAVES AND INDIAN ORIGINS

The Caves of John Brewer

Salt Lake City is blessed with two major daily newspapers—*The Salt Lake Tribune* provides the news in its morning editions from a very liberal Catholic-Protestant-Jewish perspective, while the more sedate evening *Deseret News* gives things from a strong buttoned-down conservative Mormon point of view. Thus, it came as somewhat of a surprise to *Deseret News* subscribers to read about some incredible cave discoveries in south-central Utah by a very unremarkable man in their Wednesday night, November 26th, 1975 newspapers.

Normally ridiculing such finds, the Mormon-owned paper took a more sober look at what had been discovered, while still maintaining a half-hearted, somewhat jocular mood in its page-wide headline banner which read: "John Brewer has a cave, but he's not giving tours!" The fascinating account opened with a brief description of a very unimpressive man: "quiet . . . in his mid-40s . . . short and frail . . . amateur collector of Indian arrowheads . . . works at a sewage treatment plant . . . does odd jobs to support his wife and five children . . . has been on public welfare at times."

Then followed a quick tirade by local university archaeologists, who felt they had "wasted their time exposing the man's works." In Brewer's particular case, it happened to be "finding inscribed tablets and plates" of very ancient origin. Between 1963 and 1975, the paper noted, he had located tablets and plates made of limestone, lead, copper, brass, and even gold!

Just to be on the safe side and not rankle ruling Church authorities or the local scientific community too much, the *Deseret News* seemed to think it was a good idea to begin with the archaeological complaints before delving into Brewer's own side of the story. The list of complaints is what you would expect from scientists who wanted very badly to go to Brewer's caves, but for understandable reasons of privacy and mistrust were politely declined by Brewer himself. Archaeologists lambasted him in no uncertain terms, concluding his plates and tablets were "the meaningless work of a forger," and giving these several reasons for their harsh condemnation:

(A) The artifacts were found in areas of a type which were not usually archaeological sites.

(B) Plate and tablet inscriptions are sharp and clear indicating modern, sharp tools were used.

(C) Metal particles were found in the 1963 limestone tablets, "suggesting that a soft steel tool such as a nail or pocket knife had been used to inscribe the stone."

(D) Fresh cotton fibers and pine pitch covered the 1970 tablets. The pitch was not cracked or darkened with age as it should have been. "Nor did it show evidence of exposure to moisture and soil for a long period of time."

A university cryptologist attempted to decipher the inscriptions and, after careful examination, "found so very few clusterings that from a language point of view he was forced to conclude that instead of a meaningful script, the work was the haphazard scratchings of a forger." To make matters worse for Brewer, this cryptologist later visited the home of a Mani cattle rancher's widow for lunch and, opening a napkin which pictured some local cattle brands, "was dumbfounded to see some of the same signs he had so carefully copied from the Manti plate and table inscriptions." Further investigation by this fellow revealed that almost 20 percent of the signs on the tablets apparently were inspired by registered Utah cattle brands.

Such simplistic explanations for Brewer's discoveries obviously satisfied heretofore intensely curious scientific and religious minds, but really never addressed the issues as they fully deserved to be. Such lackadaisical responses were similar to what a child might have said when told by his mother that he couldn't have a cookie from the cookie jar: "Mommy doesn't love me anymore!" Because Brewer had been betrayed on several previous occasions by individuals he thought were trustworthy, the man developed an obvious paranoia towards anyone who specifically asked him for a personally guided tour to his hidden caves of fabulous archaeological wealth.

A short pause here in the newspaper narrative to quote directly from Brewer's own journal will help the reader to understand better what he was up against in those days:

April 26th, 1956. I brought a guy up by the name of G... M.... up to the cave but I didn't show it to him for I didn't quite trust him. I put it to him in such a way that he had a good idea what I had. I went one way and he another and I went into the cave and I took the gold plate out and showed him and he then believed what I had told him. I made him swear to tell no one and he said that he would not but I will wait and see if he keeps his word, and if he does, maybe I'll let him in on the rest of it. If I see that he doesn't keep his word I'll just let him think that I am letting him go with me. I'll watch and see if he comes up to the cave or around it. Then I'll know whether or not to trust him.

April 29th, 1956. I didn't have long to wait for he came up today and brought someone with him but I didn't know the person that was with him . . . I should have known better. You can't trust anyone. It sure makes me mad as hell at them and myself for letting someone in on this for all they want is the money end of it . . . . Later on today I met him (G... M....) down in Rick's Cafe and I talked to him and I asked where he had been and he lied through his teeth and said that he had just gotten back from Mt. Pleasant.

April 30th, 1956. I went to the cave and hid it so that no one would find it, only me. I will have to be more careful from this day on for there will be G... watching all the time. Boy! I must be awfully dumb to pick a partner. Never again will I trust anyone until I put them to the test. I then went over west to do a little arrowhead hunting and to think things out. . . . I found a good arrowhead grounds and, if I look, I can see the place where the cave is. I wonder if the Indians knew of that place and what went on there. But I think that the people that lived there were before the Indians so I guess that they wouldn't know of it as I do for they let the old be where it was. I guess they were just too busy getting something to eat to think of anything else." (Photocopied typescript of John Brewer's journal in possession of the author).

Returning to the *Deseret News* interview of John Brewer, this is what he told reporters in regard to his spectacular cave finds:

I found the cave (his second cave discovery came years later) about 20 years ago, when I was 22. George Keller, a Negro that lived in Manti, Utah showed it to me after I gave him a couple bottles of wine. Inside the cave are big boxes with plates in them, two mummies (male and female), and a lot of gold stuff and figurines and stick-like things.

After the natural entrance to the cave fell in a few years later, Brewer said he dug his own 30-foot tunnel, which is now beset with natural booby-traps for anyone who might discover it. He feels it's a private place, his own little work area, and says he spends hours tinkering around in the cave, widening it, bringing plates out into the open.

For years there was a snag—the cave was on private property. But the "old man" who refused to sell died, and his son now has sold Brewer 10 acres, including the cave site, Brewer claims. Dr. Paul Cheesman of Brigham Young University's Religion Dept. has been trying to get Brewer to show him the cave, but Brewer has balked.

"Whenever I don't understand anything, I stall," Brewer said, and his actions verify that. He has put Cheesman off for four years and, in fact, hasn't shown a single person the cave—including his wife and children.

"Most people don't understand why I keep it a secret," he noted. The three reasons he gave this reporter were: "I value my privacy highly. Who gets the credit for finds like this? Always some professor working on his master's thesis, never the guide that showed him the place. I have three boys, and I don't have much money. I want to leave something for them."

Brewer maintains that at least three private collectors have "offered me six and seven place figures" for the cave . . . and its contents. I'm deep in debt, but so is everybody else. I just won't sell."

"I don't expect anybody to believe me," Brewer says. "And I'm not worried, either, because I know what I've got," he said, with an emphasis on the "I." . . . Meanwhile, Cheesman has mixed feelings. "They could be real," he stated.

Until now, the proximate location of Brewer's original cave has never been publicly divulged. But excerpts from his personal journal give the reader a better idea of where such a fantastic find was made and the interesting way he came about it.

March 30th, 1955 . . . I met a Mr. George Keller (a Negro) and we got to talking about the fair (Sanpete Country Fair held annually in Manti). I mentioned that I was going to try and set up an arrowhead collection to put on display. He then told me about a cave in back of the temple hill (the one on top of which sets one of the Mormon temples—the Manti Temple). He told me there were lots of arrowheads there.

May 10th, 1955. I went and looked for the place but I couldn't find it so I went and ask him again where it was but all that I could get was a laugh from him. I thought that he was pulling a fast one on me so I let it go at that. I told Jack about it and he said to offer him some wine and I might get him to tell me then.

May 19th, 1955. I went out to the Keller place and offered him some wine with the promise that he would show me the place he had told me about a while back. He said that he would not only show me the place but he would show me the spot himself if I would get him another bottle. I got the bottle and he showed me the place. No wonder I couldn't find it, I was on the wrong hill. It wasn't on the temple hill at all but the one in back of it. I went into the cave and found 30 arrowheads right off. I went back to the truck and thanked the old man. I then asked how he came to know of the cave and he said that he and an Indian boy played there as an old hideaway. He said he had a lot of fun there.

Now the previously cited newspaper article gives a more full account of what transpired after this. Suffice it to say, Brewer in the process of time brought forth considerable artifacts of very ancient origin that any archaeologist might be inclined to kill for. But Brewer had a problem with trying to determine their origin and the precise identity of the two well-preserved mummies entombed therein. The photographs on the next several pages are first pen-and-ink sketches of the two mummies made by Brewer himself, looking downward into each of their stone coffins. Note the strong Mongolian features of the Chinese-style dragon motif symbolism depicted in Figures 1 and 2. Figures 3-5 represent specimens of lead and copper plates which he brought out of his original cave. In the upper right-hand corner of the lead plate in Figure 3 is a symbol reminiscent of a 19th-century Plains Indian or Sioux medicine wheel. Note the rather curious-looking feathered head-dresses worn by the "Indian"(?) caricatures shown in the center plate of Figure 4 and on the half-moon plate at the extreme right edge of Figure 5. Note also directly adjacent to it the figure of a scorpion in the next half-moon plate to its left. Apparently some of the ancient civilizations about whom we know so little utilized the scorpion to symbolize the drama between life and death and possibly even more than this. Brewer had the plates shown in Figures 3-5 professionally photographed by a private studio. The author of this book can attest to their genuineness and authenticity, for he has some in his own private collection which were given to him by Brewer some years ago.

Figure 1

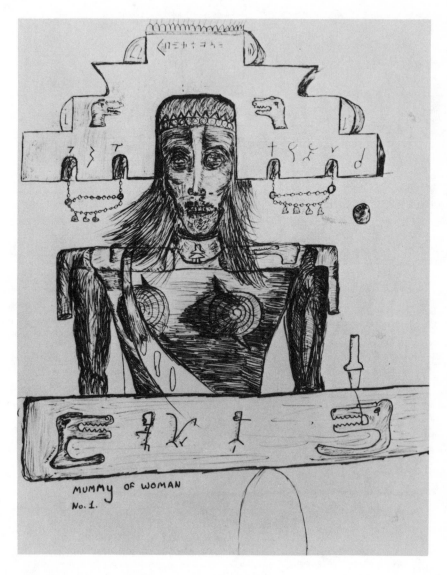

Figure 2

Figure 3

Figure 4

Figure 5

In attempting to solve the cultural identity problem facing him with regard to his artifacts and mummies, Brewer was drawn more and more to the *Book of Mormon*, that sacred record of those who once inhabited this entire Western Hemisphere in ancient times and has now become one of the four canonized scriptures of The Church of Jesus Christ of Latter-Day Saints (abbreviated to LDS Church). Brewer's November 17th, 1955 diary entry mentions that "while reading the *Book of Mormon* I read that the Jaredites and the Nephites both came to the north but I don't think that it was the Nephites. . . ."

His June 17th, 1956 journal entry is even more explicit in the archaeological quandary he faced and informs us of the decision he finally reached concerning to whom such things once belonged:

"I wish I could find out why some of these things are here. It just doesn't fit into the puzzle that I have here for there have been Indians here, that I know. Now the things on the bottom must be the early generation and the ones on the top must be a later generation so I have that much straight now then who left the ones on the bottom? All that I have found have been on the bottom or pretty close to the bottom. Now what does that give me—not too much. I don't think I am missing the main part of the puzzle. . . . I seem to come to the Jaredites. I don't know the reason that it comes to me this way but it seems to stay with me."

Asiatic Origins

The Brewer cave findings have done several things during the years since their discovery. First, they have helped many members of the LDS Church appreciate more fully the historical value of their *Book of Mormon*. Secondly, they further confirmed an Asiatic origin for the predecessors of the American Indians—something already pretty much accepted by scientists in general. Thirdly, they support the idea put forth by the *Book of Mormon* that the original and true Native American culture was derived from a genetic amalgamation of several different ancient American societies over an extended period of time.

But first, who are the Jaredites and from whence did they come? An ancient American Jaredite prophet by the name of Ether kept a faithful record of the final destruction of his people between 600 and 300 B.C. In the beginning of his narrative (appropriately called "The Book of Ether" in the *Book of Mormon*) he tells about two brothers who lived somewhere close to the Tower of Babel in what is now central Iraq. Realizing that God was going to punish mankind by breaking the universal mother tongue into a variety of languages soon, they pleaded with him to spare them, their families, some friends and their families of this linguistic disaster.

Their petitions were granted and they proceeded to migrate in a northerly direction, taking with them many different kinds of animals, including elephants, species of fish in an animal skin tank, and even honeybees (which they called in their ancient tongue, "deseret"). They also took with them many types of plant seeds, iron implements of every description, wheeled wagons and carts, clothing, and so forth. In short, it was one massive relocation effort to say the least.

Reaching the Caspian Sea, they turned in an easterly direction and crossed the wind-blown steppes of central Asia. In some places they had to construct makeshift rafts and boats to ford the occasional inland seas before them. At last they reached the coast of mainland China, somewhere on the shores of the Yellow Sea of China in the Shandong (Shantung) Peninsula and not too far from Mount Tai, China's holiest of her five holy mountains.

While led by a man named Jared (from whom they eventually derived the name of their later great civilization in the Americas), they were spiritually guided by a man known simply as "the brother of Jared." Ether describes him as "being a large and mighty man, and a man highly favored of the Lord." Whenever Jared needed divine inspiration, he would simply ask his brother to go and check it out with the Almighty. One might infer from this that this "brother of Jared" was the group's shaman or spiritual advisor.

It wasn't long before Jared asked his brother how they were going to cross the vast ocean which lay before them to reach the proverbial New World that God had promised them earlier. So his brother inquired of the Lord and was shown in vision a detailed diagram of a rather unique sailing craft which was capable of floating on top of the water or submerged beneath it at times. Without a doubt these must have been the world's first recorded submarine prototypes.

Sometime thereafter, it occurred to the brother of Jared that they would need light for their vessels, since glass windows were out of the question. He withdrew himself from the society of others to an exceedingly high mountain, taking with him sixteen small stones which he had made out of molten rock. By supernatural means, each of his small transparent-like stones was touched by the finger of Deity, causing them to emanate light continually. A pair of each of these stones was then placed in every one of the eight vessels.

In 1980 I went to mainland China with the American Medical Students Association. While there I received special permission from the Ministry of Archaeology to visit Taisan (the city located at the base of Mount Tai). It took two days of considerable red tape to grant me this, since Taisan wasn't included with our group's original travel itinerary. My desire in going there was to investigate further local legends which stated that the first Chinese emperor ascended Mount Tai many, many centuries ago to converse with the Chinese god, and upon his later descent brought with him gems that glowed in the dark, which were eventually placed in various temples throughout the land. From this historical experience came the reputation for the mountain's absolute holiness.

I discovered that much of the local folklore had disappeared as a result of Mao Tse-Tung's takeover of the country in 1949. However enough fragments had survived in some of the older people to convince me that something of supernatural significance had taken place in ancient times with a shaman-type leader. Several crucial parallels between the old legends and the account given by Ether strongly suggest that this was the mountain to which the brother of Jared went for his special needs.

The rest of Ether's narrative is pretty much mundane and routine: migrants entered vessels with their livestock and belongings; had an exceedingly rough trip across the angry, tempest-tossed ocean, sometimes being on top of and at other times below the water; and finally landing their crafts somewhere on the shores near what is now Acapulco, Mexico. From there they spread out all over the face of the land, building an empire that rivaled if not exceeded many of those in the Old World. In fact, as historical and traditional evidence suggests it was the Jaredite empire that a ship of Phoenician sailors lost at sea came in contact with and later took back reports about to Egypt and Greece—from whence came Plato's legends concerning Atlantis the "lost continent."

After some 1,600 years as sole rulers of the Western Hemisphere, the Jaredites started a campaign of deadly genocide among themselves which eventually terminated in the complete and utter destruction of their entire glorious culture. Various survivors in time made their way back down to Central America from the last great battles fought in upper state New York, where they soon linked up with a group of strangers who had recently emigrated to that region from the Holy Land in the Old World. These few Jaredites intermarried with the Mulekites, who took upon themselves the name of their leader, Mulek. This Mulek was the only son of King Zedekiah to escape from the terrible destructions wrought upon Israel by the Babylonians.

About this same time too, another group made an ocean voyage across the Pacific from southern Arabia and landed near Valpariaso, Chile. This group of fleeing Israelites soon divided themselves into two distinct groups, taking upon themselves the names of their respective leaders—the Nephites (after Nephi) and the Lamanites (after Nephi's wicked brother, Laman). A couple of centuries later the Mulekites (now known as the people of Zarahemla, because of their great leader by the same name) moved southward and occupied the country now called Colombia. While fleeing from their marauding tormentors, the Lamanites, the people of Nephi, or Nephites as they were then called, met the people of Zarahemla.

Both cultures soon merged into one with the latter taking for themselves the identity, language, and learning of the Nephites. However, the people of Zarahemla had managed to maintain certain cultural and genetic traits of the old Jaredite race. For one thing, the stronger genes of surviving Jaredites seem to have predominated over the weaker Israelitish genes of the former Mulekites; so much so that later generations appear to have had a definite Mongoloid look to them, while, curiously enough, not having the same genetic blood factors common to most East Asiatic Orientals. The people of Zarahelma or old Mulekites were somehow able to retain their own distinctive bloodline, while at the same time maintaining many of the outward physical features of the by then extinct Mongoloid-looking Jaredites. In time, some of the ferocious Lamanites in the south towards Ecuador, made peace with these newly merged cultural groups and joined them as well.

Basically what we have here then is a short synopsis of the *Book of Mormon* version of how the present Native Americans came about. I have purposely omitted citing all of the necessary scriptural and Mormon historical references in support of this; but they can be had within the literature of the Mormon religion and are readily available to those familiar enough with such things as to be able to search them out of their own accord. Since the ultimate purpose of this work is to cover Native American spiritual values and temporal health matters, it was deemed unnecessary to burden the reader with a lot of information not pertinent to the themes of this book.

However, we can briefly summarize the *Book of Mormon* origin for present day Native Americans this way:

1. Jaredites emigrate to coastal China from central Iraq.

2. Acquire or already have in their genetic makeup certain proto-Mongoloid physical characteristics.

3. Most Jaredites emigrate to America via a very historic transoceanic crossing, with some remaining behind in China however to eventually become the Chinese race. Scientists seem to think and the evidence bears them out, that additional land crossings via the Bering Straits to this hemisphere occurred sometime later.

4. Jaredite survivors from the great internecine wars fought some 1,600 years afterwards escaped from North America and returned to their ancestral homelands somewhere in Central America. Then they met and joined an Israelitish emigrant group called the Mulekites, later to be referred to as the people of Zarahemla. Inter-marriage keeps the stronger Jaredite genetic physical traits alive and well for many generations to come.

5. It is with these people of Zarahemla that the first distinctive features of the classic Native American "look" become evident. Later cultural mergers and inter-marriages between first the Nephites and secondly, converted Lamanites, further refined this model of noble bearing and behavior into the actual ancestors of all later Native American cultures throughout the Western Hemisphere.

Of course, there will always be those skeptics who maintain that as elegant and lovely as this sequence of real historical events might seem, yet, for them, a trans-lated version of an ancient American record of such things is not good enough. They will obviously take the typical attitude of so many in regard to the truth: "I'm from Missouri—show me!" Matters involving supernatural experiences, such as Joseph Smith's own profoundly "channeled" efforts in bringing forth the *Book of Mormon*, simply cannot be matched up word-for-word with what science has discovered. But (and this is very important to understand), certain basic ideas promulgated by Smith's translated record can be verified scientifically enough to lend considerable credence to the *Book of Mormon* version for the origins of all Native Americans dwelling in this hemisphere. The remaining pages of this opening chapter explore some of the evidence available in this regard.

To start with, the *Book of Mormon* advances several significant ideas relative to the populating of the Western Hemisphere. Briefly summed up, they are as follows:

(A) First emigrant stock originated from the coasts of northern China somewhere near the Yellow Sea of China. (The footnote references by Elder Orson Pratt, an early Mormon Apostle, in editions of the *Book of Mormon* before 1920 for "The Book of Ether" section bear this out. Also Pratt's additional sermon comments as found in the *Journal of Discourses* occasionally lends further credence to this idea).

(B) Two additional migrations followed from relatively unknown points of origin somewhere in the Near East.

(C) All three migrant groups came by way of sailing vessels across different oceans to this hemisphere instead of by land routes.

(D) Over an extended period of time there were genetic, linguistic, and cultural amalgamations among all three groups or among survivors from each of them.

Considerable scientific evidence exists to support all four of these principal points advanced by the *Book of Mormon* and elaborated on further by some early Mormon Church leaders, such as Apostle Orson Pratt. Each point will be treated separately.

Native American Origins

Point A: First progenitors came from somewhere in northern China. *Natural History* (March, 1987) observed that the Na-Dene family of Native American languages is genetically closest to Sino-Tibetan and the now extinct Sumerian languages. *Science* (Vol. 62, no. 1607, p. xii, October 16, 1925) quoted the famous Canadian anthropologist, Dr. Edward Sapir, as being convinced of the identity of the language of certain Indian tribes with that of the primitive Chinese. Sapir observed that the Nadine (now termed Na-Dene) American Indian language group, which stretches from northern Mexico to the southern boundary of Alaska, has unmistakable parallels with primitive Chinese. Not only do the Nadine groups speak with a tonal accent, raising or lowering of the voice to give certain meaning to words, in a manner similar to the tonal peculiarities of the early Chinese, but also that the meanings of certain words are absolutely identical. The Indians have retained certain prefixes and suffixes that long ago had disappeared from the Chinese language, but which were clearly discernible in the early forms.

In the book *Ancient North Americans*, edited by anthropologist Jesse D. Jennings, contributing archaeologist Stephen C. Jett cited numerous parallels between China's first dynasty (the Shang, circa 1800 B.C.) and Middle America's first empire (the Olmec, circa 1450 B.C.) in his chapter on "Precolumbian Transoceanic Contacts." Both cultures possessed ideographic writing and enumeration systems. Both were skilled workers in jade. Both practiced elaborate methods of water control and had long distance trade networks. Both cultures were distinctly hierarchical with capital and administrative and religious centers whose buildings were often built on artificial earth platforms with a north-south orientation to them. Furthermore, both he and recently deceased Smithsonian Institution archaeologist,

Betty J. Meggers noted that the Olmec culture began at a very technologically advanced level in southern Mexico, instead of evolving upwards over a lengthy period of time in the conventional prehistoric fisherman/hunters-gatherers and later pottery makers' sense of the word. This sudden importation of a high civilization supports the basic idea of Shang influence on the Olmec, they argued.

In the book *Transpacific Echoes and Resonances: Listening Once Again*, the famous Cambridge University scholar on ancient Chinese technology and culture, Professor Joseph Needham makes his own well-proven points for an Asiatic origin for the ancestors of all Native American tribes. In referring to the Maya method of writing, he recalled how much the squareness of the Maya glyphs resembled those of ancient Chinese characters. Also, the order in which they are read, usually downwards and occasionally right to left, and even the indentations, are quite similar to Chinese methods. Needham likewise points out that the pictographic writings from the Shih-chai Shan culture bear strong resemblance to those found in some of the Aztec codices. The same may also be said for Mesoamerican cylinder-seals, which bear an uncanny resemblance to those frequently used in ancient Babylonia. Another equally strange relationship between Southeast Asian and Mesoamerican Indian cultures may be found in the lokapala motifs. Figures occasionally dressed in armour are often depicted walking on demons or evil spirits. Such scenes adorn different ancient Maya temple walls throughout southern Mexico, Guatemala, and Honduras as well as Chinese Buddhist temple walls at Tunhuang and Yunkang in mainland China. In fact, Needham was almost overwhelmed with surprise and disbelief at what he found in the Tabasco Museum in Villahermosa some years ago. There in a large display case were Chinese-looking figurines and statues with Thang-like lokapala motifs, but actually belonging to the Maya culture instead!

Dr. Needham's feels that one of the strongest evidences for an Asiatic origin for early American Indian cultures is the Mesoamerican "hot-cold" version of the Chinese "yin-yang" concept. For instance, the Nahuatl word "tona" compares favorably with "yang" because of its various meanings: heat, life, dryness, maleness, and energy. Its counterpart or the female force of cold and wetness found in earth and water also occurs in the Nahuatl language as well. But rather than being seen as opposites, they are envisioned as complementaries.

There are several other excellent scientific references to point to an Asiatic origin for Native American ancestors. A Stanford University team of geneticists stated in the April, 1981, *Proceedings of the National Academy of Sciences* that major migrations to America must have started from Asia, respectively from the northeastern parts. And Gordon E. Ekholm, formerly the Curator of Anthropology for the American Museum of Natural History wrote an intriguing article entitled, "Is American Culture Asiatic?" for the October, 1950, issue of *Natural History* magazine in which further evidence was given to this same effect. Many other studies could be cited as well, but these few are sufficient to prove adequately the first point made in the *Book of Mormon* relative to the Jaredite-Native American ancestral connection.

Point B: Two more ancestral migrations followed centuries later. There is a growing body of scientific evidence from the anthropological, dental, genetic, and language fields to support the *Book of Mormon* position of three distinct migrations from Asia to the New World. One team of scientists writing in the *American Journal of Physical Anthropology* (66: 1-19, 1985) presented pretty solid genetic evidence for such, although they differed with the *Book of Mormon* view in having all three groups cross the Bering Land Bridge instead of coming by water. Since the data presented is quite complicated, the reader will not be burdened by a lot of confusing statistics. Suffice it to say that the report assigned a northeast Asian location for the origin of all three waves of emigrants, pointed out that there were at least two distinct migrations with the third later migration experiencing some type of genetic admixture with its predecessor groups, and that each migration sprang from an original "mother population" that had three basic genetic haplotypes shared by all three migratory groups.

Another group of scientists took the same approach in yet a different publication—*Current Anthropology* (27:477-97, December 1986). In their paper they suggest that North China is the ultimate ancestral homeland for all Native Americans, citing the Chinese broad facial form, straight black hair, Mongoloid sacral spot, and numerous other anatomical and biochemical features as evidence. They also mention that dental variations in the New World form only three clusters and that all Native American languages in this hemisphere fall into just three linguistic divisions. In addition they cite the reference in the preceding paragraph having to do with only three distinct genetic groupings of Native American populations as further evidence of the three migrations idea.

Still another proof for three migrations of Native American ancestry to the New World may be found in Joseph H. Greenberg's *Language in the Americas*, a book I recently reviewed for an international linguistics newsletter (LOS or *Language Origins Society Newsletter*, Fall 1988). Dr. Greenberg is a Professor of Anthropology and Linguistics Emeritus at Stanford University and has distinguished himself in his particular field by devoting over a quarter of a century to the study of Native American languages in this hemisphere. Greenberg cites the oldest migratory group from Northeastern Asia as being the Amerind. They were possibly connected with the Paleo Indian or Clovis culture, he conjectures. The second group to arrive to the New World were the Na-Dene, coming much later than the Amerind. Greenberg believes the linguistic evidence shows that Eskimo-Aleut is the most recent of the three migrations. His book is very complex and difficult to understand except to those with scientific backgrounds in Native American linguistics, yet it shows that all Native American Indian tribes throughout North and South America originated from three distinct genetic and linguistic groups in Asia.

Point C: All three migrations were accomplished by transoceanic crossings to the New World. Here the available evidence supports only part of this *Book of Mormon* idea: transoceanic crossings were indeed a reality. But further proof is wanting that there were just three such migrations by water. Navigational scholar J.

G. Nelson in his article on "Drift Voyages in the Pacific," which appeared in the quarterly journal of maritime history, *American Neptune* (April 1963), set the tone for such occurrences taking place anciently. His comments in this regard become even more interesting in light of what "The Book of Ether" in the *Book of Mormon* has to say about the Jaredites' own transoceanic crossing experiences. Ether 6:5; 8 are especially noteworthy, since they describe "a furious wind" blowing across the Pacific towards the Western Hemisphere. This ancient American historian recorded that these Jaredite barges were continually being driven across the mighty sea by this terrific gale of wind, until their final landing somewhere south of Baja, California and near Acapulco.

Nelson's own observations parallel those of Ether's, only in more precise details. Maritime disasters seem to be frequent along the Japanese coastline every January due to the powerful northwest monsoon winds. These winds usually blow anchored ships into the Kuro Siwo current, which runs from the Japanese Sea to the American west coast. This current is only one of several different 'river of oceans,' which flow with consistent regularity in an easterly direction. The diffusion of many cultures and resettlement of man throughout the great Pacific rim is believed to be attributed mostly to such currents.

Nelson relates how some of these northwest winds blowing out from Japan, change course and assume first northerly and then northeasterly positions as they eventually merge with the steady trade winds coming down from the northeast. Ships venturing into this part of the wind pattern would soon reach Hawaii. Still other of these northwest winds emanating from Japan, become westerly and then southwesterly trade winds, as they gradually move out into the central and eastern part of the Pacific Ocean. Here they split, some going upward towards the coast of British Columbia, while others take a downward turn along the coastlines of southern (Baja) California and Mexico, from about Mazatlan down to Acapulco.

The speeds of such winds usually are greater than 13 miles per hour. But if they're combined with fierce gale winds, could easily steer a number of Japanese junks off course and onto some part of the California coastline.

The account in Ether and Nelson's descriptions of winds and currents in the Pacific are quite compatible with each other and strongly suggest that at least the Jaredite portion of Native American ancestry left Southeast Asia anciently, undoubtedly sometime in their calendrical equivalent of our month of January.

Apostle Orson Pratt in his original footnote references to editions of the *Book of Mormon* printed before 1920 (when his were extensively revised) that the Jaredites launched their vessels somewhere in the Yellow Sea of China. A simple map showing some of the ocean currents that Nelson spoke of in his own article appeared in the book *Early Formative Period of Coastal Ecuador: The Valdiva and Machalilla Phases*, written by three archaeologists and published by the Smithsonian Institution in 1965. The map has smaller, lighter arrows pointing in a downward direction from the Shandong (Shantung) Peninsula towards the East China Sea, with other much bolder and bigger arrows pointing in an easterly direction just beneath Japan.

These same large, bold-print arrows, representing Nelson's ocean currents, continue all the way across the Pacific well above Hawaii and then start a gradual, curving descent towards Baja, California and the western coastline of Mexico. Undoubtedly it was this route along which the Jaredites were taken to their home in the New World.

Another maritime expert, Otto Sitting, wrote on "Compulsory Migrations in the Pacific Ocean," which appeared in the *Annual Report of the Board of Regents of the Smithsonian Institution* for July, 1895. Sitting made this significant statement relative to land and oceanic migrations:

"If we look still further eastward, we shall see that Bering Strait does not form the sole bridge between the Old and the New World. Migrations from Asia to America have undoubtedly taken place in more southern latitudes."

He then proceeds to show how oceanic voyages eastward from Asia depend as much on the prevailing winds as they do the water currents. A very detailed map in his article indicates the particular wind currents that Nelson referred to and clearly shows how vessels from the Asian coast could be brought to the shores of California or Mexico very easily. Two other very pertinent articles of more recent origin appeared in the March 20th, 1981, *Journal of Geophysical Research*. Written by experts in the geophysical and oceanographic sciences from Princeton University and Texas A&M University, both papers cover these same types of ocean currents and prevailing winds in great scientific detail. Here again, they reconfirm and support the idea that the Jaredite forefathers of today's Native American races came by water to this country.

At the January, 1981, Conference on Underwater Archaeology held in New Orleans, a paper was presented by Larry J. Pierson of San Diego, California entitled, "New Evidence of Asiatic Shipwrecks off the California Coast." In his paper, Pierson mentioned the discoveries of several ancient stone anchors dating to around 3,000 B.C. at two separate California locations—the first being some 150 miles southwest of Point Conception and the second site off the shore of Palos Verdes. A possible quarry source for both stones was suggested by a Chinese geologist familiar with the type of rock used in both anchors. The *Anthropological Journal of Canada* (Vol. 18, no. 3, p. 20, 1980) as well as Pierson's conference paper identify the Shantung and Liaotung peninsulas on mainland China's north coast as being the quarry sites for, these anchors. And in private correspondence to this author, dated October 25th, 1981, Pierson also made mention of "an entire Chinese Junk discovered in recent sediments in San Pedro" as well as different Oriental jade figurines found in the sands of Catalina Islands, Long Beach, and Huntington Beach. Clearly; all of this evidence more than supports at least one major nautical migration (the Jaredites) mentioned in the *Book of Mormon*.

Point D: All three major *Book of Mormon* migratory groups (or survivors from them) experienced a series of cultural, linguistic, and genetic mergers over an extended period of time. To begin with, the prevailing view of *Book of Mormon* geographical sequences among Mormon Church leaders in the 19th century was that Chile, Peru, and Ecuador constituted the original homelands for the Nephites and

Lamanites, until the Nephites moved further northward and eventually united with the people of Zarahemla in what is now Colombia. The only river ever mentioned in the *Book of Mormon* —the river Sidon—was identified by Orson Pratt, George Reynolds, and others as being the River Magdalena which flows through Colombia today. And, as was stated previously, the southern half of Mexico and much of Central America were believed to have been the original homelands of the ancient Jaredites. This brief summary from an early Mormon perspective is essential in order to show amalgamations taking place among the various cultural identities involved.

The first piece of rather unusual evidence to emphasize this point comes from a remarkable paper written by a linguistic graduate student, Brian Stubbs. Appropriately entitled "Elements of Hebrew in Uto-Aztecan: A Summary of the Data," it discusses the large predominance of Hebrew words in what is otherwise a very large language family comprising many different Native American tribes: Paiute, Shoshoni, Hopi, Pimi, Papago, Tarahumara, Yaqui, and, of course, the Nahuatl or Aztec. Extending all the way up from Mexico City to southern Idaho and over to the California coast, this broad group of Indian tongues apparently has a strong Hebrew element running through it. Stubbs assigns an approximate 2,500-year period of time for the presence of this Hebrew morphology in Uto-Aztecan. Since the Aztecs themselves, like all other Middle American Indian races, bore strong Mongoloid physical features indicative of Asiatic origins, then where, pray tell, did the Hebrew element in their native tongue come from? Could this not be suggestive proof of an amalgamation between the Hebrew Mulekites fleeing Jerusalem, landing somewhere around Yucatan, and the last few Jaredite survivors of the great wars in North America returning to their own deserted homelands in the same peninsula region of southeastern Mexico? This, at least, is what the *Book of Mormon* portrays as happening, and Stubbs' original research merely gives further credence to this historical event.

This apparent Jaredite influence upon the Mulekites (later called the people of Zarahemla) is strengthened even more if we correctly assume that the Olmecs and Jaredites were one and the same civilization. In his classic work, *The Olmecs—The Oldest Civilization in Mexico*, French archaeologist Jacques Soustelle says almost this very thing. He assumes the Olmecs were American Indians and probably lived alongside another AmerIndian group. This second group, in turn, may have inherited from the Lomecs and perpetuated some of their distinctive physical features, he noted.

By way of interest, Soustelle mentions that the ancient Olmec city of San Lorenzo (in the Mexican state of Veracruz) appears to have experienced "an extraordinarily violent revolution," judging from the "brutally shattered" monuments, "decapitated and buried" statues, and extremely vandalized colossal stone heads lying around in terribly ruined condition. Ether informs us, in his narrative within the pages of the *Book of Mormon*, that his people ended up destroying each other with such intense violence and passionate hatred as had never before been known.

Elsewhere, a number of scholars have cited various Olmec (read Jaredite) contributions to Maya culture (read people of Zarahemla first, followed later by admixturing with Nephites and some Lamanites). Writing and counting systems, jade manufacturing, and even the language to quite an extent, were bequeathed to the Maya from their Olmec predecessors. *Adam's Origins of Maya Civilization*, Ferguson's and Royce's *Maya Ruins in Central America in Color*, and Hammond's July, 1982, National Geographic article bear these things out. And Grove's *Olmec Paintings of Oxtotitlan Cave, Guerrero, Mexico* speaks of both Maya and Peruvian cultural influences present in these Olmec cave paintings in one of Mexico's largest, remotest, and mountainous states. In this latter example, we can certainly see evidence of civilization blending at its grandest from three separate cultures!

The evidence in favor of the *Book of Mormon* proposal for all three civilizations borrowing the best (and sometimes the worst) from each other, besides intermarrying, is so abundant as to almost boggle the mind. Even a simple and ingenious device like the blowgun supports this idea very well. The Autumn, 1952, issue of *Southwestern Journal of Anthropology* related how the blowgun originated in Colombia and eventually made its way up through Mexico and into the Southeastern part of the United States, while another route took this same implement from somewhere by the isthmus of Panama across the Pacific to the Polynesian Islands. The very last chapter of "The Book of Alma" in the *Book of Mormon* speaks of "an exceedingly curious man" named Hagoth, who launched a series of ships near the isthmus and traveled with a great company of people far across the ocean, never to be heard from again. Mormon Church leaders have interpreted the Polynesians and even the Hawaiians as being descendants from those who accompanied Hagoth on his adventuresome quests.

When the people of Zarahemla (formerly Mulekites) traveled southward and set up operations in Colombia, they eventually united with the Nephites and some righteous Lamanites pushing northward from Ecuador and other points south. In time, these groups (by now collectively called Nephites) started emigrating towards the north again to those same regions once occupied by the ancient Jaredites and later-arriving Mulekites. The same last chapter in "The Book of Alma" makes clear reference to this event.

Consequently, it should come as no surprise to those who understand these sequential migrations in the *Book of Mormon* to realize why there is a strain of Mayan influence in the ancient Peruvian art work of the Chavin culture (which was contemporary with the Jaredites). Or for them to wonder why essentially Middle American residing birds such as the toucan or very noisy paroquet, should appear in the art work of the mound-building Hopewell Culture which once occupied much of the Mississippi Valley in the eastern United States. Lathrop's chapter contribution ("South America as Seen from Middle America") in *The Maya and Their Neighbors* and Hensha's fascinating piece ("Animal Carvings from Mounds of the Mississippi Valley") in the *Second Annual Report of the Bureau of Ethnology* (1880-81) point these things out.

In summary, we can view present-day Native Americans as being essentially a composite of three different cultures—the Jaredites (from northeast Asia) and the Mulekites (people of Zarahemla), and the Nephites/Lamanites (from the Near East). *The Book of Mormon* advocates such an idea and, as we have seen, the scientific evidence bears this point out rather well.

The Maya Factor

It is important to close this chapter with one last point, if we are to understand better the spiritual wisdom and power inherent in Native American races. That is the undeniable influence of the ancient Maya on most American Indian tribes. Much has been written by scholars on the cultural impact which the Maya made upon many other lesser Indian cultures. But M. L. Crimmins' observations in the September, 1933, *Bulletin of the Texas Archaeological and Paleontological Society* pretty well sum up all other prevailing views in this regard:

Dr. Paul Radin of the University of California says that our North American Indians owed the fundamental and basic traits of their civilization to the direct or indirect influence of the Mayas. Our Indians undoubtedly developed their agricultural, pyramidal mounds, ceramic art, and other evidences of culture through the influence of the Mayas. Radin believes the Mayas or a people completely transformed by the Mayan culture, actually invaded the lower Mississippi Valley and laid the foundation of the Mound-Builders. The Mound-Builders in turn doubtlessly influenced the culture of all the tribes east of the Mississippi to a very great extent, and some of their culture evidently spread to eastern Texas as shown by recent finds of the University of Texas.

During the several years that I became well acquainted with John Brewer, the man who found the first cave mentioned at the beginning of this chapter, I learned from him of the existence of an ancient stone map indicating the location to a second cave somewhere within Sanpete County, Utah. After months of figuring out the points of direction given on it, Brewer eventually found what he had been looking for. In time, when he had gained enough confidence in me, he invited me to go with him high up in the mountains just south of Wales, Utah, where this second cave was. From it were taken different artifacts bearing a striking similarity to Maya art work from Mexico and Guatemala. Again, as with the first cave behind the Manti Temple hill, heavy cemented stone boxes weighing approximately ninety pounds each and highly decorated with ingenious art work, were removed. Within these boxes were also found ancient metal plates of curious workmanship.

The stone box depicted in Figure 6 is representative of how the boxes appeared when first discovered in each of the caves. They had been carefully enclosed in a juniper bark wrapping with pine pitch smeared all around so as to make them relatively waterproof. This particular box shown in Figure 6 is in the possession of Dr. Paul Cheesman, now retired from his professional duties in the Department of

Religion and Brigham Young University in Provo, Utah. Dr. Cheesman is one of only a very few scholars besides myself who has never ridiculed Brewer and, as with the rest of us, believes that his discoveries are genuine and authentic.

On the succeeding pages are illustrations of additional stone boxes. The one in Figure 7 is of more ancient origin and comes from the first cave, that the Jaredite mummies and plates shown in Figures 1-5 came from. The scorpion symbol and a horse and a chariot with its rider are evident on the top of the lid. On the other hand, Figures 8-9 represent a different kind of box removed from the second cave. Maya features pretty well adorn the entire box.

During the period of my close association with Brewer, I never knew the man to lay claim to reading or interpreting any of the ancient symbols or writings that appeared on the outside of these stone boxes or any of the plate inscriptions either. As for myself, I can only say that they are of very ancient origin (with those in the second cave being some centuries "newer" by reason of their "fresher" appearance) and that the artifacts in Cave No. 2, found with the help of the stone map in Cave No. 1, strengthen the evident cultural links which existed between the Jaredites (Olmecs) and the amalgamated Zarahemlites/Nephites/Lamanites (Maya).

Beyond this, however, one cannot venture too far lest ridicule from the academic profession and Utah's major religious entity be heaped upon him. Brewer had more than his share of it, and later on when I became temporarily affiliated with him in his archaeological extravaganzas, I too received the blunt end of criticism from jealous ecclesiastical and academic authorities, who felt that as a devout member of the Mormon Church and an active participant in the scientific community, I had simply "wandered off track" and needed to be reined in. Since my religious membership and academic livelihood were involved, I was "persuaded" (read nicely forced) to leave well enough alone and tend to my own business of medical anthropology.

Whatever happened to Brewer after this fateful 1980-81 ultimatum was handed down, I never learned. Nor have I been in touch with the man since then, although still retaining in my private collection enough artifacts from both caves to convince the most doubting skeptic that in those hidden caves laid precious treasures and sacred records which rightfully belong to those of Native American ancestry.

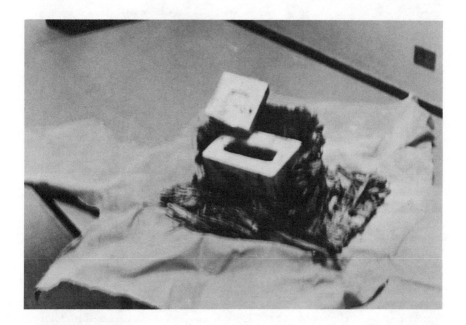

Figure 6

Figure 7

Figure 8

Figure 9

CHAPTER TWO

THE MAYA PHILOSOPHY OF LIFE

"Within you there is a stillness and a sanctuary to which you can retire whenever it pleases you in order for you to be yourself."
Words of wisdom from an ancient Maya high priest to a young man as found in the old *Annals of the Cakchiquel Maya.*

Supreme Beings

Anthropologist William H. Holmes wrote in 1985 in his *Archaeological Studies Among the Ancient Cities of Mexico* that of all the Native American races, the Maya were the most intensely religious and profoundly moved by mystical ideas. As archaeologist Daniel G. Brinton observed in 1890 in his *Essays of an Americanist*, "to the Maya, the woods, the air, and the darkness are filled with mysterious beings who are ever ready to do him injury or service. . . ."

Even the rocks, soil, grass, trees, and water were filled with minute particles of an unexplainable power emanating from somewhere else within the Universe. This is probably what led author Ruben E. Reina to state in his *Shadows—A Mayan Way of Knowing* that these people had achieved an integration with Nature unlike anything he had ever encountered in his own lifetime. This respetar, as he defined it, was an incredible respect for nature which inclined each person "to be cautious with each step and to be in peaceful coexistence with many things of Nature." Everything had its right place in the Maya view of nature, and man had no business interfering with the ways of the earth, he wrote. Man only moved with nature, never against her.

Among these ancient people, writes Yale University archeologist, Michael D. Coe in *The Maya*, there existed a pantheon of interesting deities. First and foremost was a one-and-only god (Hunab Ku) who was incorporeal and omnipotent. Essentially, it was the god of all Mayan gods—the one from whom all of the other deities drew their ultimate strength and sustenance. Without Hunab Ku, there could be no other gods.

Hunab Ku was the equivalent of "the light of Christ" in Mormon theology—that force which was in all things, through all things, and round about all things. Or as Mormon Apostle Orson Pratt termed it, "The Great First Cause" which consisted of innumerable self-moving particles of magnetized intelligence constantly moving through time and space. The ancient Jaredites conceived this power as having no emotions to speak of, but needing organized intelligences with personalities such as ourselves in order to move through to acquire feelings, whether for good or evil, for its own eventual advancement or retrogradation, as the case may be.

Next in line of actual authority and power was Itzamna and his wife Ix Chel, the "Rainbow Lady." As Morley and Brainerd explain in the third edition of *The Ancient Maya*: Itzamna was Lord of the Heavens, and Lord of Day and Night. Originally, he was thought to have been mortal, serving as the first Maya priest to name the places in Yucatan and to divide the lands there as well as inventing writing and books. He is depicted in the old Maya codices "as an aged man with Roman nose." Sometime after his death, he inherited that glory to which all gods belong.

This concept parallels a similar one for Father Adam in early Mormon theology. Brigham Young, second leader of the Mormon Church following Joseph Smith's cold-blooded murder at the hands of "born-again" Christians and angry apostates in June, 1844, taught from the pulpit that Adam and Eve were really our Heavenly Father and Heavenly Mother, who previous to this life were exalted mortals and that they once lived on a mortal world very much like our own somewhere else in the Universe. By faithfully fulfilling their mortal obligations to their own god, Adam (then a blacksmith) and Eve (a busy mother and dutiful wife) eventually qualified themselves in the course of time to become deities themselves. Later, they descended from their thrones of power and glory to come to earth and reacquire temporary mortality in order that all their spirit children might have physical bodies of flesh, bone, and blood. After completing this necessary assignment they then re-entered the Garden of Eden, partaking of the divine fruit of the Tree of Life enough so as to purge out of themselves all traces of human blood. Once accomplished and renewed by divine spirit, they ascended into Heaven and returned to their thrones of glory and power. Such then in a nutshell is the "Adam-God Doctrine," which early Mormons believed, but church leaders have forced the members to reject as being erroneous.

According to Francis Robicsek's *The Maya Book of the Dead—The Ceramic Codex*, in very early Maya mythology there were two God K's; an 'old god' (likely the offspring of the old one). Though his role has never been fully manifested in surviving Maya records, could we not assume a distinct parallel here between the older and younger God K's and God the Father and His Only Begotten Son, Jesus Christ?

In each of the four corners of this world stood a benevolent Chac or Rain God. Regarded not only as a single god but also as four separate deities, Chac was a universal deity of first importance, Morley and Brainerd noted in their book. Each Chac was assigned a specific color and part of the earth in which to reside: Chac Xib Chac, the Red Man (Chac of the East); Sac Xib Chac, the White Man (Chac of the North); Ek Xib Chac, the Black Man (Chac of the West); and Kan Xib Chac, the Yellow Man (Chac of the South).

Working closely with them were four other gods known as the Bacabs. These were consulted to determine a propitious day for honoring the four Chacs with an elaborate celebration. During this particular ceremony, held once a year, the idols and incense burners were renewed and, if necessary, the Temple of the Chacs was rebuilt. A tablet commemorating the event was set into the temple wall.

In some ways, Chac exceeded Itzamna in importance of duties: pictures of Chac occur 218 times in the only three surviving Mayan codices we know of, while Itzamna occurs only 103 times in just two of them! Since this rain god was associated with creation and life, he became an all-important deity for the average Maya farmer.

In his book, Coe mentions that the Maya believed in various degrees of hell, each presided over by a different kind of devil. Chief among such wicked gods was Death itself, being variously identified as Cumhau, Ah Puch, and Cizin. This is the modern Christian equivalent to Lucifer, the "Son of the Morning," the "old dragon," "Beelzebub," or the more familiar "Satan."

Itzamna, the "Lord of the Heavens," wasn't the only god in the Maya religion, who was married, in this case to Ix Chel, the "Rainbow Lady." The farmer god K'ax-ix (originally called T'ak) and "lord of the sixth heaven" was married to Chak Kit the "Great Goddess" who sent crop-destroying storms when ungrateful farmers offended her by not remembering her husband for the bounteous harvests he gave them, or by conducting themselves in wicked and immoral ways so as to incur her wrath and vengeance.

This unique marriage relationship between K'ax-ix and Chak Kit is highlighted in Yuri Knorozov's *Maya Hieroglyphic Codices*. Knorozov also speaks of other goddesses residing within Maya mythology: the virgin goddess Sak-ch'up, who represents maidens and appears paired with the thunder god Tox; the nameless goddess Ch'up with no distinctive attributes represents women and was often depicted in the embraces of the cultivator god; and several other goddesses of different responsibilities.

What all of this demonstrates, however, is the high degree which womanhood attained within the ancient Maya culture. According to Victor von Hagen in his *Ancient Sun Kingdoms of the Americas*, Maya women were on an equal par with their men to quite a degree. This is reflected not only in the belief that women who departed this life could become goddesses in the Maya Hereafter in company with their exalted husband gods, but also in mortal affairs as well.

No matter what her title may have been von Hagen observes, the wife of any Maya lord was herself lordly. She enjoyed the utmost respect and shared in the same great honors accorded her husband. This is readily evident from clay models of Maya women belonging to the upper classes. For instance, in the Bonampak murals a wife of a Maya nobleman can be seen with her head flattened and ears pierced, wearing earrings and a necklace. In the mural her hair has been styled into a swirling coiffure. She is adorned in exquisite red and white materials and in her hands may be found a folding fan. There is a queenly aura about her.

Unlike the majority of Christian, Moslem, or Jewish sects today which severely limit the roles of religious activity for many women, the ancient Maya, as with modern Latter-Day Saints or Mormons, believed that women were an integral part of the entire religious process. One only need look at the way the Catholic Church places some of its women in subordinate ecclesiastical positions as nuns or the way some Jewish and Moslem factions isolate their women from the men in worship services or expect them to cover their faces and heads to understand just how pervasive such cultural belittlement of females really is in different societies today.

Built into the ancient Maya religion was an intrinsic respect for women. Women were never put on a pedestal by their Maya men, but rather treated as equals in all things and given the same high regard in their particular sphere as wives, mothers, and homemakers as the men expected in their own circles as husbands, fathers, and providers. The Maya believed, and rightfully so, that they could not advance to any of the higher degrees in their multi-storied version of heaven without their women beside them.

Additionally, the Maya imagined that the family unit was an eternal thing, which took a lot of earthly preparation in order to keep it together. Different gods and goddesses had to be appeased, various rituals had to be attended to, and worthy couples had to live lives emulating the same high moral values and virtues reflected in the gods and goddesses they worshipped. Only then could a Maya couple expect some kind of high exaltation into a level of godhood satisfying to them and their posterity. Which probably explains the necessity for so many temples within their culture; these undoubtedly were for the purpose of performing endless ceremonies and rituals for couples to guarantee them such a thing hereafter.

The principles and practices of Mormonism parallel many of these same ancient concepts, only without much of the extreme heathen exaggerations that eventually crept into the Maya belief system over many centuries of time. Mormonism is the only Christian religion which emphasizes a Heavenly Mother, for example, or which places woman on an equal footing with man in all things. And though only men can hold the Priesthood, yet women can share in this Priesthood in connection with their faithful husbands. And, of course, as many already know, Mormon couples married in temples for time and all eternity have their children "sealed" to them, and undergo sacred initiation rites (called "taking out your endowments"), hopefully to place them in exalted positions of godhood hereafter, assuming that they live exemplary lives of worthiness here to qualify for that over there.

Without burdening the reader with further historical proof of what the Maya believed in regard to deities or even themselves becoming such, suffice it to say, as von Hagen so correctly noted in his classic work: "Religion pervaded everything . . . the whole of Maya life was religiously oriented—birth, death, agriculture, time count, astronomy, and architecture; life itself was bound up with religion and its rituals." An eloquent poem written by a 19th century Mormon poetess pretty well sums up both the corrupted Maya beliefs and the more clear Mormon views regarding the final destiny in eternity of selected good and faithful and virtuous men and women in this life. Entitled "The Ultimatum of Human Life," it was written after a visit from some seraphic being and later published in her *Poems—Religious, Historical and Political* (Salt Lake City: LDS Printing and Publishing Establishment, 1877). Several pages in length, only the three most pertinent verses are cited here as basically summarizing ancient Maya and early Mormon beliefs:

> Adam, your God, like you on earth, has been
> Subject to sorrow in a world of sin:
> Through long gradation he arose to be
> Cloth'd with the Godhead's might and majesty.
> And what to him in his probative sphere,
> Whether a Bishop, Deacon, Priest or Seer?
> Whate'er his office and callings were,
> He magnified them with assiduous care:
> By his obedience he obtain'd the place
> Of God and Father of the human race.
> Obedience will the same bright garland weave,
> As it has done for your great Mother, Eve,
> For all her daughters on the earth, who will
> All my requirements sacredly fulfill,
> And what to Eve, though in her mortal life,
> She'd been the first, the tenth, or fiftieth wife?
> What did she care, when in her lowest state,
> Whether by fools, consider'd small, or great?
> Twas all the same with her—she prov'd her worth
> She's now the Goddess and the Queen of Earth.

> Life's ultimatum, unto those that live
> As saints of God, and all my pow'rs receive;
> Is still the onward, upward course to tread—
> To stand as Adam and Eve, the head
> Of an inheritance, a new-form'd earth,
> And to their spirit-race, give mortal birth—
> Give them experience in a world like this;
> This leads them forth to everlasting bliss,
> Crown'd with salvation and eternal joy
> Where full perfection dwells, without alloy.

A clear parallel to this Mormon concept may be found in J. Eric S. Thompson's classic, *Maya History and Religion*. In the book, he noted that the idea of a single creator God (as is common to much of Christianity) is very much out of step with the Maya notion of a pair of creator beings who people this world through a conjugal relationship. Furthermore, he says, just as a Maya bachelor is despised when young and pitied when old, so to is a wifeless Maya God not given much respect by his mortal worshippers. Hence, the ultimate achievement for any worthy Maya couple in ancient times was to have earned an exaltation in the highest realm of Maya heaven then believed to be attainable by worthy men and women.

Mayan Hereafter

The majority of Christendom and Jewdom conceive heaven and hell as being essentially two different planes of existence with no additional levels in either. The Apostle Paul, however, in his writings made reference to an unnamed person whom he had known "who was caught up unto the third heaven." And the Mormon Prophet, Joseph Smith, Jr. had a great vision in company with his friend, Sidney Rigdon, in which they saw at least three distinct divisions of glory: the telestial (being likened unto stars of varying brightnesses), the terrestrial (being compared to the glory of the moon), and finally, the celestial (comparable to the sun in its brilliance).

The ancient Maya shared similar views with Paul and Joseph Smith. Thompson made several interesting observations in his own book which parallel ancient Christian and early Mormon viewpoints concerning the Hereafter. Thompson reported 13 divisions in the Maya heaven and 9 separate levels for their netherland. These 13 celestial layers were arranged like 6 steps ascending from the east to a zenith point or 7th, from which 6 more steps led down to the west. By the same token, 4 other steps led down to hell in the western horizon to the lowest point possible, with 4 remaining steps ascending out of the infernal pit to the glorious eastern horizon. In reality, then, there were just 7 celestial and 5 infernal layers or glories, he noted. He also hinted at the possibility that the Maya may have divided each of their days into 13 hours and their nights into 9 hour segments as well, to match these numbers of celestial and infernal steps.

Within the ancient Maya religion, there existed the belief that to the extent of just how faithful and devoted a couple were to their respective gods determined a lot just which degree of glory they would inherit later on; similarly, the extent of their wickedness and unrepentant ways would determine which basement of hell they were eventually to be imprisoned in for a millennium or so. In other words, unlike the Far Eastern religions that espouse the doctrine of reincarnation, the Maya held no such notions or silly fancies. For them, this life was it—here was where you either succeeded or failed; there was no second chance to get things right in another mortal sphere or coming back in some other life form.

Thompson's book reports that continual struggles exist between the 13 Gods in heaven and the 9 Gods of the underworld. The powers of light and goodness were forever contending with those forces of darkness and evil in the daily battle for the souls of men and women. But the Maya gave this common Christian understanding a new twist of lemon: they imagined this antagonism to be more a sexual drama with masculine light and female darkness having a mystical intercourse together by which life was able to enter this world. The Mormon temple rituals to some extent depict this though in their own parallel interpretations of good versus evil. This concept may be thought of as a type of religious/sexual yin-yang.

Another aspect in the Maya religion concerning the Hereafter which parallels a similar doctrine in Mormonism was this idea as expressed by Thompson: "The Maya recognized three abodes of the dead: the underworld, final resting place of most persons; a paradise located in one of the heavens; and a celestial home to which were admitted warriors who had died in war or on the sacrificial block and their feminine counterparts, those who died in childbirth." Mormons believe in a Spirit World, which is kind of a "halfway house" between exaltation in one of the higher kingdoms of light and joy or temporary banishment to a spirit prison filled with darkness and misery.

Still another wonderful idea expressed in the *Book of Mormon* as well as in Mayan religious philosophy was that children under the age of eight, who died, went into a heaven of happiness being considered blameless for whatever wrongdoings they may have done in mortality. Thompson reported in his *Maya History and Religion* that the unweaned children belonging to the Tzotzil May of Chamula, who died at birth, were snugly wrapped in solt fabric and tenderly placed in a great ceiba tree in the heavens. The Maya believed that this tree had many breasts like unto a nursing woman on which the children constantly sucked for their daily nourishment.

When one considers the Maya version of Hereafter, it is so much more fraught with opportunities to progress and go forward if you've lived a good life (or retrogress and go downward if you've been bad) than what most Christian denominations and Jewish and Moslem sects depict in their own narrowly defined and severely limited interpretations of an afterlife for man beyond the grave.

Worshipping the Gods

Unlike the lascivious and licentious gods of the pagan Greeks and Romans, the Maya deities were considered as a whole to be quite moral and extremely virtuous. Thompson notes in his book that the lascivious and licentious conduct imagined for their immoral gods by the ancient Greeks and Romans, was simply unthinkable by the Maya for their own deities. Maya gods were expected to lead noble and virtuous lives and set the proper examples for their earthly admirers. In fact, no Maya petitioner could even think about approaching any of his respective gods without first of all becoming ritually clean, which meant *no* physical acts of sex and *no* mental preoccupation with the same either. Also, the Greek belief that the gods sometimes committed adultery with married mortals or entered into homosexual relationships between themselves was entirely out of place in the Maya religion, Thompson declares.

As the Maya imagined their gods' lives to be conducted, so too did they seem to think that the same examples were expected of them and more so. "To be pure in mind and heart like the gods" was an old Maya saying committed to memory and actively applied by every Maya man and woman. One didn't dare think of approaching the gods until he or she had first put his or her spiritual house in good order. This is certainly something that many people today could apply within their own lives, especially those in the New Age movement who seem to think that one can tap the higher realms of knowledge and inspiration without doing anything about their sordid habits of avarice, deceit, lust, or perchance.

Next in order, as Thompson notes, was abstinence from sexual intercourse and heavy food. Mild food fasting was often implemented to sharpen the spiritual senses more and to quicken the mind. Occasional sweat baths were employed to drive out any evil influences lurking somewhere within the recesses of the body itself.

Now for those under considerable stress, the Maya had a remedy for helping to relax the nerves and put the mind at ease, which, when one thinks about it for a while, does make a lot of sense. As Francis Robicsek of the Museum of the American Indian in New York City mentioned in Volume 7 of the *Aztecs du XLII Congres International des Americanistes:* The Maya probably smoked as an activity of religious or ceremonial importance rather than only just an act of daily pleasure.

Robicsek later expanded his research into a well-researched book entitled *The Smoking Gods* (published by the University of Oklahoma Press in Norman). In it, the author points out from considerable pictorial evidence found on Maya vases and temple walls painted during the Classic Period, that these ancient people (especially the men) would roll fat cigars and slowly puff on them (usually seven times to correspond to each level of the upper worlds) as an act of courtesy and submission to their respective gods. It was their way of relaxing the troubled mind and calming the distraught soul before petitioning their respective gods.

To some this may seem a bit silly, especially to those who cannot stand cigar smoke. Yet there is a decided placebo effect which this act has upon the mind. I have at different times in my life tried the same thing with very relaxing results. Of course, on the whole "good Mormons" do not smoke, because our religious laws strictly prohibit this, as well as drinking alcohol, coffee or black or green tea. However, I can attest to a genuine peace of mind and real calmness which has settled over me after I have stretched out on a couch or on some lawn grass or on a sandy beach and very slowly and casually puffed away on an expensive Havana cigar. There is a profound tranquility which settles in one rather than over one—more of a mood, I would say, than an actual surrounding environment of peace which one might experience in the presence of a holy influence. But this sublimity of mind and heart can certainly prepare the soul for entrance into higher spheres of consciousness more safely than hallucinogenic drugs might. And this short testimony comes from one who himself dislikes cigarette smoke and smoking in general, despite its obvious therapeutic value with cigars so far as an agitated mind or distressed heart may go.

By far, though, the best account I have ever read of the positive effects on jangled nerves with cigar smoking comes from the journal entries of a deceased Mormon Apostle, Elder James E. Talmage, once an active member of the Quorum of the Twelve Apostles of The Church of Jesus Christ of Latter-Day Saints until his demise over half a century ago. What makes his never-before-published testimony so striking is that he personally abhorred the use of tobacco in any form at any time and as a high LDS Church official had repeatedly counseled thousands upon thousands of Mormons from the pulpit never to use tobacco, reminding them that it was a sin in the sight of God and so forth. More remarkable still is that he was ordered by the Prophet of God in office then (President Wilford Woodruff) to take up smoking cigars for the benefit of his nerves. His remarks demonstrate why the ancient Maya smoked cigars before petitioning their gods and why this author has himself resorted to them from time to time for his own peace of mind.

"March 12th, 1896 . . . I was requested by the Presidency to remain after the business referred to was terminated for the day. To my surprise the brethren began to question me in detail regarding my bodily health. I learned that some well-meaning friends had spoken to the brethren on the subject and that the opinion of physicians who were well acquainted with me had reached the ears of the brethren. They had learned that my health has been jeopardized and as they said, my sanity, and life threatened by insomnia and other evidences of nervous disorders. It is true, that overwork or rather worry over my work has affected me in the manner described, and other bodily weaknesses have developed at intervals. President George Q. Cannon speaking in behalf of the First Presidency (of the LDS Church), told me that it had been reported to them that the moderate use of tobacco would have a good effect upon me. This opinion has been expressed to me by some of our foremost physicians, who have on several occasions specifically advised me to smoke, on the opinion that my system is particularly responsive to the effect of tobacco. . . . I have reason to think that their opinions have by direct or indirect communication reached the ears of the authorities in the Church. Today President Woodruff, President George Q. Cannon, and President Joseph F. Smith gave me combined counsel to try the effect of moderate smoking: indeed said President Cannon, 'We give you this rather as an instruction than as counsel.' Apostle Heber J. Grant was present, and expressed his acquiescence. Brother George F. Gibbs was also present.

"This was unusual counsel and to me very surprising. I have long taught the ill effects of the tobacco habit, and have had no thought of becoming addicted to it myself. Nevertheless I have long known that tobacco produces an unusually strong effect upon me—even the odor of tobacco smoke produces a soothing effect upon me: and affects my bowels as does no ordinary purgative—marked by few of the injurious effects which follow in my case the use of cathartics. . . . On the eve of my departure for the east last month, one of the general church authorities—Elder George Reynolds of the Council of the Seventies, having knowledge of the physicians' advice, and of my then weak state of bodily health—I was suffering from loss of sleep,—came to me with the counsel that I test the effect of tobacco while away; and that I did conscientiously as he advised. To my surprise, I suffered no nausea or other ill effects, and while I took no pleasure in the act of smoking, a good cigar produced a marvelous quietening of my over-wrought nerves. Of course the brethren in counseling me as they did today, warned me against contracting the smoking habit to injurious degree." (*Journals of James E. Talmage*, Special Collections, Harold B. Lee Library, Brigham Young University, Provo, Utah).

All Native American tribes in the western hemisphere employed the smoking of tobacco for either religious or social functions. Among the Plains Indians, for instance, said A. Hyatt Verrill in *The American Indian*, the calumet ceremony was in vogue, and this became widely known and was the origin of the universal idea that most Indians smoked the 'pipe of peace.' According to him, smoking the pipe was often done as a supplication for rain, or when the Indians desired to win the favor of their deities.

In Susanne and Jake Page's masterpiece simply entitled *Hopi*, a brief description of the strong role which tobacco plays in religious pilgrimages to sacred mountain shrines is given at the end of their book. At one shrine in particular, Hopi priests are shown smoking ceremonial tobacco in clay pipes. The smoke is a blessing and prayer that reaches the kachina spirits. A simple ritual is then performed over the shrine by the medicine men placing prayer feathers in the ground, sprinkling sacred cornmeal over them while at the same time praying and blowing smoke directly into the shrine. (The prayer feathers are made of eagle down). By doing this, the priests make sure that the place they are at remains a good home for the kachina spirits and, through offering of prayer in company with tobacco smoke, they seek guidance and wisdom from such spirits. Certainly then, there are useful spiritual and temporal purposes for using tobacco in moderation, but more so when smoked in the form of occasional cigars or pipes than in the nastier, uglier habit of cigarettes.

Author Norman Hammond observes in his *Ancient Maya Civilization* (published by Rutgers University Press), that the Maya have another intriguing aspect to their curious religion, namely that of "veneration of ancestors." Now if this isn't a clear indication of the Asiatic Jaredite (Olmec) influences on later Maya (people of Zarahemia/Nephite/Lamanite) thought and culture, then just what is? Hammond says it is uncertain whether such ancient Maya ancestors were venerated as Gods or possibly considered as intermediaries between divine beings and mere mortals. He refers to the great ruler Pacal at Palenque who appeared to have been worshipped as semidivine following his demise. To the Maya, death seemed more a change of status rather than a final separation, which allowed ancestors further contact with their living descendants on earth.

Apparently caves were a good place to make contact with departed relatives. Hammond cites archeological evidence to support this assertion. He points out that caves were considered to be direct links to the underworld, ("pathways to Xibalda," as he terms them). Evidence of such ritual activities has been found in parts of caves that ordinarily would never be penetrated for shelter or just collecting water. It seems that the Maya have been using caves to make contact with their dead since the

Middle Preclassic period. The western foothills near Poptun, Mexico, for example, yielded a spectacular find in 1980 in the form of several murals deep within the recesses of one such cave. Hieroglyphic writing accompanied scenes of musicians playing a drum and conch trumpet, seated figures making offerings, and a ball-game player—efforts made for penetrating that thin veil which separates this life from the next.

Not only were immediate, deceased relatives venerated, but also more distant ancestors were honored by sometimes invoking their names in order to receive channeled communications from beyond. This was especially so with the ancient Maya priesthood. A newly confirmed priest who had entered into all of the necessary endowments and rituals then obtained a new name—one pertaining to the holy priesthood he held. The new name was usually more ancient than the receiver was. It would be the name of a man long before him who enjoyed the same priesthood privileges.

Along with this were given four penalty signs and four penalty tokens, involving the maneuvering of the hands, fingers, and arms to certain upheld positions. Whenever the newly initiated priest desired to know things of an ancient or past origin, he would invoke his new name and a particular token sign. However, if he wished to know of present matters instead, he would just use his own given mortal name. And as for tapping the future, he would use a third name which referred to the first token of his greater priesthood. Essentially then, with his ancient, modern, and future names, he could inquire concerning events past, present, or future, according to his pleasure.

Channeled Knowledge

The hottest thing going these days in the New Age movement, it seems, is "channeling"—a process by which selected men and women become conduits of inspiration provided by disembodied spirits or exalted beings in other dimensions of time and space. Well, the Maya subscribed to this in a big way, but with a few cautionary provisos thrown in for good measure.

Rule Number One was that the one doing the channeling had to have his or her own moral life in perfect order and be a person of good character, heart, and mind. Otherwise, if said channeler was corrupted with any of the vices of this world, then he or she could be easily deceived by a similar corrupted spirit or evil being. Thus, it was important for ancient Maya to investigate closely the moral conduct of those to whom they went for channeled information.

Rule Number Two was that only channeled information given free and without any cost to the receiver could reasonably be expected to be from an authentic and good source. Otherwise, if channelers charged fees or demanded payments, such knowledge transmitted from the other side would invariably be from evil and deceiving sources.

Rule Number Three and this was the most important of all: there had to be a very legitimate reason in mind for wanting such-and-such information or asking for specific knowledge and wisdom from the other side. If it were for mere speculation or out of simple curiosity, the chances were quite good that a wicked instead of benevolent influence would respond to the seeker's demands through the respective channeler consulted. The Maya understood that their gods and friendly spirits had better things to do with their time than just to satisfy the mere whims and pleasures of idly curious and fussy mortals.

Rule Number Four implied that both the channeler being consulted and the seeker himself or herself had to be on the same wavelength of faith and in tune spiritually, so as to exercise the greatest amount of penetration possible through the veil which separates this life from the invisible world on the other side.

Therefore, it seems that those wishing to pursue a course of channeling for themselves, either alone or with the aid of a gifted seer or seeress, ought to first consider each of these points well before engaging in such actions. Only then can they be reasonably assured that those speaking from the other side are friendly, helpful beings with good intentions in mind and not malevolent spirits bent on deceiving and destroying the human soul with their wicked lies.

Mirrors and crystals were and still are favorite devices which ancient and modern Maya have relied upon to give them the knowledge they need for specific matters. Archeologist Gordon F. Ekholm gave a paper some years ago at the 40th International Congress of Americanists in which he referred to special concave mirrors used in ancient China and among the Olmec in Mexico for divination purposes. Anthropologist Robert Redfield touched upon simple divining crystals in modern times in his classic study, *Chan Kom, A Maya Village* (published by the University of Chicago Press): These "zaztuns" or "stones of light" as they are called in that part of the Yucatan are usually translucent stones or often pieces of glass, say from a Coca-Cola bottle, for instance. The shamans who handle them (called "h-men") generally keep such relics in leather pouches. The h-men can find lost objects with them and sometimes discern the activities of mischievous spirits as well. Prior to using zaztuns, h-men will plunge them into bowls of some type of strong liquor (balche or rum) to purify them and help to awaken their inner powers. They then consult these sacred objects by candlelight. In the reflected glow the h-men can read the will of the Gods.

The *Book of Mormon* speaks of such devices, commonly called "seerstones" in Mormon jargon. In fact, Joseph Smith, Jr. used a special pair of them, mounted in a unique frame by the Brother of Jared in ancient times, when he commenced translating the Gold Plates from the Nephite reformed Egyptian into the colloquial English common to upper state New York in the 1820s and '30s. The Nephites themselves possessed such seerstones, which in times of war gave them a decided advantage over their enemies, the Lamanites. According to the Prophet Joseph Smith, Nephite warriors only needed to look into their seerstones to discover where their enemies were hiding, so as to gain a more strategic position over them, winning the conflict (*Utah State Historical Quarterly* 10:180).

Probably no other Christian denomination has placed so much importance and interest in seer crystals as has The Church of Jesus Christ of Latter-Day Saints. Several scholars from Brigham Young University (BYU) in Provo, Utah have already written extensively on such devices. Dr. Richard Lloyd Anderson, a professor of ancient scriptures at the Mormon-owned school, wrote an article on such things in the Fall 1986 issue of *BYU Studies*, in which he quoted the Prophet Joseph Smith as saying that "every man who lived on the earth was entitled to a seer stone, and should have one, but they are kept from them in consequence of their wickedness, and most of those who do find one make an evil use of it." More recently, Dr. D. Michael Quinn, a Yale University history graduate and former professor of American history at BYU, covered such religious seer crystals in his book, *Early Mormonism and the Magic World View*. Quinn relates the story of a Mormon mission president using such a seer stone in the 1940s to assist him in speaking by inspiration in many Church meetings. He said that when he rubbed this stone it gave him the spirit of inspiration to speak.

Two of the most famous seerstones in Mormon history are those discovered by Joseph Smith, Jr. himself and the one eventually found by Edwin Rushton. Smith was shown his in a vision as being located some 30 feet beneath the earth at a well site he soon dug for Clark Chase, near Palmyra, New York. The stone he obtained was a chocolate-colored, somewhat egg-shaped object. Quinn mentions in his book (p. 148) that former Church President Wilford Woodruff once remarked that the seer stone discovered by Smith had been previously used in *Book of Mormon* times and possessed an ancient name by which he and others called it—the name being "Gazelem." This same President Woodruff later placed Smith's Gazelem stone on the prayer altar during the dedicatory services of the Manti Temple (*Comprehensive History of The Church* 6:2320). Gazelem is now kept inside the locked vaults located in the offices of the First Presidency of the Church, along with other valuable artifacts, some being of ancient origin as well.

But it is with the Rushton Stone that considerably more is known. The reason for taking you, the reader, on this somewhat circuitous route, is to help you better understand things of an ancient nature by discussing what we know of them in modern times. Since both stones were apparently used by ancient Native American ancestors, some added details with regard to the one found by Rushton, a devout Mormon living in Nauvoo, Illinois in the early 1840s, should help readers to appreciate the spiritual significance and value attached to such sacred objects.

Returning to the journals of Mormon Apostle James E. Talmage (which were cited several pages ago), we find this entry made February 22nd, 1893 by him:

"Later in the day Brother Rushton called upon me and gave me a history of the stone. He found it in Nauvoo, associated with a valuable record, and with a store of gold, but neither the record nor the gold could he obtain. He claims that the location of the stone was revealed to him in a day vision thrice repeated, and at first it was under a seal, the nature of which he declined to explain. He says the stone possesses a celestial and a terrestrial side, and is capable of revealing matters connected with this world and the spirit land. One surface of the stone is devoted to the Ten Tribes, and in that the Seer can perceive the place and circumstances of that people beyond the ice. Brother Rushton says the stone served him to locate the burial places of several of Joseph Smith's kindred, the prophet having placed several of the brethren under covenant to bury his dead together. Since that work was accomplished, Rushton has lost his gift, but lives in hope that it will be restored to him. The stone he believes will be of service in the vicarious work (for the dead in) the Temples, by revealing the condition and desires of those behind the veil."

A day prior to this, he carefully examined the Rushton Seerstone from a scientific perspective, he (Talmage) being a trained geologist by profession. Of his findings, he wrote:

"During the afternoon I made a careful examination of the stone. It is transparent, of a greenish tint, low fusibleness and hardness, specific quantity of 2.5, contains silica and the alkalies in fact appears to the eye and under test to be a piece of glass, plain and simple. It weighs 66 grammes (nearly 2 1/4 oz.). . . . I believe the Lord could endow a piece of brick with the properties of a seer stone, and endow his chosen servants with power to use such. . . ."

This last expressed opinion of his is most noteworthy in light of what Redfield had to say about the quality of stones used by Maya seers or h-men in the Mexican village of Chan Kom: The zaztun is a translucent stone, perhaps a bit of glass such as a bottle-stopper. Here is where an important point must be made: it's not so much the quality or type of substance employed for viewing purposes, as it is the quality of the material comprising the seer! In other words, Talmage was correct in assuming that a common brick could be used provided that the one using it was right before God in his or her heart. I have personally witnessed deep in the jungles of Yucatan, an old wrinkled Maya seer of many years divining up future events from nothing more than broken pieces of green glass belonging to, of all things, an empty Coca-Cola bottle! Hence, it is the user more than the object used, which determines the success or failure of such objects.

This business of needing an expensive or fancy crystal is for the birds. I have attended enough New Age conferences to know that many people get "ripped off" by having others suggest to them that they need a pretty and costly gem in order to enhance their spiritual powers. That is sheer nonsense to say the least! Proof that almost anything will work so long as the user is right with God has just been presented in the foregoing paragraphs.

Several other true incidents connected with the Rushton Seerstone will give the reader additional information concerning the variety of uses for such sacred objects. In Volume 7 of *Our Pioneer Heritage* (published by the Daughters of the Utah Pioneers) this was found on page 576. She said that a quarter of a century ago, a son-in-law of Mr. Rushton's by the name of Christensen, took the stone to a Mormon church party. Two sisters by the name of Barnes thought it would be fun to gaze into the crystal for awhile. Later they emerged from the room in which they had been studying it and appeared as if they both were in a state of shock from what they had just seen. They soon confided to Mr. Christensen that the stone showed them their local ward bishop crying over an open grave. Since Bishop Duncan's wife was then seriously ill, they decided to say nothing of the matter to him. Later, however, after his wife died, they related the affair to him at the cemetery grave site.

An even more profound discovery was made with its assistance in 1930, when a Western Airline's mail plane, flown by Maury Graham, crashed in a blinding snowstorm in a canyon 22 miles south of Cedar City, Utah. William E. Perkes, Mormon patriarch of the Fillmore, Utah Stake, related the rest of the story to me by phone, Friday, October 25th, 1985:

"One of our family members, Zella Scott, borrowed the seerstone that once belonged to Edwin Rushton in the hopes of locating it herself, since all other search-and-rescue efforts had failed. After concentrating a few minutes, a vision opened up before her eyes within the stone. She saw the plane go down in the blizzard. She saw the pilot get out and walk a short distance where he attempted to make a small fire in order to keep from freezing to death. She tried to describe the location as best she could to others, but without avail. The following spring though, they found the plane. It appeared as if the pilot had managed to escape and had made several fires before perishing from the cold. But the circumstances in which they found the downed aircraft and his fires were precisely as Zella had described them from what the seerstone showed her."

Patriarch Perkes also related a second episode with regard to the stone's use:

"When we lived in Salt Lake City some years ago, we kept the Rushton seerstone in our home. My sister's girl friend, who was visiting us at the time, happened to be a very religious person. Her name was Anna Johnson and she had fulfilled an honorable Church mission to the Hawaiian Islands. One day we were talking to her about it, and she asked if she could see it.

"Placing the stone in her hand, she looked into it. We were watching her facial expressions at the time, and could tell she was witnessing an event of some kind in it, which apparently kept her quite engrossed. Suddenly she turned deathly white as a ghost, and immediately shoved the stone back into my hand. When we asked her what she had seen, she promptly retorted in an agitated tone of voice, 'I don't care to ever talk about it!' We never learned what it was that she had seen, but she did have the gift to use it. Apparently whatever she saw, she didn't like!"

Maya and Mormons are not the only ones to have enjoyed the use of seerstones for investigating the past or prognosticating the future. The Sioux Indians of North America kept their own sacred stones, which served them in different ways. Frances Densmore spoke about them at rather great lengths in the Smithsonian Institution's Bureau of American Ethnology Bulletin 61 entitled *Teton Sioux Music* and published by the U.S. Government in 1918.

"The stones were the native brown sandstone, usually spherical in shape, though oval stones and stones slightly flattened were also used, the principal requirements being that they should be regular in outline and untouched by a tool.

"It is said that a medicine-man, in demonstrating his power to acquire information by means of the sacred stones, sends them long distances. After a time the

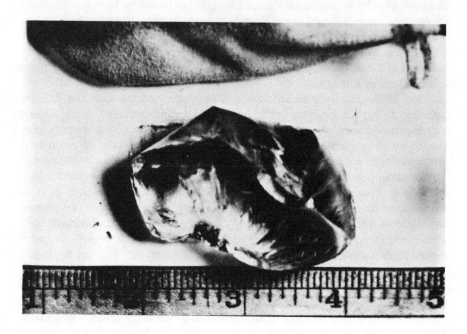

Figure 10.
The Seer Stone Found by Edwin Rushton

stones return and give him the desired information. He is the only person who can understand what they say, and therefore he repeated their message to the man who requested him to make the inquiry. . . . This power of the sacred stones to move through the air is connected in the mind of the Sioux with Ta'kushkayskay' . . . one of the native Dakota (Sioux) gods. This god is too subtle in essence to be perceived by the human senses. . . . He lives . . . in 'the four winds.'

". . . The man whose use of the sacred stones is most open at the present time is Brave Buffalo, a prominent medicine-man of the Standing Rock Reservation. He was born near the present site of Pollock, North Dakota, and at the time of giving his information was about 73 years of age. His father was a leading medicine-man of the tribe. In describing his dream of the sacred stone Brave Buffalo said:

"When I was 10 years of age I looked at the land and the rivers, the sky above, and the animals around me and could not fail to realize that they were made by some great power. I was so anxious to understand this power that I questioned the trees and the bushes. It seemed as though the flowers were staring at me, and I wanted to ask them, 'Who made you?' I looked at the moss-covered stone; some of them seemed to have the features of a man, but they could not answer me. Then I had a dream, and in my dream one of these small round stones appeared to me and told me that the maker of all was Wakan'tanka and that in order to honor him I must honor his works in nature. The stone said that by my search I had shown myself worthy of supernatural help. It said that if I were curing a sick person I might ask its assistance, and that all the forces of nature would help me work a cure.

"Soon after this dream Brave Buffalo found on the top of a high butte his first sacred stone, which is still in his possession. About a month later he found several others, one of which is in the possession of the writer (Frances Densmore). This is almost a perfect sphere. On one side is a number of dots, the grouping of which suggests a tiny face, a characteristic pointed out by Brave Buffalo. The stone is dyed red with native dye. The color, which is a favorite color of Brave Buffalo, has no significance. The stone, surrounded by eagle down, is kept in a wrapping of red cotton cloth. It was said that 'there is something between the eagle down and the stone, because when surrounded by eagle down, it cannot get away.' The stone can be sent on errands of observation by its owner, and when not in use is imprisoned by the downy eagle feathers.

"Concerning the nature of the sacred stones, Brave Buffalo said: 'The earth contains thousands of such stones hidden beneath its surface. . . . Some believe that these stones descend with the lightning, but I believe they are on the ground and are projected downward by the bolt. In all my life I have been faithful to the sacred stones. I have lived according to their requirements, and they have helped me in all my troubles. I have tried to qualify myself as well as possible to handle these sacred stones, yet I know that I am not worthy to speak to Wakan'tanka. I make my request of the stones and they are my intercessors.'"

Acts of Supplication

Distinction from worship but still connected therewith is the act of supplication. *Webster's New Collegiate Dictionary* for 1959 defines worship, which had already been covered, this way: "1. Courtesy or reverence paid to worth; hence, honor; respect. . . . 4. Act of paying divine honors to a deity; religious reverence and homage. . . . Worshipped; worshipping. . . . 1. To pay divine honors; to adore; venerate. 2. To idolize."

On the other hand, we find supplication or, more specifically, its verb intransitive form "supplicate" to mean this: "To make a humble entreaty; especially, to implore God. 1. To entreat for; to ask for earnestly and humbly. 2. To entreat as a supplicant.—Synonym. See beg."

Essentially then, that's the difference between the two. Earlier we explored a little how the Maya honored their gods: living godlike lives themselves; relaxing the mind and paying homage to their gods with tobacco smoke; and venerating their ancient ancestors through rituals and taking upon themselves some of their ancestral names or actually asking specific departed ancestors when desiring to receive channeled information. Or, as I once explained it to two young teenage friends of mine, Matthew and Jason Fountaine, "Worship is when you tell God what a great guy He is and remember all the wonderful things which He has done for you, but in which you do not ask for very much, if anything at all. Prayer, however, is when you specifically go to Him with many wants and needs, in a contrite spirit with a heart and soul filled with humility, begging as it were for His divine favor and grace to shine upon you." Hence, both brothers have two separate forms of communication with their Heavenly and Eternal Father: they often spend a few minutes several times each week, praising Him and thanking Him for all of His goodness over them; and always every day at different times, they will invoke His holy name again to bless their food, themselves, their family and friends, their home, and so forth.

It seems fitting, therefore, to close this chapter with a particular Maya prayer. President Herbert Hoover, once speaking before the public school superintendents of America sometime in February, 1926, said:

"The dangers of America are not economic or foreign foes; they are moral and spiritual. Social and moral and spiritual values outrank economic values. Economic gains, even scientific gains, are worse than useless, if they accrue to a people unfitted by trained character to use and not abuse them" Reverend Edwin A. McAlpin's *Prize Sermons* (NY: Macmillan Co., 1932, p. 114).

The prayer to follow in the last paragraph is a sample for the reader to adapt for himself or herself, that thereby a greater sense of humility may enter one's own heart by a deep realization of personal unworthiness when in the act of supplicating God.

Found in J. Eric S. Thompson's book, *The Rise and Fall of Maya Civilization*, it pretty much summarizes the entire attitude of the Maya toward the divine powers ruling them. The supplicant starts off by calling attention to the offering he has made to them, and then asks, in return, that they should send him game to hunt as he has nothing to eat but his tortillas. As a good Maya he does not ask for more than he needs, for he will be content with one trogon bird, which is equivalent to the size of a grouse. He acknowledges that he is in the hands of the divine powers who are to him as a father and mother, thus recognizing the existence of an eternal father and mother in Heaven, who protect him wherever he may be. He makes his act of adoration in the beautiful and eloquent expression, "I am beneath humility which he feels at the time he is supplicating both." Finally, he renders thanks that his sins have been forgiven him. It is a prototype of what all prayers should be like and resembles the Lord's own prayer as given in the New Testament Gospels; but here, in this instance, the petition came from an ancient Maya who apparently knew nothing of Jesus Christ or Christianity as such, yet truly had religion in his soul when he uttered it:

"Thou, O God, Thou lord of the mountains and valleys. I have given thee a morsel for thee to eat, for thee to drink (in the copal incense). Now I pass beneath thy feet, thy hands, I a traveler. It grieves thee not, it troubles thee not to give me all kinds of great and small animals, thou my father. Thou has many animals—the trogon bird, the pheasant, the wild boar. Show them, therefore, to me. Take them and set them on my path. Then I shall see them, behold them.

"I am beneath thy feet, beneath thy hands. I am fortunate, thou lord of the mountains, thou lord of the valleys. Everything in abundance is possible to thy power, to thy name, to thy being. Of all I may partake. Today, it may be, I was forced to eat my tortillas, yet I am in good hunting lands. It may be that God does not see that there are any living beings here. Perhaps I may bring hither, I may carry back, a small trogon bird.

"Now I see, and behold thee my god, thee my father, thee my mother. It is only that of which I speak which I intend. What I have brought you is in truth not much and of little good for thy eating and for thy drinking. Whether it be so or not, what I say and what I think, O God, is that thou art my father, thou art my mother. Now I shall thus sleep beneath thy feet, beneath thy hands, thou Lord of the mountains and valley, thou Lord of the trees, thou Lord of the liana vines. Tomorrow is again day, tomorrow is again light of the sun. I do not know where I shall then be. Who is my father? Who is my mother? Only thou, O God. Thou seest me, thou protectest me on every path, in every time of darkness, from every obstacle which thou mayest hide, which thou mayest remove, thou, O God, thou my Lord, thou Lord of the mountains and valleys.

"It is only that which I say, which I think. Whether it should be more, whether it should be less than I have said. Thou dost tolerate, thou dost forgive my sins.[1]"

1 J. Eric S. Thompson, *The Rise and Fall of Maya Civilization* (Norman: University of Oklahoma Press, 1966).

CHAPTER THREE

HEALING SOUNDS OF SWEET MUSIC

A Universe Filled with Music

Music is all around us. From the apparent warbling of song birds, babbling of brooks, and rustling of tree leaves to the less obvious singing of fishes, whistling of planets, and humming of cells, music surrounds us everywhere in some form or another. But just in case you may have missed the last part of the foregoing sentence—yes, it is quite true that fish sing, planets whistle, and cells hum! From what telescopes may detect, microscopes reveal, or the naked eye discern, all forms of life emanate rhythm and harmony to some extent.

No one was closer to these phenomena or understood them better than did the early Native American himself. To the Indian then, as with many of his descendants now, everything in nature was vibrant with life. Even the soil and the rocks could speak their own language if one listened carefully. This seems to be what author Ruben E. Reina had in mind when he wrote *Shadows—A Mayan Way of Knowing*. Referring to the present-day Maya farmers inhabiting the archaeologically rich El Peten-Itza area of northern Guatemala, he said that they were incredibly alert, quick on their feet, and sensitive to all noises around them. He explained that the reason they were such skillful forest men was because the forest was part of them. They had achieved an integration with Nature. In other words, the sublime harmony in Nature dwelled within their bosoms and her subtle melodies beat within their breasts. They were, quite literally, in tune with Mother Earth!

Now, what about these singing fish, whistling planets, and humming cells, the casual skeptic may be inclined to ask. Well, they really do exist, believe it or not. Science says so, but of far greater import is that a special kind of intuition suggests so. We often speak of "a woman's intuition" for being able to detect those things which a man might not be readily inclined to reveal, but what of that type of intuition or "sixth sense," if you will, that allows only a very few of us to hear the "silent" parts of Nature cascading with delicious sounds that nourish the starved soul so well?

In 1982 Mark Ferguson worked as a senior aquarist for the Thomas Wayland-Vaughn Aquarium Museum, located at the famous Scripps Institution of Oceanography in La Jolla, California. One day while he was taking a look around a neighboring research building (the adjacent Physiological Research Lab), he entered the research room of an ethologist who was then studying the electrical location and behavior patterns of a species of knife fish. While Ferguson watched, an electrode was lowered into the tank. It was wired to an amplifier and speaker to help evaluate the field intensity. But Ferguson heard something else in the sounds that were produced. It sounded like an orchestra tuning up, he recalled for the April 1982 issue of *Omni* magazine, which covered his subject. He became quite fascinated with what he had just heard, especially since his interest had always been in music and electronics, as well as aquarium keeping. Within minutes he saw a "perfect fusion" between all three.

In time, he was able to adapt current electronic technology to record these small freshwater "singing" electric fish. "The rhythms may be decidedly alien," he admitted with a chuckle, "but it was music to my soul the first time I ever heard it." A reporter, Jim Mastro, who slipped on some headphones months later and became one of Ferguson's first listeners, discovered an entirely new world of wonderful sound as the electrodes were lowered into the water. The aquarium full of these musical electric fish teamed with vibrations of sound, some of which would be instantly recognizable to any trained musician. For instance, there was definitely a dominant note, A minor, "interwoven with complex harmonics and subtle beats." Background crackle had a somewhat orderly and intermittent staccato beat to it. In fact, Mastro noticed that each movement of the fish was reflected in tonal alterations. The reporter concluded from what his ears had just experienced that it was partly music and partly "a collective, melancholy haunting" wail of the boundless universe itself.

For his part, though, Ferguson saw it "as intelligent creatures communicating" with each other through the medium of music. Two additional years of experimentation enabled him to develop a workable "orchestra" piece with just the right alto, tenor, and bass waves and pulses to it. Appropriately enough, it is called "Finnish Scales."

Now the question may be asked with certain purpose in mind, "Can the average person pick up such mysterious but uniquely wonderful sounds on his own simply by placing his ear next to the goldfish bowl or the office aquarium? Better still, would dropping a water-resistant microphone into either enable one to pick up such intriguing harmony on a nearby speaker system?" I think not, for the simple reason, that the souls of most average lay people are just not in tune with the fundamental spirit emanating from Nature herself.

I believe one cause of this has been modern television. Another is much of the rock, jazz, and country western noise beamed across the land via the radio, both of which have severely cankered the soul of man and woman and desensitized them to the point that they cannot even hear the hushed yet audible lullabyes of a passing breeze. The harmful health effects of these obnoxious sounds will be discussed later.

An illustration or two will suffice for my point to be effectively made. My family and I own a large cattle ranch in southern Utah, south of the incredibly beautiful Bryce Canyon with its lovely limestone formations and red sand buttes. A couple of years ago, I had working for us one summer several ranch hands, only at different periods of time. The first hired help was a typical loud-mouth, arrogant teenaged drifter named Joe Roper, who in spite of his unpleasant ways was a hard enough worker when the boss hung around long enough to see that things got done the way they were suppose to have been.

Now through that part of the country many gentle breezes and mild-tempered winds incessantly blow. One time, I asked the kid if he had ever paused long enough to listen to the harmony in the wind. To which he matter-of-factly responded with a mouthful of chewing tobacco, "Nope, an' I don't really care to." He spat a dark stream of the juice on the ground and said, "It's all the same to me—jest plain wind that blows fuckin' sand in yer face or else sends your hat a-tumblin' quite a ways."

Roper and his cousin, Tony, eventually walked off the job, and roamed heaven knows where. Soon there came on to the place another fellow, a Navajo Indian, named Joe Red Dog. He had hitched a ride from somewhere in northern Arizona to as far as the junction turnoff on old Highway 89 that leads to the top of Bryce Canyon. Local people told him that there was work out on the Heinerman Ranch south of Kodachrome State Park, so he managed a few more rides and a little bit of a walk to our remote wilderness spread. He stayed with us for a while and I had a chance to form an interesting acquaintance with him in the process.

One day, both of us were up on top of one of the many high hills which dot our land, doing some surveying work on one of our boundary lines. A small breeze started up and commenced rising and falling in varying crescendos of strength. I was so absorbed in the surveying details, that I quite forgot about the occurrence of any wind to speak of. But Joe Red Dog was alert to it and began paying attention. When I finally diverted my attention away from our surveying instrument momentarily, I caught a glance of his strained features, as if in the act of trying to listen to the smallest sound possible.

"Anything the matter?" I started to ask, but was hushed into silence when he quietly laid one finger across his lips. I made no effort to say anything else and quite forgot the business of surveying for several minutes, having become curiously attracted to his strange listening stance. Finally, after what seemed to be a short eternity of silence, he looked at me with that kind of "smile" in his eyes that only Indians are capable of giving. Then in a low voice, he asked, "Did you hear it?"

I shook my head in the negative. "The wind was talking to us," he said with a certain reverence in his voice. I, who have long worked with many native cultures worldwide as an anthropologist, knew better than to laugh. Instead, I asked in a most serious tone, "What was it telling us?" whereupon he surprised me by saying that a storm was soon imminent and unless we got off that hilltop, we would be soaked to the skin. I cast my eyes skyward and saw mostly blue horizon with just a few puffy clouds hanging out here and there like so many loosely packed bales of slightly dirty wool. But knowing the unpredictable temperament of the weather in those parts, I figured Joe knew something that I did not know.

So we gathered up our equipment and trudged down to the pickup truck far below us. We had barely got back over to the cabin across the gorge, when sudden gusts of wind started whipping up. Soon the crackling of thunder could be heard rolling in the distant mountains around us. Less than half an hour later we experienced a strong but temporary cloudburst.

Naturally, my curiosity by this time increased to the point that I could not help but ask him, "Just how were you able to hear what that breeze told you up on top of the hill?" He responded with this reply: "Because I was born with a part of the spirit of the wind in me. My mother used to cradle me in her arms and sing to me outdoors a lot, when she did her weaving or fed the sheep. As I grew older, she taught me to 'listen' to different intensities of the wind. For by the strengths they blew, she used to say, you could usually tell what they were saying.   "Could you teach me, Joe, to also 'listen' to the wind as you do?" I asked. But shaking his head to mean "no," he explained why it was not that simple a thing to do. "You don't listen just with your ears," he began, "but also with your heart as well." Then bringing his right fist up to his chest, he emphasized with a thump by tapping it, "This is where the greatest listening of all occurs," he said with finality.

Further questioning of this particular Joe led me to discover that he had never watched television, seldom ever been to a movie, and only rarely ever heard any white man's music on the radio. Joe Red Dog was one of those curious anomalies that comes along every so often in most of our lives and gives us reason to pause and think about the way we are accustomed to doing things. When I paralleled this with the former Joe Roper's upbringing in a polygamist family exposed to endless hours of idiotic television, sex-and crime-ridden movies, mind-addicting "rock" music, and equally depressing country western "blues," I fully realized just how uncorrupted this Joe Red Dog's soul really was. That 1986 summer experience with both individuals, more than any other I had that year, caused me to change a lot of habits. From then on it was to be less TV, less cinema, and less Waylon Jennings and Willie Nelson. Three years later during the writing of this book, I have to confess that I still cannot "hear" the wind as well as Joe Red Dog; but I will admit that at least I can feel some of its emotional fervor in my soul these days.

And what of planets that whistle and cells that hum? Well, celestial polyphony has existed for several millenniums, as a matter of fact. The Greek philosopher Pythagoras conceived the heavens to be a grand scheme of concentric spheres whose ordered rotations through the cosmos produced music made pleasing through numerical relationships. He speculated that, as planets moved through space, the proportional distances between them, like the divisions of the strings of a lyre, produced spatial harmonies. Moving at a constant speed, each planet emitted a characteristic tone; the combination of these tones created one eternal chord audible to the divine ear.

In both the writings of Plato and Plutarch may also be found the idea that the planets of our solar system emit definite musical intonations. Even some ancient musical instruments, claim several scholars, were tuned to these planetary musical notes. A couple of clay cuneiform tablets from Ur of the Chaldees have been found to contain definite references to these planetary chants. Musicologists have discussed this intriguing discovery at greater lengths in *Revue de Musicologie* 49:3-17 (1963), *Assyriological Studies* 16:268-72 (1965), and *Iraq* 30:215-26 (1968).

This startling but highly believable notion was accepted without reservation until 1619 when the great Bavarian astronomer, Johannes Kepler permanently shattered its astronomical basis by discovering that the planets have elliptical rather than circular orbits, the angular velocity of each planet changing as it moves nearer to or farther from the sun. For Kepler, though, the astronomical importance of his discovery was secondary to its musical implications. Because of the planets' changing velocities, Kepler thought, the celestial music would not be a single chord but an ever-changing symphony that demonstrated the awesome beauty of God's compositional powers: "The music that God made during the Creation," he writes, "He taught Nature to play; indeed, she repeats what He played to her."

In his published *Harmonices Mundi,* or *Harmony of the Universe*, Kepler assigned a pitch for each of the six planets known to him then. He derived these by calculating each planet's angular velocity and then modulating each pitch according to the eccentricity of their individual orbits. In the modulation of these pitches, Kepler represented the changes in each planet's speed as its orbit approached or got farther away from the sun. In this way he described a six-part motet.

Finally, it was left to two Yale professors and some assistants, together with the help of some very sophisticated computer programming, to bring it all together a little over a decade ago. Yale geologist John Rodgers and rhythm specialist, Willie Ruff, an associate professor of music at the same school, made a historic recording in 1979 entitled, "The Harmony of the Worlds," based on Kepler's revised planetary chants from ancient times.

The record contains 264 years of planetary music (at a scale of five seconds per year, to put it within range of a human lifespan). It starts appropriately enough on Kepler's birthday, December 27th, 1571 and ends with December, 1835. I have listened to the album myself and find it most inspirational if not downright mystically evocative. It sure beats to hell anything ever created by New Age musicians for lifting the soul of man right into the very bosom of the cosmos itself. One may contact Willie Ruff at the Yale School of Music on 96 Wall Street in New Haven, Connecticut (06520) for a copy of the album.

I noticed, when listening, that Mercury, being the fastest and closest to the sun, makes a high chirping sound. Mars, on the other hand, with its extremely erratic orbit, has its song sliding up and down a wide range of notes. Earth and Venus, being the "twin sister" planets that they are, seem coupled in a duet in minor key. It is interesting to note here that Kepler equated our own planet's song with the mi-fa-mi minor second of the scale; to him, our sphere sang a dolorous litany of "misery-famine-misery." Jupiter is the one, though, which emanates a strong, majestic, organ-like tone, shifting slowly and weaving mysteriously with Saturn's deep growl, moving in and out of a major triad as both worlds alternately overtake each other. In some ways, the sounds emitted by these two massive heavenly bodies reminds one of a grizzly bear in deep hibernation, who is experiencing the occasional troublesome dreams that are often characterized by muffled grunts and throaty groans.

The entire concert is a constant shifting moire; melodies seem to disappear before they have time to develop fully, and the planets themselves appear to move from duets to trios to solitary wanderings. The listener, to some degree, is spiritually projected outward among the spheres themselves, until it appears as if one is at the very heart of the solar system itself. It then becomes, as Johannes Kepler himself envisioned, a variety of spiritual auditory experiences, the likes of which simply cannot adequately be described on paper.

Along with this I would like to add another small memento to further enrich our topic of the universe being filled with music. I recall while in the Soviet Union in 1979, meeting the widow of the late Soviet cosmonaut and national hero, Yuri Gagarin. Gagarin was the fellow launched April 12, 1961, in what was to become the world's first manned space flight. Difficult as it was for Valentina Gagarina to speak with me about her husband's historic trip into space, nevertheless she gathered up enough courage to answer several brief questions through an interpreter. I could tell in the occasional stifled emotions within her voice that his tragic jet crash on March 27th, 1968 in the Soviet Union on a routine training flight had not entirely been forgotten.

In asking what manner of man he had been, she replied, a very open, easygoing sort of person; one of incredibly sharp wit and keen mind; a lover of children and the simpler things in life. He had an unusual fondness for Nature and the outdoors. His emotional sensitivities were also very keen as well, she added, probably made that way in part by the atrocities he witnessed of the Nazi soldiers in World War II, who occupied his native village of Gzhatsk (since renamed Gagarin in his honor).

Among the few things I was led to ask her, I felt impelled to query her more closely on her husband's first experience in outer space—"What was it like? How did he say it felt?" and so forth. She thought a few moments on these questions before making a slow, deliberate response. An unforgettable experience, almost a feeling of being reborn were some of the descriptions which followed. But even my Russian interpreter had to momentarily pause and catch his breath, then ask her to elaborate on what she had just told him in order to make sure he had heard it right the first time. I became slightly intrigued by the arch of his bushy eyebrows and the apparent skepticism which mounted his face as he chatted with her some more before translating it into English.

"She says . . .," he began in a halting fashion, searching for the right words to use, "that when her beloved Yuri was orbiting in his Vostok spaceship, he thought he heard a low, mournful wailing noise in the distance as if. . . . "Here he stopped and quickly turned his head in her direction again, asking her another question and receiving a reply in Russian. Then turning his full attention back to me again, he continued, "Yuri told her that he thought he heard the earth in front of him make a deep, groaning noise, similar to what one might find in the funeral chant of any peasant woman attending one of our many Russian Orthodox Church cathedrals somewhere in our native land."

More conversation then ensued between my interpreter, Georgi Luchenski, and Valentina Gagarina. "She says that Yuri heard the sound on at least two separate occasions before he was brought down. And that the second time, there was no mistake he heard something distinctly odd and quite peculiar emanating from the entire planet before him. She says Yuri described it as being in front of a gigantic speaker of sorts and hearing a low, deep rumbling sound gradually pour through the system. It didn't seem to scare him so much as it fascinated and awed him beyond belief." Such then was the information given to me one hot summer afternoon on the outskirts of Moscow.

Finally, offered as evidence of musical rhythms existing within our very body cells, comes the curious piece reported by Dan Rather on the CBS Evening News for Wednesday, January 13th, 1988. Rather began by stating that a well-respected geneticist with the Beckman Research Institute in Duarte, California claims to have discovered music in the genes of humans, fish, and rabbits. "Honest!" laughed the newsman, finding it hard to suppress a smile as the cameras kept rolling.

Dr. Susumo Ohno is a scientist who specializes in DNA research—those invisible strands of chemicals that determine how we are all built. He wondered what DNA would sound like if each chemical on the DNA strand were assigned a musical note, and those notes strung together and played. There then followed a brief segment of music, the tune of which corresponded to the DNA in a chicken's eye. More interesting sounds followed after that: "Mouse Enzyme in C" with Marty Jabara at the keyboard and the hauntingly beautiful "Theme from Human Insulin" played by violinist Lali Breen. Furthermore, several concert musicians were astonished to hear classical echoes of Bach, Shubert, and Mozart in this delightful DNA music.

Musician Breen commented that "maybe these classical composers were feeling this music in their genes" (quite literally, too)! Using the same formula for converting DNA into music, Dr. Ohno decided to try something different and proceeded to work backwards, translating Chopin's piano concerto "Funeral March" into chemical symbols. The moody and melancholy piece emerged as nothing less than cancer. Ohno thinks that his discovery is just another cosmic clue to the ultimate unity of life. "There's a common thread to all these things," he said, indicating a presence of musical harmony in all cells of life.

For his part, though, Dan Rather found it hard to retain his composure when the news program ended. As if in the act of biting his lip so as not to burst out laughing on the air, he closed by saying, "We leave you now with the 'Mouse Antibody Duet' for violin and piano, a composition that would bring credit to any man . . . or mouse." And as the credits rolled on the screen, an unusual form of music could be heard playing in the background. Maybe a joke to some, but facts of life to the more serious-minded among us.

Walking in Harmony with Nature

Although some New Age musicians have tried hard to imitate the sounds of Mother Nature, yet few, if any, have come close to duplicating her rich resonance of flowing melodies. Comedian Woody Allen, it is said, used to listen to the New Age sounds of Ravi Shankar, but stopped after a short time, when the great Swedish film director, Ingmar Bergman, whom Allen met once, suggested something even better for the high-strung actor to relax by. Bergman said he gets up early every morning and the first thing he does is to "sit quietly for a time and just listen to the ocean," after which he has breakfast. Listening to the waves gently roll in and out reminded him of his prenatal state inside the watery domain of his mother's womb with the gentle throbbing of her heart heard somewhere overhead. When Allen cannot find time to get away to the ocean, he will slip down to his favorite New York nightspot where he enjoys playing the clarinet with friends in a small, relatively unknown band.

Many of the great composers, poets, and writers drew their inspiration from nature. Ludwig van Beethoven epitomized this in music and Ernest Hemingway did it in great literature. When Beethoven wandered off into the woods to meditate, he would very often come back with a masterpiece in mind. Many of his greatest symphonies were, quite simply, born under a tree, beside a flowing stream, or on a flowered country lane.

As Cornell University musicologist Donald Jay Grout observed in his *History of Western Music*, it was Beethoven's habit to compose out-of-doors, usually while taking lengthy walks by himself. Beethoven once answered a friend's inquiry as to how he obtained his inspiration, "You will ask me where I get my ideas? That I cannot tell you with certainty; they come unsummoned, directly, indirectly—I could seize them with my hands out in the open air; in the woods; while walking; in the silence of the night; early in the morning; incited by moods which are translated by the poet into words, by me into tones—sound and roar and storm about me until I have set them down in notes."

Dr. Grout goes on to observe that the more man's daily life became separated from Nature, the more did he become enamored of Nature. So one finds that from Rousseau onward, Nature was very much idealized, and increasingly so in its wilder and more picturesque aspects. In essence, he noted, the last century was an age of landscape painting. The musical landscapes of Haydn's "Seasons" and Beethoven's "Pastoral Symphony" were succeeded by Mendelssohn's overtures, Schumann's Spring and Rhenish Symphonies, the symphonic poems of Berlioz and Liszt, and the mighty operas of Weber and Wagner. But during this Romantic era of music, Nature was not merely a subject to be depicted. A very closely knit kinship was formed between the inner life of the artist himself and the life of Nature, so that the latter became not only a refuge but also a source of great strength, wonderful inspiration, and exhilarating revelation as well. This mystic sense of kinship with

Nature, counterbalancing the artificiality of city existence, is as prevalent in the music of the last century as it is in the contemporary literature and art. Thus, listening to classical music of the 19th century will put a person in touch more with Nature, than any other music that I know of, save for the simple, monotonous chants of many short Native American healing songs. And one of the finest classical pieces to alleviate great anxiety and stress with is Beethoven's incredibly calming "Pastoral Symphony."

The great American novelist, Ernest Hemingway, was to literature what Beethoven was to music. Early on in his writing career, he discovered that thoughts and feelings flowed more easily when he was somewhere in Nature. An avid sportsman, he enjoyed spending much of his time in the great outdoors. Unlike Beethoven though, he took some pleasure in hunting game and fishing the oceans and lakes. Forever restless it seemed when in the big cities of bustling life, Hemingway drew his greatest strength and inspiration by escaping into the bosom of Nature as often as he could. Ironically enough, it was where he finally went, deep into an Idaho woods, to end his life. There amidst the lonely silence of the forest came the report of a single shotgun blast that forever terminated his existence in mortality.

But for every creature of despair who died in Nature, there were many more who obtained life, finding it more abundantly closer to the handiwork of the Great Creator and as far away from the evidence of man's existence as possible. Reporter Don Clystrup had an interesting story along these lines for the ABC World News Tonight for Thursday, December 17, 1987. Speaking about the rare Stradivarius violins, he reported that the famous violin maker would often go into the forest and actually tap each tree to determine the resonance of the wood. Based on the particular sounds given by each tree, he then selected the tree from which to obtain wood to make his precious violins. As one well-known concert violinist has already noted, "There is an unexplainable sweetness and deliciousness to the sounds emanating from a Stradivarius"—a veritable banquet of goodies for the ears to feast on.

If the landscape scenes in Nature can be so wonderfully healing, then why cannot her music as well? Consider this medical discovery as further proof of just how marvelous can be the healing potential within Mother Nature. Dr. Roger S. Ulrich with the University of Delaware in Newark submitted a fascinating paper entitled, "View Through a Window May Influence Recovery from Surgery," which was published in the April 27th, 1984 issue of the journal *Science*.

In it he examined the restorative effect of natural views on surgical patients in a suburban Pennsylvania hospital of 200 beds. Such patients usually experience considerable anxiety, and hospital confinement limits their access to outdoor environments almost entirely to views through the windows. Views to the outside may be particularly significant to individuals who have unvarying schedules and spend a great deal of time in the same room, such as surgical patients would. Therefore, it is highly likely that a hospital window view could influence a patient's emotional state and might accordingly affect recovery.

Ulrich managed to obtain the records of patients assigned to rooms on the second and third floors of a three-story wing of an unnamed hospital between 1972 and 1981. Windows on one side of the wing looked out on either a small stand of deciduous trees or a brown brick wall. Each room of double occupancy had a single window 1.83 meters high and 1.22 meters wide with the lower edge 74 centimeters above the floor. Thus, the size and placement of each window permitted an unobstructed view out for individual patients lying in bed on either side of each room. The rooms differed only in what could be seen through each window.

Ulrich summarized his finds by noting that in comparison with the wall-view group, the patients with the tree view had shorter post-operative hospital stays, had fewer negative evaluative comments from nurses, took fewer moderate and strong analgesic doses, and had lower scores for minor postsurgical complications. Additionally, more negative notes were made on patients with the brick wall view: 3.96 percent per patient compared to 1.13 percent per patient with the tree view (almost four times a negativity increase for the brick wall view). These statistics suggest, said Ulrich, that the natural scene had comparatively therapeutic influences.

Again, the question is posed for your consideration: "If the lovely landscaping in Nature can potentiate the healing process more rapidly, then why cannot her sweet sounds of serenity accomplish the same even more so?" Were you aware that a number of highly skilled surgeons in this country and elsewhere often listen to the classical sounds of 19th century composers during very delicate and sometimes dangerous surgical procedures? They do so in order to find some relief from the enormous amount of stress and anxiety that builds up as they are probing the intricate workings of the human brains and hearts belonging to those who have committed their lives into the hands of such men and women.

Take the famous heart surgeon, Dr. William DeVries, as an example. I can recall when he performed his first mechanical heart implantation in the chest of dentist Barney B. Clark in 1982 at the University of Utah Medical Center here in Salt Lake City. He accomplished this feat against the background strains of Ravel's "Bolero." A couple of years later when he had transferred to the Humana Heart Institute International in Louisville, Kentucky, he performed his second implant of an artificial heart; this time in the chest of William J. Shroeder. Within the operating room could be heard the strains of Vivaldi, some Mendelssohn, and a little baroque lute music. As one nurse quipped to a visiting reporter, shortly after this history-making event took place, "When I'm working with DeVries, it's usually, 'Nurse! . . . Scalpel . . . Suture . . . and Schubert please!'" Or as George Atkins, Humana spokesman was quoted as saying, "DeVries likes to have music in the operating room. It breaks the tension of the procedure." A number of other surgeons nation-wide often follow similar examples, gravitating mostly towards either 19th century classical or the "easy listening" sounds of Lawrence Welk and others of the same genre.

So essentially the first step in being able to find harmony with Nature as early Native Americans did, is to recognize the potential destructiveness of the music you may presently be listening to. Consider the following evidence. Harvey Bird of Fairleigh Dickinson University and Gervasia Schreckenberg of Georgian Court College had one group of mice spend eight solid weeks exposed to the discordant drumbeats of rock music. When placed in a maze, says Schreckenberg, these mice took much longer to find the food than did others exposed to a different type of music. Those rodents exposed to rock music wandered off with no sense of direction whatsoever. And when they were eventually dissected by this physicist and neurobiologist, their brain tissue showed abnormal neuron structures in the region associated with memory and learning. It was almost as if they were lapsing into a form of mental retardation.

By contrast other mice that had spent their eight weeks listening to the inspiring waltzes of Johann Strauss performed normally in the maze. No mental confusion was evident and later autopsies showed healthy brain tissue. Get the message, rock music lovers?

Dr. John Diamond, an Australian psychiatrist, explains that much of today's rock music has what he terms an "anapestic" beat to it. That is a jolting halting in meter at the end of each measure. And, he claims, that can really destroy the symmetry between the left and right sides of the brain, thereby making rock listeners hyperactive, restless, and unable to concentrate. The most "anapestic" rockers to stay away from he warned are those like Kiss, Queen, Led Zeppelin, Alice Cooper, Motley Crue, and Twisted Sisters. Interestingly enough, he adds, the original music of the Beatles was not anapestic in tone. Even some of the tamer avant-garde stuff enjoyed by many of today's Yuppie generation has been found to cause diarrhea, stomach ulcers, and heart problems in 60 percent of the German musicians who played in Munich's three best orchestras.

But recognition of what is bad in music for you goes far beyond your own personal health. What about those around you, especially pregnant women? Dr. S. Kameswaran of the Post-Graduate Institute of Basic Medical Sciences in Taramani, India has advised expectant mothers in the daily paper, The *Hindu*, to keep off jazz, rock, pop or any other loud music in the interest of the unborn child. Damage to the fetus can result if the mother is exposed to such loud noises during the early months of her pregnancy, he insisted. In one laboratory experiment study with pregnant mice, exposure to sound of 80 decibels at a frequency of 2,500 cycles per second for just ten minutes of each hour resulted in congenital defects in all the offspring.

Undoubtedly, the best-documented scientific experiments that I have ever come across definitely showing the harmful effects of rock music appeared in Dorothy Retallack's little booklet, *The Sound of Music and Plants*. She mentioned a very interesting experiment conducted at Colorado Women's College in Denver some years ago by two music majors, Virginia Smith and her niece, Marlene Maseberg. Both women placed squash in separate Biotronic Control Chambers and tuned radios to different stations in each. One radio was tuned to a strictly rock music station, while the other was tuned to a classical station. Their experiment lasted some eight weeks and showed amazing results. The squash in the classical chamber had grown toward the radio and was beginning to twine itself around it, while in the rock chamber it had grown in the opposite direction and looked as if it was trying to climb the wall.

In the summer of 1969, Retallack decided to duplicate the work of her friends. The first chamber she hooked up to the popular rock station and the second control chamber to a semi-pop soothing music type, each being tuned to the same volume. But this time she used corn, squash, petunias, zinnias, and marigolds. Nine of each went into both chambers and three hours of music for every 24 hour period was piped into each. The corn and squash seedlings were all three inches high when started in the chambers; the petunias, zinnias, and marigolds were chosen from bench stock at the greenhouse and were as nearly uniform as could be obtained.

Each day she looked in on them with heightened anticipation. Nothing noticeable occurred for the first four days; then quite unexpectedly on the fifth day there were drastic changes. In the semi-popular music chamber the stems had begun to bend slightly toward the radio. They were all leafing and beginning to bud normally. It was an entirely different story, however, in the rock music chamber with over half the plants growing suddenly taller but with smaller leaves and the rest remaining stunted. By the ninth day it was quite apparent that about 80 percent of the stems, leaves and blossoms in the semi-pop chamber were leaning toward the radio at around a 10 degree angle by protractor measurement. The plants in the rock chamber seemed confused and were bending into grotesque shapes. The sudden growth had stopped and the leaves were beginning to yellow quite fast.

Retallack also noticed at the end of the first week that the plants in the rock chamber needed watering every other day because of completely dry soil conditions. The other chamber needed only one watering during the week's time. For some reason the plants in the rock chamber used up and required much more water.

Reactions in both chambers continued as they had commenced. By the end of the second week, nearly all the blooms of the marigolds, petunias, and zinnias in the semi-pop chamber had turned toward the radio. The plants were quite uniform and definitely lush and green. The degree of lean toward the radio was between 15 and 20 degrees.

Unfortunately, in the rock chamber the extremely tall plants were drooping, the blossoms were faded and turning away from the source of the sound. Some leaves had dropped off and the grotesque stems were leaning away at different angles from the radio. Upon entering her laboratory on the 16th day, she discovered a spectacle before her in the rock chamber that was truly unbelievable. All but a few marigolds were in the last stages of dying!

But just six feet away could be seen the beautiful blooms and leaves in the semi-pop chamber, now more abundant than ever. On the 18th day, she pulled up all of these lovely, flourishing plants in order to thoroughly examine their root systems. The roots from plants in the semi-pop chamber were so thick and tangled, it was almost impossible to count them and none measured less than two inches and the maximum measurement was five inches.

Next she unearthed the plants in the rock chamber to check out their root structures. Imagine her utter astonishment to find such sparse roots in all that she was able to count them without any difficulty. Some roots only measured 1/2" long and none more than two inches. It thus appeared that not only had the rock music affected the upper growths of the plants, but their roots as well.

Retallack later refined her experiments to include other types of music. She was particularly interested to see how they would react to Ravi Shankar's "Sounds of India" or Johann Sebastian Bach's "Oreglbuchen" (Chorale Preludes for the Church Year). The plants used, including many types of common garden vegetables such as beans and peas, seemed to "like" the East Indian music the best. By the 14th day, the plants nearest the speaker were leaning so as to almost embrace the speaker at a 60 degree angle. The growth was noticeably lush and abundant, as were the roots. The plants in the Bach chamber definitely leaned toward the speaker between 25-35 degrees, but not to the extent as seen in the Indian music chamber. It appears then that Sankar won over Bach in this instance. She also found that her plants reacted quite favorably to jazz in spite of its parenting rock music. All forms of jazz—from the earliest Dixieland bands to the latest classical Bernstein works, were favorably received by her plants. On June 21st, 1970 a nice, lengthy four-page article about her fascinating scientific experiments with plants and music appeared in the *Empire Magazine* insert of *The Denver Post*. Later that year, Walter Cronkite carried a brief report of her incredible research on the CBS Evening News for Friday, October 16th, 1970.

If recognition is the first step in finding greater harmony with Nature, then a better understanding of how negative sounds can dramatically influence your health for the worst has to be the second step. Nowhere can a finer example of such be found than in the miserable wailing tones, depressed beats and sad social themes of adultery, divorce, drunkenness, loneliness, and even murder, which collectively comprise nearly all country western songs these days.

Anthropologist James M. Schaefer, who is now the director of the Office of Alcohol and Other Drug Abuse Prevention at the University of Minnesota, designed two long-term studies of the effects of barroom environment—music, lighting, decor—on the drinking behavior of some 5,500 people in Montana and Minnesota drinking establishments. As mentioned in the March 1989 issue of *Discover* magazine, he found "a direct tears-to-beers correlation." For instance, Kenny Roger's "Lucille" and Crystal Gayle's "Don't It Make My Brown Eyes Blue" put barroom patrons under the table more often than did practically any other songs. Other singers very likely to up the downing of more brew were Merle "Misery and Gin" Haggard, Willie "Blue Eyes Cryin' in the Rain" Nelson, Hank "I'm So Lonesome I Could Cry" Williams, and Waylon "You Can Have Her" Jennings.

Dr. Schaefer speculated that the reason downbeat and down-home music combine to boost boozing has something to do with slow music's effect on heart rate or the autonomic nervous system. Looking at the lyrics of songs that stimulated rapid drinking, he soon discovered that tear-jerk lonesome blues were the primary culprits.

These songs about the sad and often abusive aspects of life among certain working-class people were more liable to encourage greater drinking. Hard drinkers, it seems, have more of a preference for slower-paced, wailing, self-pitying music as a rule, he noted.

Schaefer points out that such nasal music is found in those societies with a great deal of tension in them. And there certainly is a great deal of tension and anxiety being explored in the songs of some of the best twangy country singers like George Jones, John Conlee, and Merle Haggard. He has also found a number of variables that influence the amount of drinking that goes on in a bar. A strict, posted dress code and an even man-woman ratio contribute to moderation. Conversely though, heavy boozing seems to go hand-in-hand with dim lights, cheap drinks, and a small dance floor. A live band makes the liquor flow more than a jukebox does. Surprisingly enough, landscape scenes filled with trees, grass, flowers, geese, horses, cattle, and the like tend to slow down drinking rates, while repeated patterns, portraits, and especially action photography are known escalators of more alcoholic consumption.

Here we then find more of an understanding with regard to the ill effects of bad music upon our nervous systems. Not only does country western music depress the soul, but it can also flatten the activities of both our thymus and adjacent thyroid glands as well, leading to decreased immune resistance to some types of viral infections. Then too, these misery-invoking sounds can often interrupt the normal flow of thoughts which might otherwise proceed in an orderly fashion through our brains. I have come to experience this unpleasant sensation firsthand. When our Anthropological Research Center was located in one very large room in a downtown Salt Lake City bank building, I was able to listen quite a bit to the country western sounds emanating from KKAT Radio. Not only was it much harder for me to concentrate on the various manuscripts I had to write, but it also put members of my staff on edge as well. It seemed we had greater friction in the office as a result of my year-long addiction to this kind of music.

However, because of our need for additional space we soon relocated ourselves in another office building nearby. The extra space was more reasonably divided into three separate rooms of adequate size for our growing needs. The combination stereo record player and radio had to be put in the file room some distance away from my own private office. Consequently I was not able to tune in anymore to KKAT Country 102 as they are called out here. In no time at all, I noticed a definite improvement in my mental abilities and no longer seemed to work under the drudgery of some self-imposed druglike sounds. And there seemed to be a cheerier atmosphere for the rest of my office staff. So from my own personal experiences with country western and the recent studies of Dr. Schaefer, I was able to reach a better understanding of why I should avoid this kind of music if I wanted to have greater clarity of thought and happier relations with others around me.

Essentially then, we have the following several steps which should assist us in being able to walk more harmoniously with Nature:

(A). Recognition of the problem that some of the music we are presently listening to may be very detrimental to our overall health and well-being.

(B). Understanding just why this music is bad for us mentally, emotionally, spiritually, and physically.

(C). Determining to do something about it by changing our music preferences to that which can be more uplifting and ennobling to the soul of man.

Sanctification Through Rhythm

As mentioned in the beginning of this chapter, we live in a world and universe governed by rhythms. It was also pointed out that some of the music we enjoy listening to may be in direct conflict with Nature's own sublime and gentler melodies. And finally, we have now arrived at the state where music, at least the right kind, can help to sanctify the inner man or women in each of us.

Yehudi Menuhin, one of the world's greatest violinists, refers to music as "the universal language" that we all know how to speak somehow. "Music penetrates people's awareness more easily than any other language. It is more all-encompassing than words. . . . It is a spiritual intangible that is a key to the hearts of people—and rhythm is its most universally understood part. We are full of rhythms—our pulse, our gestures, our digestive tracts, the lunar and seasonal cycles." Finding then the correct rhythm which is the most suitable for our individual biologies should be a primary goal for each of us.

One man who has devoted much of his professional career in the pursuit of this is psychiatrist, musicologist, writer, John Diamond, M.D., who by his own admission, is also a "doctor of the human spirit." He prescribes melodies for specific maladies in much the same manner that your regular physician might prescribe pills for your problems. In a sense, he is a clinically updated version of your original Native American medicine man. This modern shaman with a medical degree and tribal roots anchored firmly in the "down under" soils of his native Australia, has helped thousands of people worldwide find their own "cantillation" or "song of the soul" as he prefers to call it. This search for a "personal harmony" adapted just for you, he points out, should be a vital part of one's own general search for true identity.

Cantillation is that activity which is unique to each individual—his or her gift or inner talent—that, when engaged in, provides a sense of joy, hallowedness, and oneness with the Supreme Creator of us all and everything else. This "song of the soul" is the primary thing each of us loves to do, an activity that provides an ultimate satisfaction. When we can do our own individual cantillations, then we have achieved just about as much peace and happiness as is humanly possible. For that period of time while we are busy with our own cantillations, we become as nearly complete and whole as mortals can ever hope to expect.

Although the physical body itself may grow old and decrepit and eventually begin to wear out in places, the continuance of our own cantillations will always breathe new life into that part of each of our beings over which mortal death has no control, namely the spirit. For one person cantillation may be painting, for another it could be drama or writing, playing the piano or building houses, gardening, raising children, doing needlepoint, learning to dance, working with the elderly and handicapped, or for countless others some type of mechanical work, poetry, bronco riding in a rodeo, solving crossword puzzles, and so forth. The list is virtually endless, but the means by which to choose from it remains the same—cantillation is that process by which one discovers his or her own unique rhythm and then figures out how to best apply it in order to obtain maximum joy in this world and the spheres beyond.

Probably one of the very best examples of someone who has found his own cantillation without really knowing it is the near-centenarian, actor-comedian George Burns. Just shy a few years from his 100th birthday, he remains incredibly alert in mind, refreshingly vigorous in spirit, and unbelievably active in body. There is about him an undefined energy and exuberance matched with a clever wit and decades of wisdom that is not found in many college kids or middle-age working class folks these days. And yet for all of this, his lifelong habits of smoking good cigars, drinking fine alcohol, and dating beautiful women have obviously taken their toll on his physical health. Who else could have survived a major heart bypass well into their eighties except this man? But what carried him through thick and thin has been his remarkable ability to do what he enjoys doing the most. By the broadest definition, this is essentially what cantillation is all about.

However, it requires music, especially sacred sounds cherished by the soul, to light the candle of harmony in each one of us. Dr. Diamond believes that the thymus gland is particularly sensitive to external rhythms. I am inclined to go along with this, but in my own field research among a number of different cultures I have come to find that the thyroid and the adrenal glands are also actively involved in the rhythm process as well. To a lesser extent, we could include the pineal and pituitary glands also. Good music can effectively elevate the energy levels of each of these glands, while bad music does just the opposite.

A case in point may serve to illustrate this better. Historian Robert Payne has revealed much about the mental, emotional, and physical states of health of one of the world's most despicable human beings. In his masterpiece biography on *The Life and Death of Adolf Hitler*, Payne brings out that Der Fuhrer suffered from chronic hypoglycemia. Besides an apparently abusive diet heavily ladened with starches, sugars, and fats, Hitler also manifested many of the classic symptoms of low blood sugar—irrational behavior marked by sudden fits of passion, extreme mood swings, and an inability to think and remember things.

This tyrant's condition became more severe whenever he attended an opera or melodrama in which tragic episodes were part of the story lines and in which very somber, near funeral-like music was required for certain scenes. But whenever he

could attend an opera written by Richard Wagner, he underwent an incredible transformation. His violence subsided, he calmed down and became more meek, submis-
sive, and humble. His gaze lost its restlessness, and his daily preoccupations were as
though they had never been. His own destiny, however heavily it weighed upon
him, no longer appeared to have any relevant importance. He no longer felt lonely
or like an outlaw residing on the fringes of a society which had booted him out of
their midst. He was in a state of intoxicated ecstasy. It is said, in fact, that when he
came to power years later and was driven through huge crowds with extraordinary
pomp and theatrical magnificence, that the very cities themselves which he frequently visited became as so many "stages for a glorious Wagnerian opera."

Or need we forget likewise the case of King Saul, who was continually troubled
by an evil spirit, according to I Samuel 16:23? He could find no rest at night nor
peace of mind in the daytime; his body and mind were often wracked by the torment
and anguish delivered up by this lingering devil. The only solution which afforded
him some relief, however temporary it may have been, was when the shepherd boy,
David, "took an harp, and played with his hand; so Saul was refreshed, and was well,
and the evil spirit departed from him."

How true the old adage, "Music soothes the savage beast." Just look at what it
does for temporarily "taming" otherwise very dangerous kinds of snakes such as the
cobra. During my one trip to India, I was astonished at how apparently docile these
deadly serpents became when charmed by the dreamy notes from a simple windpipe.
Their handlers understood and knew that the vicious natures in these reptiles could
be easily subdued when subjected to such lovely sounds of tranquility. (Psalms
58:4-5 explains how this is possible because of the near invisible "ears" which most
snakes seem to have).

We can thus see just how far the right kind of music can work in order to bring
peace and harmony to otherwise violent and disturbed existences of life. Both
Diamond and myself, independent of each other, have researched out those several
types of music which can bring the unruly spirit or rowdy soul to better terms with
itself and assist the individual in finding his or her own personal rhythm that is
bound to bring the greatest happiness possible.

For Diamond, a trained psychiatrist, it has been the singing of Jewish cantors.
Having made a study of cantors and Hebrew liturgy and listening to hundreds of
recordings, he began to employ this particular kind of music in his therapy sessions
with people whom he had designated as being spiritually dead. What he found,
interestingly enough, was that this seemed to awaken them more than anything else
he had tried up to that point.

Having met with success in his counseling practice using this music, he plunged
himself even deeper into the study of cantors. Soon he was tape recording a number
of rabbis. Later he learned to play the shofar (a traditional Jewish horn instrument)
and attended different rabbinical colleges to get more recordings. Eventually, he
found that it was not so much the words that the cantors were singing, but the
energy that the cantor imparted to the words. Strangely enough, he admitted, he

found two or three cantors who had the quality of being able to inspire and raise the life condition of those who listened to the cantor's music. It slowly occurred to him that these several rabbis had this incredible power because they themselves were experiencing great joy and fulfillment while singing. Their joy was so great, in fact, that they were able to communicate it to those who listened, thus infusing the congregation with the same identical feeling.

For myself, on the other hand as an experienced anthropologist, it has been the usually monotonous chanting of different Native American shamans. Medicine men and women never "sing with expression" as we are apt to do; instead they generally stick with one steady rhythm and keep repeating it over and over again. By doing so, the rhythm is impressed on the mind of the patient. The rhythmic pattern holds his or her attention and, in quite a few instances, may even prove to be hypnotic to some extent. Some healing songs are sung many times, while others are sung a definite number of times, usually three, four, or five. Some Indian doctors have songs for beginning and ending a treatment and others have special songs for each of the four divisions of the night.

One primary purpose of Indian healing songs is to quiet the patient. Frances Densmore, an ethnologist who made a lifetime study of hundreds and hundreds of such chants, found that the majority of these healing songs were sung slowly (d=44 to d=66). However, the general tempo of other Indian songs is a bit more rapid (d=76 to d=104) as a rule. Shamans whom I have worked with on the Crow Reservation in eastern Montana, on the Blackfoot Reservation in southeastern Idaho, on the Navajo Reservation in southeastern Utah and northern Arizona, and with several other tribes elsewhere, all informed me at various times independent of each other, that rhythms with slow tempos to them were the best to use for helping sick patients recover from hypertension, heart disease, depression, stomach ulcers, fever, diarrhea, influenza and the common cold, and related maladies.

As with Densmore and others who have preceded me in this kind of research, I too have discovered that while there are obvious differences of custom among tribes and among individual healers, yet there is a prevailing characteristic in all Native American healing songs which is an irregularity of accent. Sometimes this may take the form of unexpected interruptions of a steady rhythm and sometimes there is a peculiar rhythm pattern throughout the melody itself. At first I could not figure out the reason for this peculiar strategy common with all shamans whom I have had the distinct privilege of working with in times past. But it soon occurred to me that such small and infrequent interruptions in just one repeated rhythm was to recapture the patient's attention in case it might be drifting off somewhere.

Of all the Native American shamans that I have personally gotten to meet over the years, be they male or female, I have never known one of them to be loud or boisterous or very materialistic. To a person, they were all quiet, conservative individuals maintaining a dignity and self-respect I have yet to see much of within my own race or for that matter in the cultures of others, such as Hispanics or

Blacks. Talk about dedication! These people really prepare themselves for their special calling in life.

I especially like the description which Densmore gave concerning their individual preparations for such an honored position in their respective tribes. In Bulletin 151 of the Smithsonian's *Bureau of American Ethnology Anthropological Papers* (No. 37), she mentioned that while a "dream" to whites is associated with unconsciousness, to the Indian it implies an acute awareness of something mysterious. Dreams and their healing songs may come to an Indian in his or her natural slumber if the mind has been conditioned for such an experience. Generally though, the first important dream comes to a healer in a fasting vigil. That person isolates himself or herself in some silent place in order to make the mind more passive so as to get an impression from a mysterious source somewhere. The silence gradually becomes vibrant, acquiring a rhythmic quality to it, which in turn, soon inspires a simple melody of sorts. This is his or her "dream song"—his or her most prized possession.

Densmore recalled that an aged medicine man once recorded his dream song for her, then bowed his head with some noticeable regret. Upon asking why the sudden change in countenance, he responded in a meek, somewhat quivering voice that he said he wouldn't live long as he had parted with his most precious possession. The white or black musician composes songs addressed to his deity, but the Native American was in the habit of waiting and listening for the mysterious power pervading all of Nature to speak to him or her in song. The Indian realized that he or she was part of Nature, not just similar to it.

A study of the dream song in many North American tribes, wrote Densmore, revealed the high place that song occupied in their lives. Of course, Native Americans like so many cultures had their songs with games, dances, legends, and folk stories, but those phases of their music were separate from the primary function of song specifically—as a means of communicating with the supernatural, through which they imagined that they might secure aid and assistance in every single undertaking they pursued.

In reviewing this last section then, we can briefly summarize the important points this way:

1. Our world and universe are governed by rhythm.

2. We have surrounded ourselves by considerable negative rhythms, which produce turmoil and conflict inwardly.

3. Hence, we must undertake to "sanctify" or "purify" our inner beings with sublime and sacred melodies.

4. Since our lives and bodies are filled with a variety of naturally occurring rhythms, we should try to discover what our own "song of the soul" is and then make an effort to exercise it as often as our time and patience will permit us to.

5. True joy comes in doing what you like, not in doing that which you dislike. Consequently, we should give more time and attention towards cantillating our

personal rhythms so that our joy is manifested more often than is our necessary grinding stress.

6. The proper music makes babes out of beasts!

7. The singing of Hebrew liturgy by Jewish cantors is one way to achieve a measure of inner satisfaction.

8. Learning and repeating often a good Native American healing song is another way to obtain purification for the soul. The song below is one of the best I have ever found for this. It is an old Chippewa (Ojibwa) healing song that was frequently employed in and around the Leech Lake area of Minnesota into the first quarter of this century. This particular song was a great favorite among many of the Midewiwin or "Grand Medicine Society" of the Ojibwa nation, having been revealed to a young shaman sometime in the latter part of the 1700s or the beginning of the 1800s. The circumstances under which it was revealed were in and of themselves extraordinary to say the least. By one account alone, at least five different long deceased Midewiwin from ancient days appeared to him at once and instructed him in the proper use of this unique dream song. Having used it myself in the service of others, I can fully attest to its remarkable healing abilities, especially when it comes to binding up the wounded heart, calming the distressed mind, and reassuring the

Figure 11. Chippewa healing song, recorded by Ge miwunac.

doubtful soul. The range of its potential, if fully explored with great patience and reverence, is beyond description. And the secret to its hidden powers lies in the song's relative simplicity!

> Kimanido wihe...You are a spirit.
> Kimauido wiin....I am making you a spirit.
> Fnda nabiyan....In the place where I sit.
> Mimanido wiin....I am making you a spirit.

9. Moderate and occasional fasting, putting aside all loud noises and boisterous behavior, and gearing the mind more towards a meditative state in an atmosphere of serenity are necessary prerequisites before chanting this particular dream song.

10. Absolute silence is almost a necessity in discovering your own "song of the soul," as Diamond calls it, or having revealed to you your personal dream song the way many Native Americans before you have had.

11. Your personal dream song, which the foregoing Chippewa healing chant will help you obtain, should become your most prized possession, to be shared with one one but yourself!

For the Love of Music

Magnificent melodies convey cherished feelings of love and respect and often bring out in others the very best when at times only the worst seems apparent.

Towards the end of 1979, Edna Maie Stilwell, editor of the *Journal of Gerontological Nursing*, reported the following unexpected "breakthrough" music. As a registered nurse specializing in geriatrics, she visited a nursing home somewhere in Maryland. There she observed two elderly women sitting near each other.

"Oh, you needn't waste your time talking with her," one of them snapped matter-of-factly, pointing to her neighbor in disgust. "I've been here now going on three years, and I've yet to hear a peep from her. She's just anti-social, never speaks to a soul!"

Walking over to the silent woman, Mrs. Stilwell placed a hand tenderly on her frail shoulder and spoke to her—but to no avail. Then, she reported later, "I thought I heard a familiar melody that she was quietly humming. It took me back to my childhood. I remembered an old religious tune which my grandmother sang "When the Roll Is Called up Yonder, I'll Be There." I put my lips close to her ear and, trying to match the timing of her melody, I started to sing the words. Suddenly, to the astonishment of all, the woman turned around and looked up into my face, saying, "Oh, you know that song, too. . . ."

A deceased Mormon Church leader, President Heber J. Grant, once related this true account concerning two Mormon missionary elders proselytizing in a part of the South that formerly harbored bitter antagonism against the Latter-Day Saints. Elders J. Golden Kimball and Charles A. Welch, neither of whom could sing very well, were about to baptize some converts. A mob had assembled and both men were made to understand that if they went forward with their intentions of baptism that the mob would throw them into the river. Both Elders resolved, however, to go ahead with their plans despite whatever threats the mob made against them.

But before doing so, these missionaries decided to sing a song. The hymn they chose was an old Mormon favorite, "Truth Reflects Upon Our Senses." The song seemed to have such a powerful effect upon the mob that they were nearly transfixed with amazement. The brethren then proceeded with their baptisms and went some distance to attend to the confirmation part of the baptism ritual. A message came from the mob asking them to return and sing that song again. The request was readily complied with. The leader of the mob, Joseph Jarvis, who had previously sworn in his wrath and bitterness that "no goddamned, stinkin', son-of-a-bitchin' Mormon dogs are ever goin' ta baptize folks herebouts if I kin help it" (his exact words, pardon the profanity), later became affiliated with the Mormon Church himself. The chief reason for doing so, he confided to Elder Kimball, was the sentiments expressed in the hymn and the sweet melody they had previously sung to him. He said it was these things, more than anything else, which had pulled the poisonous darts of hatred from his heart and eventually converted him to the Restored Gospel of The Church of Jesus Christ of Latter-Day Saints.

Both examples, therefore, show the tremendous power which edifying hymns can have upon degenerate souls. Such sacred and holy strains, as with Native American dream songs, can uplift the depressed spirit of man from his dreary and forlorn existence to a much higher level of consciousness and feeling.

Decent music has always been a potent force for good, a candle in a dark room some say. It is magic and mystical, possessed of such an ethereal quality at times that I have occasionally marveled at just how well it works in transporting the human soul back to that Pre-Existent State where our spirits once were young and vigorous and the Father and Mother of all took each of us in their laps, there to cradle and press us close to their eternal bosoms with an affection that only the angels of Heaven can comprehend!

CHAPTER FOUR

CLEANSING THE INNER MAN

The Sweat Ceremony in Ancient Times

The great Native American empires of ancient times all embraced the concept of sweating for spiritual purification and cleansing the inner man of mental and emotional debris. Norman Hammond in his book on the *Ancient Maya Civilization* mentioned that sweathouses often occurred right along side temples, palaces, and ball courts throughout much of Central America. In *An Album of Maya Architecture*, the author noted that there were at least eight sweat baths among the ruins at Piedras Negras, Guatemala).

They were readily identifiable by archaeologists, having distinctive contours in their remains. One of the largest and most prominent of these sweat baths was categorized as Structure P-7. It contained a low, vaulted chamber in which was a hearth built of stone and lined with potsherds to resist the heat of fire. The entrance to this chamber was very small and was undoubtedly approached by a sunken passageway, which at the same time served as a drain to carry off the water used in the bath. The passageway continued inside between two benches on which the bathers lay, fanning about their bodies, with a bundle of leafy twigs, the steam which rose from the hot stones of the hearth when water was thrown upon them. The steam chamber is enclosed in a rectangular building divided into two rooms by a medial wall. These were probably used for dressing and for rest, as well as for ceremonies in connection with the cure or purification. The projection of the central chamber into the rear room subdivides this again into two parts, so that the building in effect has four chambers.

Sandra L. Orellana in the Winter 1977 volume of *Medical Anthropology* briefly discussed the significance of sweating among the Highland Maya who once resided in Guatemala. Steambaths were employed for ritual purification, regular cleanliness, and relaxation, as well as for some medical benefits, she emphasized. In fact, so important was the sweatbath among these people that it was even mentioned in one of their sacred books, the *Popul Vuh*. Several Franciscan friars, who accompanied the Spanish conquistadores on their several conquests of Mexico and Guatemala, made the following collective observations regarding these ancient sweats:

There is scarce any house which hath not also in the yard a stew, wherein they bathe themselves with hot water, which is their chief physic when they feel themselves distempered. When a fever becomes stronger, they entered the temazcales, which we call estufas (sweathouses), or they lay out in the rays and heat of the sun, only drinking hot water and some hot brews.

Stephan F. de Borhegyi in the second volume of *Handbook of Middle American Indians* noted that many of the sweathouses used for "ritual cleansing and curative magico-religious rites" were often located near springs or streams on the outskirts of major settlements. As a rule they were owned by the entire community or by several families. There was a lot of social interactions and exchange of religious ideas at such communal Maya sweathouses.

In his fascinating book, *The Medicine-Man of the American Indian and His Cultural Background*, physician William Thomas Corlett, M.D. mentions that the famous steam bath which we borrowed from the Russians, was in turn borrowed by them from the ancient Aztecs. Aztec sweathouses deserve a brief description here on account of their uniqueness. They were usually constructed of bricks and their forms were very similar to that of bakers' ovens, with the difference that the bottom was concave instead of flat. Their diameters were usually eight feet, their height six feet, and their entrances no longer than was necessary for men to pass through them on their knees. Opposite these entrances were furnaces with holes in their upper parts so that smoke could easily escape. The stones which separated the gates from the ovens were of a porous nature. Bathers were provided with jars of water and whips made of aromatic plants. They would then enter these ovens, the adjoining parts of which had been previously superheated, and stretch themselves out on reed mats after throwing the water onto the porous stones. Thick vapor was instantly produced, with bathers whipping their bodies with the bundles of aromatic herbs. It was not too long before copious sweats ensued.

Sage was a common herb used in those days to whip the body vigorously while in one of these Aztec sweat houses. Interestingly enough, a short description of an old Russian steam bath published in the January 1980 issue of *Soviet Life*, closely parallels the above description given for Aztec sweathouses. The Russians, however, used bundles of birch twigs instead of sage to whip their bodies. It appears that, indeed, the Russians inherited most of their methods for sweating from the ancient Aztecs somewhere along the way in history, and like the Russians after them, the Aztecs employed various kinds of massage for different ailments following a work-out in the sweathouse. For example, a swollen neck or sore throat was rubbed with the hand, a stiff neck or shoulder would have been pinched and squeezed, the throat was rubbed with just one finger to stop a cough, and sprains were treated by rubbing them very gently with the hand.

Steam heat treatments outside of the traditional steam bath were likewise employed by Aztec physicians for various other problems as well. Migraine headaches, for instance, were cured by the doctor pressing the patient's temples with hot clumps of steaming grass and then fanning the patient's head afterwards with his own hands as he invoked the Aztec gods of medicine, Quato and Cacoch. The treatment for back pain was most unusual. After heating a large stone or the griddle used in preparing tortillas, the doctor had the patient lay face down on the ground. Then dampening one foot thoroughly, he placed it on the heated stone or griddle. He did not remove it until the heat, slowly penetrating through the thick calloused coating caused by walking barefoot so much, had reached the live flesh. Then he planted it on the patient's back, pressing down with considerable pressure and manipulating his foot from side to side in a semi-circular motion at the same time. In most cases the pain would cease within a matter of minutes.

The ancient Incas also enjoyed the use of water and baths for curative purposes, as Dr. Corlett mentions in his book. He cites as evidence of this a great feast held annually, in which the men would assemble fully armed, as if going to war, in the Intip Pampa or open space in front of the Temple of the Sun. A High Priest in an elaborate feathered headdress appeared before the multitude and led them in the battle chant: "O sickness, disaster and misfortune, go forth from the land!" The men were then segregated into four equal groups of hundreds and made to face in four different directions. When given a signal by the presiding High Priest, they all bellowed, "Go forth all evils; leave us forever!" Then all four companies ran with the greatest haste in the directions they happened to be facing. Those facing west ran for some distance to the river Apurimac and bathed in it; those facing east ran over the plateau of Chita and down into the Vilcamayu Valley, bathing at Pissac; those facing north ran in that direction until they came to a stream where they bathed; and finally, those facing south ran as far as Acoyapuncu (now called Angostura) which is about two leagues and jumped in the river at Quipuisana. Since these rivers and streams eventually emptied into the ocean below, it was believed that the evil sicknesses suffered by these people were soon carried out to sea.

As Orellana points out in her excellent article on "Aboriginal Medicine in Highland Guatemala" (*Medical Anthropology* 1:139-40), the sweat baths of ancient Central American Indian civilizations were based, in part, on the old Hippocratic theory of disease, which attributed sickness to hot or cold, humid or dry conditions. In the Yucatan, however, this approached more closely the yin-yang concept of sickness and wellness long espoused by the Chinese. Thus, the Maya and Aztecs would try to cure a "cold"-caused illness with a therapy involving just the opposite quality. Hence, the steam bath, for instance, was regarded to be a "hot" cure for fevers believed to have been brought on by exposure to wind and rain.

Benefits of the Sweat Lodge

Among nearly all Indian tribes in North America, the sweat lodge ceremony played an integral role in their health as well as their religious beliefs, especially so for the latter. The following interviews with two modern-day Native American medicine men best explain how an Indian sweat lodge is the gateway to reaching their own god. I have tried very hard to keep these descriptions in their own words, so that little or none of the true meanings are lost or misinterpreted along the way.

Jose H. Lucero of Santa Fe, New Mexico is a Pueblo Indian by birth and proud of his noble heritage. These are his thoughts about the spiritual importance of the sweat lodge:

"Whether sweltering in a dark, scalding sweat lodge or worshiping in a familiar church pew, the goal is the same: to see God. The God may be the Jesus that Christians worship, the Allah to whom Muslims pray, or the Great Creator or Great Spirit that we Native Americans know.

"But the intended end is always the same. It is to find God as he is known, as Allah, Jesus, or the Great Creator. This is why we Native Americans must always have access to traditional medicine men and sweat lodges. The approaches are different, but the intended goals are really the same when you come right down to it.

"Religion is an integral part of the American Indian way of life. Compared to Western religions, the distinction between ours and commemorative religions like Catholicism, Mohammedanism, or Buddhism is they commemorate a central figure or event. But the Native American way is a continual form of religion, not just a single event."

Mr. Lucero, a Santa Clara Pueblo, belongs to the intertribal Traditional Elders Circle, and directs New Mexico's Soil and Water Conservation Division.

The second interview was with John Redtail Freesoul, a descendant of the Plains Indians, who is spokesman for the Redtail Hawk Medicine Society. A professional therapist for about a decade, he started using the sweat ceremony in counseling drug addicts and alcoholics several years ago. Presently he conducts sweat ceremonies in different New Mexico prisons for various Native Americans incarcerated therein.

"The sweat ceremony is a purification and cleansing rite for the mind, body, and spirit which precedes almost every Native American ceremony. It is one of psychological, physical, and spiritual purification and the basis of the entire Indian religious experience. One purpose of the sweat lodge is it represents going into the womb of the Earth Mother, who Native Americans see as the Great Spirit's female aspect, which includes everything that can be seen in nature. The male side is the God who cannot be seen.

"When we we enter the sweat, we close the door and look within ourselves. It applies to all human beings, not just Indians. It is a way of going to nature to purify ourselves in a natural way, to be in harmony and balance with the natural laws of life. The white man's saunas and spas simply won't do in this respect.

"The sweat lodge is built from willow branches covered with blankets or canvas. It is erected around a circle, where molten rocks are placed. Everything is circular because the circle is a symbol of God to Indian people.

"The sweat has four circles. The first is a fire outside that is seen as the fire of no end, the same as the sun of creativity, symbolizing a path of life encouraging self-discipline. Individuals who believe in the circle embrace certain behavior, including a belief that they won't walk on others.

"The second circle is the altar, which represents being centered and balanced. A person who is centered has a better perspective and focus. The third circle is the lodge's center, where sizzling rocks are placed to represent a microcosm of the universe, or the creator's center. The fourth circle is the lodge itself.

"As the ceremony begins, the lodge's door closes so participants sit in darkness. When they finish, the door opens to the east. (Author's note: Mormon temples face east, too). It represents the new light we're going to have—a new vision we've found. "As the lodge heats, participants rub their bodies with mint, garlic, and sage and breathe in the steam. (Author's note: The Gros Ventre Indians on the Fort Belknap reservation in Montana used to rub their bodies with peppermint and uva ursi. John R. Swanton in his ethnological study of *Indian Tribes of The Lower Mississippi Valley and Adjacent Coast of the Gulf of Mexico* related how the Natchez shamans would make a heavy, thick bed of Spanish moss 7-8 inches in depth and then have their patients lie down naked, covering their bodies with the same moss until only the face appeared. Next they put burning charcoal under the bed which they smothered with herbs that had been boiled and also surrounded the bed with various types of animal skin coverings. The smoke of these herbs passed through the moss producing an abundant seat in sick patients. When they emerged from this treatment later on, the shamans would run the corners of their hands over the naked bodies making rivulets of sweat run off in great abundance. Much relief was obtained this way Swanton said. James A. Teit and Elsie V. Steedman explained how the Thompson Indians of British Columbia, Canada used wormwood instead of Spanish moss in nearly similar fashion. Their description of this parallel use appeared in the 45th *Annual Report of the Bureau of American Ethnology* 1927-28).

"Physically, the body is purified as a person sweats and mucous is cleared from the lungs. The poison comes out of the body as we drink fresh water and sweat like a snake shedding his skin. Sitting naked alone, you are exposed to the creator.

"A person feels lighter after the sweat, both physically and mentally. You can get rid of a bad attitude or various behaviors such as changing your language. Others get rid of relationships or repair them.

"Participants talk directly to God as a son or daughter would speak to a parent, asking God to change their bad language, their attitude toward women or other behavior. The calmness of reflecting in the sweat allows a person to gain a clear vision of his or her inner consciousness. It is a quiet time of reflection and introspection.

"Self-realization or direct communion with God can result during the sweat. Self-realization, introspection, self-discipline, and awareness all occur, and they spell rehabilitation for inmates (in prison). It's very much like psychological group therapy or the confession to a priest. The feeling is universal.

"It's the epitome of group therapy. I didn't plan to use the sweat in therapy. I was using it in my personal life and sharing it with friends. After I saw the value, I took it to my clients. If I'd lost my temper, shot someone, and got five years, I'd need the sweat lodge more than ever. It would be the only way to go inside myself and see why I did it.

"And speaking practically, the sweat can assure sobriety in people who have used alcohol or drugs for years because they cannot enter unless they've been drug free for at least 48 hours. The key to the sweat ceremony is personal accountability and responsibility to God for one's own behavior. Your behavior can spark behavior in me and it is the same with the spirit world."

Is Mr. Freesoul correct? Does the sweat lodge actually help those taking abusive substances kick their addictive habits? Roberta L. Hall, an anthropologist at Oregon State University in Corvallis seems to think it does. In an interesting paper published in Volume 472 of the *Annals of the New York Academy of Sciences*, which was devoted entirely to the subject of alcohol and culture in Europe and America, she concluded that the sweat lodge may have a major role in preventing alcohol abuse and in creating a new Indian identity. The sweat lodge program should aid in rehabilitation.

Sweat ceremonies have also helped to cure or relieve certain forms of muscle paralysis, as mentioned by Orellana in her paper (previously cited). Likewise did Ralph Roys refer to the occasional use of sweating as a means to help crippled people regain some use of their limbs in his book, *Ethnobotany of the Maya*.

However, those seriously considering a sweat lodge ceremony of some kind for inner cleansing and purification should be aware of several possible contra-indications in a few cases. Pregnant women and elderly people with weak hearts ought to avoid it. But as for most everyone else, the great benefits to be derived from entering a sweat lodge are many and certainly more spiritually than physically advantageous as the evidence clearly indicates.

The Maya Enema Ritual

Another form of internal purification once practiced among the ancient Maya of Central America was the administration of enemas. Oh, these were no ordinary run-to-the-bathroom kinds of enemas, but elaborate rituals that involved not only the injection of "holy" substances into the rectum but also great musical fanfare as well. As the two authors of *Maya Ruins in Central America* in Color pointed out, enema rituals in classic Maya times were accompanied with an orchestra that included trumpets, carapaces (turtle backs), drums, flutes, and rattles, not to mention some fancy footwork as well. Quite literally, an enema in those days was one heck of a glorious experience, attended by wandering minstrels, beautiful dancing girls, and some herbal concoctions that really opened up the mind to an entirely new kaleidoscope of colors beyond the realms of mortal vision.

Yale University archaeologist, Michael D. Coe and his co-author, Peter T. Furst, elaborated at some length in the March 1977 issue of *Natural History* magazine on such a remarkable cleansing ritual. They mention plenty of historical evidence to show that enemas were quite popular for both cleansing as well as religious purposes. From ancient Egyptian pharaohs who had court-appointed "Guardians of the

Royal Bowel Movement" to administer enemas, to King Louis XIV of France who received some two thousand of them in his lifetime (even while conducting business with foreign dignitaries), enemas have often been administered with a certain amount of flair and style to them. Unlike today's mundane colonic experiences, enemas in ancient times were in and of themselves really special events marked by considerable fanfare and personal preparation.

Coe and Furst noted that early Native Americans discovered just how quickly the rectal administration of intoxicants could radically change one's state of consciousness and with less undesirable side effects like nausea that generally accompany oral intake. The physiological reasons for this are relatively easy to understand. Substances introduced into the rectum enter the colon, the last segment of the large intestine. Now the chief activity of the large intestine is the reabsorption of liquids into the system and the storage of wastes until they can be evacuated. The absorbed liquid immediately enters the bloodstream, which carries it to the brain. An intoxicant or hallucinogen administered rectally closely resembles an intravenous injection in the quickness of its effects.

Such traditions have survived even in modern times, although in rarer instances. Both authors cited the accidental discovery by ethnographer Tim Knab, while he was doing linguistic research among the Huichols of western Mexico as proof of this. Knab was shown a peyote enema device employed by an old female shaman in the village of Santa Catarina. The bulb was made from a deer's bladder and the tube out of the hollow femur of a small deer. She prepared her peyote by grinding it to a fine pulp and diluting it with water. Instead of taking the mixture by mouth, which the Huichols usually do, she administered it rectally, experiencing its effects almost at once while avoiding its bitter, acrid taste and the nausea that most Indian peyoteros feel when chewing the stuff outright.

Although I don't personally recommend a hallucinogenic enema ritual, yet for some this may be a practical and very useful experience in cleansing both body and mind at once! A brief case study will serve to illustrate what I mean by this. A man in his mid-thirties, whom I will simply call Tim, approached me a couple of years ago after I had given an herb lecture at a Whole Life Convention in Los Angeles. He wanted to know what herbs he could take to correct his occasional chronic constipation and at the same time help him to overcome what he described then as "a very minor drug problem." But when I pressed him for details about his drug habit, he refused to be more specific than this, so I had to be content to just work with the information he'd volunteered.

I recommended the following enema concoction for him with the appropriate instructions on how to administer it. And at the same time I asked him to respond back in writing as to the success of it when he was able to. He promised me he would. I soon forgot about the episode until several months later, when the following letter was received. Except for the obvious name and address changes to conceal his true identity and residence, everything else remains intact:

January 11, 1988

Dear Dr. Heinerman:

You may remember me from the WL Convention here in L.A. sometime back. I'm the guy who asked you for something for my constipation and drug urges. You gave me a formula to use and said you wanted to know how it worked for me.

Well, sir, I can tell you that it really helped a lot. At first, I mixed too much of the buckthorn and senna together and got bad diarrhea, but cut back on the amounts and things went fine after that. I can tell you for sure, though, that those spices really did the trick. Maybe the catnip had something to do with it also. But they gave me the 'highs' I needed until I could quit my dependency on the other stuff, which I figured was destroying my health anyhow.

That's about all I have to say. Hope this is what you wanted.

Tim
Los Angeles, California

What Tim did was this: He brought a quart of Perrier mineral water to a boil (no other type of water will work as well). Then he added one tablespoon each of coarsely cut buckthorn bark and senna leaves (no powders here). After which he reduced the heat, covered the pan with a lid, and simmered for about five minutes. Then the pan was removed from the heat and uncovered. To this mixture was added two heaping tablespoonfuls of powdered nutmeg, cinnamon, and powdered catnip herb. The mixture was stirred thoroughly and then the pan recovered, its contents being allowed to steep for an hour or until the liquid was lukewarm. Then it was strained through a coarse wire sieve into a glass jar, making sure that the powdered ingredients were included in the strained liquid. This was then poured into a hot water bottle with a hose and syringe attached to the bottom and injected into the rectum in small amounts over several minutes and retained for as long as possible. At other times, the buckthorn and senna would be omitted, and just the powdered spices and catnip taken by him instead. Appropriate "New Age" or more traditional classical Richard Wagner types of music can be played in the background for a more heightened cleansing experience if one so desires.

CHAPTER FIVE

TRADITIONAL INDIAN FOOD AND MEDICINE

Asiatic Origins of Indian Medicine

In the opening chapter of this book, considerable evidence was presented for an Asiatic origin for the ancestors of all Native American races which have inhabited this Western Hemisphere. Since the Jaredites (who were contemporary in time with the American Olmecs) emigrated from somewhere near the Tower of Babel in central Iraq to the western coast of Mexico, it only seems reasonable to assume that they must have brought with them some of the Old World healing traditions.

One of the more notable customs they imported from the Near East was the wearing of feathered masks for special occasions. These appear to have originated from Syria and were quite common in ancient Assyrian art from the Middle Assyrian period onwards. Cylinder seals, foundation boxes, vases, and temple walls were often decorated with figures of men adorned with elaborate winged griffin headdresses. In those days, the griffin was a mythical monster who was part lion and part eagle. According to Volume 20 of *Sumer* (a journal of Iraqi archaeology and history), griffins performed many beneficial services, including protecting the kind and deities and driving away evil spirits. The first plate following some historical notes on the griffin on page 57 show three temple priests clad in griffin headdresses. Many eagle feathers are very apparent in all three representations and bring to mind similar headdresses worn by a number of early Native American medicine men. As a further example of the uncanny similarity, Dr. Eric Stone's detailed description of an Apache medicine man's headdress with all of its elaborate trimmings (including eagle feathers and mountain lion claws) in his little work *Medicine Among the American Indians* is well worth reading. One cannot help but be amazed at the near likeness of Near Eastern griffin head gear worn by ancient temple priests to the eagle-feathered headdresses employed by most American Indian shamans several millenniums later.

As one follows the ancient route of the migratory Jaredites further eastward across the many steppes and seas of Central Asia, additional evidence becomes available to show more parallels with Native American medicine. The use of the bearskin is one of these. The April 1943 issue of the *Journal of the Royal Asiatic Society* contains some fascinating information about an incredible archaeological find near the city of Honan, China. Among the relics discovered were a number of bone fragments with pictographic inscriptions on them. The texts have been dated to at least three thousand years ago by scholars. One of them depicts the stick-like figure of a man with some type of bulky headgear covering the top part of him. Although somewhat difficult to translate, the accompanying inscriptions seem to suggest that the role of the human figure depicted was as some kind of chief exorcist who, covered with the hood of a bear's skin, would then explore dwellings and expel the pestilence therefrom. Is this any different from the numerous bear skins and bear masks worn by early American Indian medicine men when attempting to drive evil spirits or sicknesses from the bodies of their suffering patients? I think not.

Further proof for Asiatic origins for many aspects of Native American medicine may be found in John A. Grim's fascinating study *The Shaman* in which he shows strong resemblances between the healing patterns of western tribes and that of the Ojibwa Indians.

Ceremonial Gathering of Herbs

Today many of those who still gather herbs from the wild or harvest them from domesticated plots of ground, do so in the usual laborious way without any thought or regard for the plants themselves. But not so with Native Americans, either past or present, as the evidence is about to show. These people, who are one with Nature, have an inherent respect for all life forms around them and consequently act in such a manner as to show proper consideration.

Eric Stone, M.D., mentioned this peculiar trait in his *Medicine Among the American Indians*: "Even the medicines commonly used were only collected after appropriate offerings to the gods along with prayers and chants. In some tribes, he continued, elaborate rituals were occasionally required, as in the case of the highly effective anti-rheumatic medicine made by the Little Fire Fraternity of the Zunis in Arizona. A four-day-long ceremony is essential for the preparation of the six special herbs which go into this particular formula.

In his treatise on "Sacred Formulas of the Cherokees," ethnologist James Mooney gave us an interesting insight into the ritual surrounding the gathering of herbs by these people. His description was published in the 7th Annual Report of *The Bureau of Ethnology* of the Smithsonian Institution for 1885-1886 and is as follows:

"In searching for his medicinal plants the shaman goes provided with a number of white and red beads, and approaches the plant from a certain direction, going round it from right to left one or four times, reciting certain prayers the while. He then pulls up the plant by the roots and drops one of the beads into the hole and covers it up with the loose earth. In one of the formulas for hunting ginseng the hunter addresses the mountain as the 'Great Man' and assures it that he comes only to take a small piece of flesh (the ginseng) from its side, so that it seems probable that the bead is intended as a compensation to the earth for the plant thus torn from her bosom. In some cases the doctor must pass by the first three plants met until he comes to the fourth, which he takes and may then return for the others. The bark is always taken from the east side of the tree, and when the root or branch is used it must also be one which runs out toward the east, the reason given being that these have imbibed more medical potency from the rays of the sun.

"When the roots, herbs, and barks which enter into the prescription have been thus gathered the doctor ties them up into a convenient package, which he takes to a running stream and casts into the water with appropriate prayers. Should the package float, as it generally does, he accepts the fact as an omen that his treatment will be successful. On the other hand, should it sink, he concludes that some part of the preceding ceremony has been improperly carried out and at once sets about procuring a new package, going over the whole performance from the beginning."

A different variation of the same essential theme was presented by anthropolgist Arthur C. Parker in his book, *Parker on the Iroquois*. Parker himself was part Seneca having been raised on the Cattaraugus Reservation and had interviewed a number of old Seneca shamans as he entered adulthood. He later became the curator of the New York State Museum in Albany. The ritual described in his book was revealed by supernatural means to an old Seneca visionary named Handsome Lake.

When a Seneca shaman desired to gather medicinal plants, he would retire to the forest where they grew and there build a small fire. When a sufficient quantity of glowing embers was ready, he would then position himself before them and as he spoke in intervals, would toss pinches of tobacco on the hot coals. In this way he would be addressing the spirits of the medicines themselves, telling them that he wanted their healing virtues to cure his people of their ailments. "You have said that you are ready to heal the earth," he would then chant in his native tongue, "so now I claim you for my medicine. Give me of your healing virtues to purge and cleanse and cure. I will not destroy you but plant your seed that you may come again and yield fourfold more. Spirits of the herbs, I do not take your lives without purpose but to make you the agent of healing, for we are very sick. You have said that all the world might come to you, so I have come. I give you thanks for your benefits and thank the Creator for your gift." When the last puff of tobacco smoke had dis-appeared, the shaman began to dig up the various plants from their respective roots, making sure to break off the seek stalks and dropping the pods into the holes and covering them over with fertile leaf mold so that they might in time replace what was removed. "The plant will come again," he chants, "and I have not destroyed life but helped increase it. So the plant is willing to lend me of its virtue." These several examples illustrate the profound respect which has always gone into the preparation of herbal remedies by Native Americans everywhere.

Indian Materia Medica

The rest of this lengthy chapter consists of numerous medicinal and food plants previously employed by many Native American tribes residing throughout the continental United States and portions of Canada and northern Mexico. A number of important reference volumes were consulted. Some date from the 19th or early 20th century are either personal adventure narratives or else specific treatises of Indian materia medica. John D. Hunter's *Manners and Customs of Several Indian Tribes Located West of the Mississippi* (Philadelphia, 1823) and M.R. Gilmore's *Uses of Plants by the Indians of the Missouri River Region* (Washington, D.C., 1919) are examples of these. In all, the information from many books too numerous to mention here was gleaned and put into the author's own words for the readers benefit. Plants have been listed by their Latin binomials first and then by their common names.

Achillea millefolium (Yarrow). The Bella Coola made a burn dressing by chewing the fresh leaves and then applying this green saliva-herb mixture directly to the burn itself. The Chehalis made a decoction from the leaves to stop bloody diarrhea. Among the Cherokee this herb found many uses too: infusion given for fevers and insomnia; poultice for hemorrhoids; tea made for various types of internal hemorrhaging; dried and smoked in a pipe for simple inflammation of any mucous membrane.

With the Plains Indians, such as the Cheyenne, it worked wonders as well: tea made of the fresh leaves and flowers for congestive heart failure and chest pains (angina pectoris) related to cardiac problems; infusion of the fresh or dried plant for clearing up colds, subduing coughs and getting over nausea; infusion for inducing perspiration while inside a sweathouse; small poultice of the crushed leaves placed in the nostrils to stop nosebleeds quickly; tea of the fresh or dried plant for tickling of the throat; tea made of leaves for tuberculosis. With the Chippewa nation, a decoction of the roots was used externally for various types of skin eruptions, or the dried root was well chewed and then the spit rubbed on sore leg or arm muscles as a stimulant. A decoction of the leaves and stalk was similarly used on horses to make their legs stronger. The Cowlitz Indians used a tea made of the leaves as a wonderful hair wash and a decoction of the roots as a digestive aid. The Creek Indians whom the early American frontiersman Davy Crockett once fought singlehandedly, mashed the fresh plant into a tiny poultice and then put it next to an aching tooth to relieve the pain and misery.

The Delaware-Oklahoma of the Southwest found that an infusion of the entire plant was ideal for treating liver and kidney problems. On the other hand the Gitksan gargled with a decoction of the young plant or root for relieving sore throats. The Gosiute made poultices of the plant to rub on stiff joints affected by rheumatism and to reduce the swelling and discoloration of bumps and bruises. The Iroquois had their own particular uses for yarrow: poultice of plant or leaves for neuralgia; infusion of leaves for worms in young children; decoction of the plant for stopping convulsion in infants; infusion of the crushed plant for diarrhea and sunstroke and soreness throughout the muscles and joints (such as is common with influenza); decoction of the plant, root, and rootbark for purifying blood; decoction of the plant for abdominal cramps; cold infusion administered internally and externally for unconscious epileptics coming out of seizures; and a decoction of the plant, root, and rootbark for venereal disease.

Both the Karoh and Klallam Indians made poultices of the soaked stalks and leaves for treating wounds and sores. The Northwest Coast Kwakiutl made a poultice of the leaves for chest colds or to soften hardened breasts after childbirth and lengthy nursing. The Lummi made a decoction of yarrow flowers to prevent childhood illnesses such as mumps. The Mahuna rolled yarrow leaves and then inserted them into a cavity to stop toothache. The Mendocino Indians of California made an infusion of the leaves and flowers as an eyewash for sore, aching eyes, and similar infusions for treating indigestion, ulcers, migraines, and tuberculosis and emphysema. The Menominee crushed the fresh flowers and rub them on eczema and rashes. With the Mohegan, cold infusions were drunk to stimulate the appetite and as a tonic for the liver and kidneys, especially after heavy meals consisting of a lot of deer or fish meat. The Arizona Navajo have used an infusion of the plant as an external wash for cuts and saddle sores, and internally by the men for increasing their sexual prowess. The Ojibwa placed yarrow flowers on hot coals and then inhaled the smoke to break up a fever.

The Okanagan found yarrow quite handy as a decoction for washing chapped hands, pimples, rashes, and insect or snake bites. The Potawatomi, like some of the other tribes already mentioned, found the flowers, when they were smudged on live coals for a short time to be quite useful for reviving comatose patients. The Quileute made a strong decoction of the leaves as an aromatic bath to help weak and sickly infants regain their strength. The Northwest Coast Sanpoil Indians made a decoction of the stems and leaves in the hope of causing abortions, but whether it was successful is unknown. The Shuswap made an infusion of the leaves for poison ivy and poison oak rashes. The Swinomish made a bath from the entire plant for adult invalids. The Winnebago found a wad of the fresh leaves or an infusion of the same quite handy for putting into the ear to relieve an excruciating earache.

Allium species (Wild and domesticated garlic, onion and leek). The Cherokee employed wild garlic for treating poor urination, accumulation of phlegm, scurvy, asthma, fluid in the lungs, deafness, worms, croup and colic in children. Here I would like to briefly digress to bring in other materials to support the Cherokee use of wild garlic for deafness. The May 1977 issue of *Chinese Medical Journal* (3:204-5) carried a short article about doctors using a thin slice of garlic to help repair an eardrum perforation. And the September 1986 *Journal of Laryngology and Otology* described how either a slice of warm onion or several drops of warm onion oil put into the ear canal could help relieve an excruciating earache. This same medical journal explained how some of the bactericidal principles in garlic and onion might positively affect middle ear disorders. Finally, a detailed article in the August-September 1988 issue of the *Catalyst* (a Salt Lake City holistic health bimonthly publication) explained from both a pediatrician's and parent's point of view how garlic oil therapy helped to save a 10-month-old child from a very serious inner ear infection. In all three instances the validity of using garlic for ear-related disorders such as deafness by the Cherokee Indians has been fully confirmed.

Both the Mohegan and Shinnecock tribes made a syrup of chopped onions to get rid of colds and flus. Rappahannock medicine men often mashed raw onions and then applied them as poultices to remove fever from inflamed injuries. The Mahunas rubbed wild garlic juice on their bodies and also took it internally to treat insect, lizard, spider, and snake bites and scorpion stings. The Rappahannock also chewed raw root bulbs of wild garlic for shortness of breath and hypertension.

Ambrosia artemisiifolia (Common ragweed). The Cherokees used the crushed leaves of this common field weed on insect stings, hives, and infected toes. Infusions of the leaves were taken for pneumonia and fevers. Among the Dakota Indians an infusion of the leaves and plant tops was quite useful for stopping bloody diarrhea and vomiting. The Delaware-Oklahoma tribes made poultices of the entire plant to prevent blood poisoning and tetanus at an infected site. The Iroquois discovered that an infusion of the roots of this common weed was excellent for heart problems. The California Mahunas made an infusion of the plant as a wash for minor skin eruptions and scalp diseases. Cheyenne found that an infusion of the leaves and stems was quite good for abdominal cramps, bloody stools, and constipation. The Gosiute made a poultice of steeped ragweed leaves for sore eyes. Clearly, the many uses derived from this ordinary weed elevate its medical importance to quite a degree.

Angelica species (Angelica). The California Costanoan burned the roots and inhaled the fumes to relieve migraines; chewed the root for indigestion; heated the juice from the leaves and rubbed it on sores. The Creeks of Davy Crockett fame found the roots to be a wonderful analgesic for upset stomach and lower back pains, to expel worms from the intestines of children, and to calm down those in hysterics. The Mendocinos used the roots for nightmares, colds, sore eyes, colic, fever, allergies (like hay fever), and rattlesnake bites. The Paiutes employed a hot decoction of the roots for lung problems, sore throats, coughs, and kidney ailments; whereas a salve made out of the mashed roots was good for applying to cuts, sores, and swellings. The Shoshone used a decoction of the roots for washing venereal sores and rashes.

Arctium lappa (Burdock). With the Cherokee burdock root was valued for getting rid of kidney stones, clearing up scurvy, and strengthening weak female organs. The Menominee, Micmac, and Ojibwa made poultices out of either the boiled leaves or boiled buds and roots to treat skin sores. The Delaware-Oklahoma nations found that a poultice of leaves bound to the body would reduce intense pain from swelling and inflammation; and that an infusion of the roots made a great blood purifier. The Fox Indians gave their squaws in labor burdock root tea to make childbearing easier for them. The Mohegan liked an infusion of the entire plant for curing colds in the winter. The Ojibwa used the root for ulcers, indigestion, and gas. The Iroquois made poultices of the mashed leaves for relieving migraines, drawing out purulent matter from surface infections, getting rid of pimples on the face, reducing the swelling and itching of bee stings, and stopping bleeding cuts. They also made decoctions of the roots for increasing urination and of the leaves as drops for earaches.

Artemisia species (Wormwood and big sagebrush. Official wormwood, *A. absinthium*, came from Europe to this continent). A Gros Ventre squaw of the upper Missouri in 1833 cut off one joint of her little finger as a sign of mourning and held the bleeding stump wrapped in some prairie wormwood leaves. The Potawatomis of Forest County, Wisconsin slowly burned the foliage and flowers over glowing coals and then directed the resulting fumes into the nostrils of a comatose patient by means of a paper cone in order to revive him. A decoction of the leaves has been used by the Nevada Paiutes for malarial fever. The journal called *Science* for May 31, 1985 reported that Chinese doctors isolated a compound from *A. annua* called *qinghaosu* (QHS or artemisinin) and were able to treat 2,099 cases of malaria; while investigators at the Walter Reed Army Institute of Research isolated the same antimalarial component from this species of wormwood growing in and around the Washington, DC area.

The Navaho-Ramah have made cold infusions of the leaves of sagebrush to use as a lotion for cuts on their sheep and to give internally as well for intestinal worms. The *National Institute of Animal Health Quarterly* (22:138-43), a Japanese periodical, reported in 1982 that the powdered shoots of *A. herba-alba* successfully eliminated experimental *Haemonchus* worm larvae from the intestinal tracts of some Nubian goats between the ages of 7-14 months. The Navaho-Ramah also sometimes prepare a bitter decoction from sagebrush to drink with heavy meals consisting of a lot of mutton. Another Japanese publication, *Chemical & Pharmaceutical Bulletin* (31:352) reported that the buds of *A. capillaris*, a popular wormwood in Oriental folk medicine, contain at least four bioactive agents (esculetin 6,7-dimethyl ether, capillarisin, and capillartemisin A and B) which encourage the secretion of bile from the gall bladder (bile aids in the emulsification of ingested fats).

The Northwest Coast Salishan made a cold infusion of big sagebrush (*A. tridentata*) and rinsed their mouths with it after a meal. Both *A. herba-alba* and *A. tridentata* have been shown to be decidedly antibacterial, with the former being used in parts of China and Japan to prevent tooth decay by inhibiting the adherence of *Streptococcus mutans* to tooth enamel which eventually leads to caries (*Phytochemistry* 22:1057-58, 1983). The Shoshone applied hot poultices of big sagebrush leaves to the forehead and temples to relieve migraines and hot poultices of branches to various aches and pains.

In my best seller, *Heinerman's Encyclopedia of Fruits, Vegetables and Herbs*, I recount a historical incident from the life of Joseph Smith III, son of Mormon Church founder Joseph Smith, Jr., which involved the use of wormwood tincture in a rather dramatic way. While still a teenager, he and his mother, Emma Smith, were traveling in a carriage together somewhere near their hometown in Nauvoo, Illinois. At one point, the boy accidentally had two of his fingers caught in the carriage door and badly crushed when it was slammed shut by mistake. His mother dressed the wounded fingers as best she could, but the throbbing pain became almost unbearable for the lad. Whereupon she took from her trunk a small bottle of whiskey and wormwood and poured the liquid directly upon the tips of his two injured fingers. In the words of Smith himself: "For the first time in my life I promptly fainted, for it seemed as if she had poured the strong medicine directly upon my heart, so sharply it stung and so quick was its circulatory effect!" Suffice it to say, however, when he regained consciousness a few minutes later, the excruciating pain had nearly subsided.

A total of 12 pages are devoted to just the *Artemisia* species alone in Moerman's classic work. Many more uses could be cited, but space does not allow it. However, those applications which have been mentioned here are, for the most part, followed by some clinical or scientific evidence to show that Native Americans really understood the medicinal advantages to many plants even though they probably did not know the biochemical reasons as to why they worked so well.

Asclepias syrica (Common milkweed). Infusion of root for backache (Cherokee); milky sap rubbed on warts to remove them (Cherokee); tea made of plant for laxative (Cherokee); milky sap rubbed on bee stings and cuts (Iroquois); infusion of leaves for stomach problems (Iroquois); decoction of plant taken after childbirth to prevent hemorrhaging (Iroquois); infusion of leaves for kidney failure (Iroquois); young buds eaten or decoction of root drunk for respiratory problems (Menominee); milky sap used for ringworm (Rappahannock).

Berberis aquifolium (Wild Oregon grape). Root decoction for indigestion or internal bleeding (Blackfeet); steam bath of the leaves and roots for yellow fever (Karok); decoction of tips of stems to stop vomiting (Sanpoil); root infusion as eyewash (Sanpoil); infusion of roots as a gargle for strep throat and tonsilitis (Squaxin); bark infusion as a wash for skin sores and inside the mouth for cold sores (Cowlitz); and a root decoction for nagging coughs (Quinault).

Berberis vulgaris (Barberry). The Micmac, Mohegan, and Penobscot used either the dried, powdered bark and root for treating ulcerated gums and sore throat or made a cold decoction of the berries to reduce fevers and heal swollen tonsils. The Northeast Shinnecock, on the other hand, made a strong decoction of the leaves and administered them three times daily as an effective cure for yellow jaundice.

Betula species (Birch). The Cree first boiled the bark of white birch, then dried it out before rendering it into a powder to be used on chafed skin. The Iroquois made a strong decoction of the bark of yellow birch to relieve rashlike itching. And the Menominee made a decoction of the bark tips of that birch used to make their canoes, as a general tonic for the body. It is interesting to note that, in the November 1979 issue of the Soviet medical journal *Vestnik Khiurgii Imeni*, a 20 percent tincture of birch buds in a 70 percent alcohol solution was used successfully to treat superficial, deep, and cavity wounds in 108 patients. Apparently the above three Indian tribes knew about birch's wonderful skin and tissue applications, which until now only the Russians seem to have discovered.

Capsella bursa-pastoris (Shepherd's purse). A cold infusion of the leaves and stems was used by the Cheyenne for relieving headaches. The Chippewa took comfort in a decoction of the whole plant for dysentery cramps and diarrhea. The Menominee found that the same decoction was excellent as a skin wash for poison ivy rash. The Mohegan found than an infusion of the seed pods themselves was good for getting rid of intestinal parasites and relieving stomach pains.

Capsicum frutescens (Cayenne pepper). Although not indigenous to North America but rather a product imported by early white settlers from either Africa or Central America, it found some interesting uses among a few Indian tribes. The Cherokee and Navaho-Ramah seem to have used it the most. Poultices of red pepper were applied to the soles of feet for mild fevers or elsewhere on the body to treat gangrene. The powder has been taken in some kind of juice, water, or whiskey for colds and flus. Some Indian women have even rubbed the powder on their breasts to wean nursing children away from further sucking, and on a few occasions some men have even mixed a little red pepper with some petroleum jelly and rubbed it on their chests to break up mucus and congestion in their lungs.

Chrysothamnus nauseosus (Rabbitbrush). In making my selections for this chapter, I have tried wherever possible to include those plants, which while extensive in some parts of the country, are not always mentioned in the traditional herb books. Thus far, ragweed and sagebrush have been covered, followed now by a close relative of goldenrod. Rabbitbrush is one of the most familiar plants of the California Mohave Desert and covers tens of thousands of square miles of arid, gravelly plain and mesa and mountain slopes throughout much of the great intramontane basin of Nevada and Utah. This rather low, roundish bush is often heavily scented, attracting large numbers of bees to its usually white or gray felted stems lacking adequate foliage but adorned with clusters of yellow flowers.

In their *Rubber Plant Survey of Western North America* (published by the University of California Press in 1919), Hall and Goodspeed related an incredible discovery made by the Paiute Indians. Judge Davidson of Inyo County, California happened to see some of these Indians chewing some gum, which they told him came from thoroughly chewing the inner bark of rabbitbrush. A later lab analysis indicated the presence of rubber, which prompted the U.S. government to consider seriously it as a potential source of rubber during World War I. Rabbitbrush has been extensively employed by various western Indian tribes for a number of health problems as the following list indicates:

Flower infusion drunk or smoke from burning plant inhaled for colds (Cheyenne).

Flower infusion for coughs (Cheyenne).

Leaves and stems infusion as a skin wash for smallpox (Cheyenne).

Flower infusion for tuberculosis (Cheyenne).

Twig infusion for chest pains and bronchitis (Coahuilla).

Poultice of mashed leaves and stems for blisters (Klamath).

Lotion of leaves for headaches (Navaho).

Root decoction for menstrual pain (Navaho).

Root decoction for colds and flus (Navaho).

Salve of branches and leaves for horses to keep annoying horseflies and pesky gnats away (Sanpoil).

Roots and tops decoction for bloody diarrhea (Shoshone).

Leaf infusion for stomach disorders (Shoshone).

Cirsium arvense (Canadian thistle). I deliberately bypassed *Cimicifuga racemosa* (Black cohosh) in preference to this. The latter has been treated extensively in many herbals, but this noxious weed has not. Ask any farmer in the United States what he thinks of this problematic weed and he is apt to turn the air somewhat blue with profanity. While understandably a curse to agriculturists, Canadian thistle has some valuable medical applications which deserve mention within these pages, since nothing much on it can be found elsewhere. The Mohegan used an infusion of the leaves as a mouthwash for yeast infections and cold sores and to drink for lung problems. The Montagnais likewise found a decoction of the entire plant helpful for consumption. The Ojibwa made a tea out of the entire plant and drank it cold for moving the bowels. The Gosiute in times past employed the plant for healing cuts and sores. The Southeast Houma made an infusion of the leaves and root in whiskey to clear mucus from the lungs and the back of the throat. The Navaho-Ramah sometimes rely upon a cold infusion of the root as a wash for eye diseases afflicting humans or livestock. The Arizona Zuni employ, from time to time, the entire plant as an infusion for treating syphilis; this is accomplished by increasing perspiration, urination, and bowel movements of the patient. Their neighbors the Hopi make a decoction of the entire plant to wash the skin in cases of severe itching or to gargle to relieve a tickling throat. Clearly then, this noxious plant from which tumble-weeds eventually originate has some practical value in health care maintenance, although one might have a mighty hard time convincing your average farmer of that.

Clematis ligusticifolia (Clematis or Western virgin's bower). This again is one of those entries which you will not find in most herbals. An exception would be Michael Moore's *Medicinal Plants of the Mountain West* in which he recommends a tablespoon of the plant in a pint of water as a tea for excruciating migraines, such as are common in those withdrawing from alcohol or drugs. Throughout much of the West and Southwest clematis may be found. You really do not have to be much of a botanist to recognize it if you happen upon it in midyear when the vine is setting seeds. Then the tousled seed clusters, each seed with its long curling plume of a tail, are like a myriad of silvery-haired, miniature Skye terriers, tumbling about over shrubs and clambering into trees. In fact it is the most common vine in the mountainous regions out West and in the Southwest. Clematis has opposite leaves that are formed by three to seven stemmed leaflets and underlying tendrils for grasping. One kind of flower has small cream-colored blossoms in dense clusters; the other has single downturned four-petaled flowers which are showy and bluish blue-red to purple in color.

Some of the California tribes scraped the end of a clematis root and then applied it to the nostrils of their horses, promptly reviving the tired animals. The braves would also chew some of the peppery leaves and stems for curing sore throat and colds. The Arizona Hopis enjoyed making a tea of the hairy seed clusters in the fall and then rubbing it into their scalps to induce luxuriant hair growth. I am informed by several reliable witnesses (a Baptist missionary couple and an Anglo trader) that such really works in some cases of beginning baldness. A lotion has also been made of the plant for backache, sore leg and arm muscles, and sore feet. The plant also makes a good wash for dandruff, scabs, and eczema. The Shoshone made a nice poultice of the mashed, moistened seeds for treating severe burns. The Navaho-Ramah will sometimes scrape a piece of the root and then hold it up to the nose to relieve the misery of head congestion.

Cucurbita maxima and *C. pepo* (Squash and pumpkin). Many of the Southwestern Indian tribes such as the Hopi, Navaho, Havasupai, Papago, Pima, Apache, and Yuma grow plenty of squashes and pumpkins. In fact, both are some of their favorite foods, besides having medical applications. The Oklahoma Cherokee sometimes eat the oven-browned seeds to stop bedwetting and to expel intestinal worms. They also make a nice tea out of the browned seeds for kidney stones and scalding urine. (All of the foregoing applications are mainly for pumpkin seeds). The Navaho make a tea of pumpkin leaves for indigestion and heartburn. The Pima grind pumpkin seeds to a paste for cleansing and softening rough, dirty skin. The Zuni find that a poultice of pumpkin seeds and blossoms is good for cactus scratches. The Cheyenne will sometimes make an infusion of squash rind for relieving arthritis, increasing urination, and promoting bowel movements. They also use the same infusion for venereal disease, heart problems, and earaches.

I like the way the White Mountain Apache in southern Arizona fix their pumpkin. They cut the pumpkin into pieces and boil it until soft, after which they peel and mash it. Then they salt to taste and mix in about three tablespoons of yellow cornmeal for every cup of pumpkin. The Pueblo Indians of New Mexico make a delicious squash dish by cutting the kernels off three ears of corn, slicing an onion, and mincing a garlic clove. They add this to a little water in a covered pan and cooked on low heat for five minutes, after which some sliced summer squash is added and cooked another ten minutes. Then two sliced tomatoes are added and cooked until warm but not long enough to become mushy. A small handful of coarsely shredded yellow Monterey jack or crumbled white goat cheese is added. Everything is then lightly stirred in the pot before serving. The Arizona Havasupai remove the seeds from pumpkins and dry them in the sun on flat cookie sheets. They then transfer the seeds to a large wooden bowl and pour just enough corn oil over them to lightly coat them. Everything is then thoroughly stirred together and a pinch of salt added for taste. These oiled seeds are then put back on the same cookie sheets and slowly cooked in a 250-degree Fahrenheit oven until they start turning brown. Occasionally, they are stirred during the roasting process so that all sides are baked.

Echinacea angustifolia (Echinacea). This is one of the most popular herbs in both American as well as European herbal products. A number of scientific papers have been published in different European journals indicated its strong immune-stimulating properties, including increasing the production of white blood cells to help fight infection better. However, there is another side to echinacea to which none of the popular herbals refer. Melvin R. Gilmore was born in 1868 in Nebraska and grew up around Plains Indian tribes. Later in life he worked for the Museum of the American Indian (Heye Foundation) in New York City and eventually became curator of ethnology at the Museum of Anthropology of the University of Michigan. In 1919 the 35th *Annual Report of the Bureau of American Ethnology* dealt with his fascinating study, *Uses of Plants by the Indians of the Missouri River Region.* Much of the valuable data obtained for this scarce, long out-of-print work, came from Native Americans themselves—the daughters of Chief Iron Eye of the Omaha nation, Penishka of the Ponca tribe, Fast Horse, Joseph Horncloud, Otto Chief Eagle, Mr. and Mrs. Knife-Chief of the Pawnee nation, and so forth. What they and others revealed to him about the heat-enduring properties of echinacea are well worth sharing here in his own words.

"Echinacea seems to have been used as a remedy for more ailments than any other plant. It was employed in the smoke treatment for headache in persons and distemper in horses. It was used also as a remedy for toothache, a piece being kept on the painful tooth until there was relief, and for enlarged glands, as in mumps. It was said that jugglers (a special type of Indian shaman) bathed their hands and arms in the juice of this plant so that they could take out a piece of meat from a boiling kettle with the bare hand without suffering pain, to the wonderment of onlookers. A Winnebago said he had often used the plant to make his mouth insensible to heat, so that for show he could take a live coal into his mouth. Burns were bathed with the juice to give relief from the pain, and the plant was used in the steam bath to render the great heat endurable."

Back a few years ago when firewalking was very popular as a test of one's own endurance and personal ability to put mind over physical matter, I mentioned this Native American use of echinacea to someone in southern California after a lecture. The individual decided to give it a try for himself and obtained sufficient fresh echinacea for this purpose. While he never actually walked on coals to try this out, he did rub enough of the crushed plant on his hands so that he could juggle some hot, live coals in midair without ever burning himself!

Equisetum arvense (Horsetail or shavegrass). The Cherokee used an infusion of the stems and leaves for strengthening weak kidneys, while the Cheyenne gave the same infusion to their horses for coughs. The Iroquois found it to be a wonderful analgesic for rheumatism, aching joints, lower backache, headaches, and pain in general. The raw stems were sometimes chewed by their babies to relieve the pains of teething. The Potawatomi liked to drink an infusion of the entire plant to cure lumbago. The Costanoan and Cowlitz tribes made decoctions of the stalks to wash scalps and hair infested with vermin such as lice. Braves of the Northwest-Plateau Quileute who loved to swim would sometimes rub the crushed plant over their entire bodies to make them feel stronger, especially so with the arms and thighs. The Northwest Thompson Indians burned stalks of horsetail, then mixed the resulting plant ash with bear grease to apply on severe burns with good success. The Menominee of the Northeastern United States made a poultice of the rough leaves and stems to staunch the bleeding from cuts and open wounds.

The chief mineral which makes horsetail work so well is silicon. According to the ninth edition of V. E. Tyler's *Pharmacognosy*, the stems contain large amounts (5-8%) of silica and silicic acids, thereby explaining its historical use in much of medieval Europe as an effective scrubber for pots and pans. Recent research has determined that silicon is present in the body as a silanolate (an ether derivative of silicic acid) and is an essential component of certain mucopolysaccharides (most notably hyaluronic acid, chondroiton 4-sulfate, dermatan sulfate, and heparan sulfate). These particular mucopolysaccharide substances are principal constituents of connective tissues and skin. Hence, silicon functions as a biological cross-linking agent contributing to the architecture and resilience of connective tissues, such as those found in shoulder, elbow, wrist, hip, knee, and ankle joints. So said the October 1978 *American Journal of Clinical Nutrition*.

Some years ago I helped to develop an excellent skin-bone-muscle-cartilage formula based in part on Native American use of horsetail for many of these same things. In time it became very popular with many chiropractors and naturopathic doctors in the U.S. and Canada, who work with many patients suffering from skin rashes, weak or fractured bones, atrophied muscles, and stiff, sore joints. Called Q34, this herbal formula may be obtained from its Canadian manufacturer, Quest

Vitamin Supplies Ltd. (1781 West 75th Avenue, Vancouver, B.C. V6P 6P2, (604) 261-0611). About two capsules daily with meals is recommended.

Fraxinus americana (White ash). In consulting half a dozen well known herbal works by prominent American herbalists, I could only find a small reference to white ash in Jethro Kloss' *Back to Eden*, where he said that it was excellent for reducing. I know this to be true for I have long recommended a tea to be made of the inner bark and drunk by obese subjects so they could become thinner. Two heaping tablespoons of the coarsely cut, dried inner bark is first simmered on low heat for five minutes in one pint of boiling water and then removed from the fire and steeped another 30 minutes. An obese person should drink one cup of the cold tea twice daily in between meals. The slimming results are absolutely unbelievable and have to be actually experienced in order to fully believe! The Cherokee used the inner bark as a liver and stomach tonic. The Delaware-Oklahoma made a bark decoction for getting rid of excess bile in the intestinal tract. The Iroquois mixed in some of the crudely powdered bark with feed as a laxative for their horses.

Galium aparine (Goose grass or bedstraw). The Cherokee made an infusion for constipation. The Chippewa used a cold infusion of the stems as a lotion for dermatological problems. The Iroquois found that an infusion of the plant was good for poison ivy and general itching. The Micmac made a tea of the stems to stop internal hermorrhaging. The Ojibwa employed an infusion of the entire plant for kidney stones and the inability to urinate. The Penobscot used an infusion of the entire plant for venereal disease. The Choctaw made a tea out of the whole plant for curing measles. The Fox Indians made an infusion of the whole plant for treating raging fevers and extreme chills. The Navaho-Ramah made an infusion of the plant and used it as an external lotion for those headaches which accompany colds and flus. In combination with licorice root, bedstraw has been used by both the Southeast Cherokee and the Northwest Kwakiutl as an infusion for chest pains and bronchitis. The Iroquois have made a decoction of the plant and then soaked cloth material in it to poultice swollen testicles or ruptures. In fact, one of the best rupture medicines I ever ran across was made by an old Cheyenne Indian in the eastern part of Wyoming. Henry Red Cloud brewed together equal parts of bedstraw, horsetail, and marshmallow root (one large handful of each) in one and a half quarts of mineral water (he preferred Perrier). After initially bringing everything to a boil, he would then reduce the heat considerably and allow everything to steep, covered with a lid, for about an hour or until the contents had been reduced to about half. Then he would strain it several times into a small fruit jar and refrigerate until needed. He would administer about four cups of this daily to those bothered with hernias. Out of some 17 people who had tried this stuff, 11 of them informed me that his brew had helped to heal their ruptures.

Geranium maculatum (Cranesbill or wild alum). It was some of the Indian uses for this particular herb that eventually led me to include it in a special formula for canker sores and hemorrhoids. The Chippewa found it to be an excellent antidiarrheal on account of its strong astringent properties. They also washed children's mouths with a decoction of it to cure fungal infection or thrush. The Fox Indians made an infusion of the root to treat neuralgia of the face and toothaches. The Fox also made a poultice of the smashed root and bound it to the anus by means of leather tongs to cause hemorrhoids to disappear. The Fox made an infusion of the root as a mouth rinse to ease pain in teeth and gums. The Iroquois made a poultice of either powdered or chewed roots to apply to the unhealed navels of newborns. The Iroquois also employed decoctions of the root in several different ways to treat mouth sores, trench mouth, and cankers. Q32 is the unique formula that I created for Quest Vitamins Ltd. of Vancouver, British Columbia, based on these Native American uses. It can be ordered directly from them (1781 West 75th Avenue, V6P 6P2 (604) 261-0611).

Hamamelis virginiana (Witch hazel). I shall spare the reader a litany of interesting Native American uses for this remarkable plant and instead focus on just one aspect of it. The Menominee made a strong decoction of the twigs which was then used as a lotion to be rubbed on the legs during sports events in order to keep them limber, and on sore back muscles to make them feel better. The Potawatomi employed the twigs in their sweat baths to create a steam that brought relief to sore muscles. When I go to a local health spa here in Salt Lake City to work out, I generally rub my body with Pierce's brand Tincture of Witch Hazel before entering the sauna. I can personally testify to just how great it makes the muscles feel!

Helianthus annuus (Sunflower). Poultice of crushed plant parts on snake bites (Apache); flower infusion for chest pains (Dakota); powdered seeds made into energy cakes and taken on war parties to overcome fatigue with (Gros Ventres); poultice of boiled seeds and plant parts as an application for spider bites (Hopi); warm decoction of root to soak tired feet in or else warm poultice on the lower back to relieve aches and pains (Paiute); leaf decoction for high body temperatures (Pima); powdered leaves mixed with lard or grease for leg ulcers and skin sores (Thompson Indians). Florida Seminoles once used the dried leaves in place of tobacco in rolled cigars, the flavor said to resemble mild Spanish tobacco to some extent.

Hens go crazy over sunflower seeds and will usually lay two or three extra eggs when it is fed to them, while honey bees often swarm to these giant yellow flowers on account of their deliciously sweet nectar.

Pimas and Maricopas of the Salt River Reservation in Arizona once made a tasty chewing gum by pounding the inner pulp of sunflower stalks. A darned good coffee can be made from the seeds. Simply brown the empty hulls in a heavy cast-iron skillet, making sure they do not burn. Then grind them to a fine powder. For every cup of brew, steep one and a half teaspoons of ground hulls to a cup of boiling water for about five minutes. The Zunis make an interesting pudding. With a sharp paring knife scrape off enough kernels from immature corn cobs to yield about a cup; then put them through a food grinder retaining all of the juicy matter. Then put it into a pot with a cup of finely ground raw or roasted shelled sunflower seeds and a cup of finely chopped zucchini or yellow crookneck squash. Add two cups of water and a pinch of salt; cover and simmer an hour, stirring every so often. Remove the cover for the last 10 minutes so the mixture can thicken. It tastes great served warm or cold.

Humulus lupulus (Hops). Infusion of the fruit (scaly, conelike things growing from the female flowers) taken for kidney stones, bladder inflammation, breast and womb problems, intestinal pains, fevers, nervous tension, influenza, cold, coughing, and pneumonia (Cherokee, Dakota, Mohegan, Navaho-Ramah, and Shinnecock). Poultices of heated herb in muslin bag applied to relieve earache and toothache (Delaware-Oklahoma) and of soaked hops to reduce swellings and bruises (Great Basin Round Valley Indians).

Hydrastis canadensis (Goldenseal root). A very popular cancer remedy among the Cherokee nation and an infusion of the powdered root for liver disturbances among the Iroquois. The latter have also made a crude fluid extract of the root in whiskey for heart problems or overall fatigue. Both tribes have also employed it often in numerous other infectious ailments with good success. But like cayenne pepper, garlic, and onion, goldenseal root may cause adverse reactions in those suffering from low blood sugar on account of their strong hypoglycemic properties.

Juglas cinera (Butternut). The Cherokee made infusions from the inner bark to check diarrhea and promote bowel movements. The Iroquois drank a decoction of the bark for painful urination and intestinal parasites, as well as liver disturbances. Both the Menominee and the Potawatomi made a syrup from the bark sap as a useful "physic" when constipation prevailed. I helped to develop one of the gentlest and most effective intestinal cleansers ever marketed using a lot of butternut rootbark. I found that it minimized the cramping caused by stronger laxatives such as cascara sagrada and rhubarb root. And Formula Q12 is not habit-forming as so many laxatives are. It can be obtained from: Quest Vitamin Supplies Ltd., 1781 West 75th Avenue, Vancouver, B.C. CANADA V6P 6P2 (604) 261-0611.

Juniperus communis (Juniper). This evergreen shrub prefers dry, rocky soil as a rule and ranges from the Arctic Circle on the north to central Mexico on the south. Because of its widespread abundance and extreme popularity among many early Native American tribes, ample space is devoted to it here as was the case with yarrow. Dan Moerman devotes eight full pages in his book just to this herb alone, which indicates the importance it has played in American Indian medicine.

Scorched twigs are rubbed on the body to stop convulsions (Apache). Infusion of leaves for coughs and colds (Apache). Infusion of leaves for pregnant women to relax uterine muscles prior to childbirth (Apache). Decoction of roots, leaves, branches, and bark for stomach pain (Bella Coola). Infusion of juniper boughs taken internally or used externally as a steam bath for colds (Cheyenne). Infusion of leaves for coughs and tickling in the throat (Cheyenne). Decoction of twigs and leaves for asthma and bronchitis (Chippewa). Infusion of twigs, leaves, and berries used as a disinfectant for external wounds (Cree). Decoction for extreme fevers and chills caused by flu (Iroquois). Decoctions made of the stems for washing hair, of the gum to heal wounds and open sores, and of the cones to disinfect skin ulcers (Micmac). Infusion of the twigs as an eye wash for pollen or dust allergies (Okanagan). Juniper berries consumed for kidney infection and kidney stones (Okanagan). Infusion of dried berries for purifying blood and for lumbago (Paiute). Cold decoction of twigs taken for venereal disease (Paiute). Small limbs boiled and the fumes inhaled to relieve migraines and tight congestion in the chest (S. Carrier Indians). Decoction of twigs for stomach problems (Thompson Indians). Heated twigs rubbed on measles eruptions to relieve itching (Shoshone). Poultice of leafy twigs for sprains or bruises (Tewa). Poultice of twigs to draw out pus from boils or slivers (Paiute).

Larrea divaricata (Chaparral). This foul-smelling, tangle-branched evergreen shrub is common to the West and Southwest. It stands erect about two to feet tall, has brittle stems and small, resinous leaves with olive-green branches that emit a tarry odor. Chaparral will generally grow where nothing else grows and because of the nordihy-droguaiaretic acid (NDGA) secreted into the soil by its root system, no other plant including other chaparral will grow in its presence for a perimeter of several feet!

In the January 1959 *Arizona Highways*, environmentalist author, Doug Rigby said chaparral was like a corner drugstore for desert dwellers because of its multitude of functions. The California Kawaiisu tribe made a decoction of the leaves to heal collar sores on their plow horses and mules, as well as making a poultice of heated leaves to relieve aching limbs. The Nevada Paiute first made a decoction of the leaves, then mixed in some badger oil to make a nice salve for severe burns. They also made an infusion of the leaves for colds and as a skin wash for chicken pox. The Shoshone used a decoction of leaves for veneral disease. The Coahuilla Indians gave the shrub to their horses to treat distemper and runny nose, while the Mahuna tribe made an infusion of the plant for dandruff and body odor. The Papago often chewed the leaves and then laid them on insect bites, snake bites, and scorpion stings as a poultice to help draw out these venomous poisons. The Pima often made a decoction of the branches for upset stomach, gas pains, dysentery, and abdominal cramps, as well as for high fevers, sore throat, and influenza. The Pima would sometimes also hold an infusion of the plant in their mouths to relieve toothaches. The Chiricahua Apache used to fashion special "stay well" amulets from chaparral and hang these around the necks of their children so they would not get sick.

The most efficacious and well-documented use for chaparral has been in the treatment of cancer. And since everyone loves a good story, especially if it is true, then the case history of one former Mesa, Arizona resident may be worth relating. I spent several years in tracking down those who knew Mr. Ernest Farr in order to make this narrative as complete as I could. For instance, Helen Schlie, who owned a bookstore in Mesa, told me in an April 18, 1980 interview that she often saw Mr. Farr in the Mormon Temple there, usually acting in the capacity of a witness to the ceremonial sealings which frequently go on inside. At that time she noticed several half-dollar sized spots had started to evolve on the side of his face and neck. An affidavit supplied to me by a nearby Tempe resident, Kay Windes, who also knew him, related in Mr. Farr's own handwritten words what happened next:

"I had a black spot on my right cheek for about 15 years, but it never bothered me. About two and a half years ago it started to get sore. I went to my local doctor and he operated twice. Each time it became worse and a lump developed under my right chin. He wanted to cut my juggler vein in some manner as there was some interference. I didn't want to undergo another operation, but my daughter in Salt Lake City, Melissa Beckstead and Maybeth Reimann prevailed upon me to go to SLC and see Dr. Cowan at the University Hospital. He wasn't there, so a Dr. Smart took care of me instead.

"About 4 or 5 days before leaving Mesa, I started to take tea made out of creosote leaves. I would take a large tablespoon of leaves and pour hot water on it. I knew about chaparral being used by the Indians so I just decided to use it. I was taking 3 cups of 8 oz. each per day when Dr. Smart operated. When he finished he told my daughter that it was melanoma cancer and that he didn't think I would last too long as it was very active. I came back to Mesa and continued taking the chaparral tea. After I had been home about 2-4 months my daughter called from Salt Lake City and said she feared for me, expecting me to be in very bad condition. But I told her my face was all healed up and I was feeling 100% better. She was so elated. Then Dr. Smart sent for me and my face has been healed ever since. In the meantime I was still taking 3 cups a day, but today I only take 1 cup every other day. I've never had kidney trouble with it now or any toxic reaction. This is my experience and I make this affidavit on November 15, 1969.

Ernest Farr
418 So. 2nd St., Mesa."

The November 1970 *Rocky Mountain Medical Journal* carried a synopsis of Farr's interesting case. It reported that when the melanoma expanded in size for a fourth time (after having been surgically removed on three previous occasions), the patient had become weak and pale and lost considerable weight. Sometime in the month of November, 1967, the journal went on to say, the patient started taking 'Chaparral Tea,' an old Indian remedy. By February, 1968, the medical report noted, the facial lesion had decreased to the size of a dime. The neck mass had disappeared, he looked better, and had begun to gain weight and strength. He looked greatly improved in color and general health."

A major Utah newspaper, the *Salt Lake Tribune* neatly summarized Farr's recovery this way in its January 12, 1969, early morning edition: An 87 year-old man from Arizona with extensive malignant melanoma in his face and neck tried chaparral, which he had heard about from the Indians. Doctors were amazed that his cancer virtually disappeared. A tumor mass the size of a lemon had shrunk to the size of a matchhead!

This old Indian herb just happens to be one of the main ingredients in a fantastic tea for staying fit and trim. Called "Mon Cheri Special Dieter's Tea," it contains, besides chaparral, cassia, marshmallow, bearberry, ginseng, feverfew, moon daisy, papaya, citrus peel, and exotic spices. Not only does it help get rid of unwanted pounds, but it also gently cleanses the system. Some of these aforementioned herbs in it were likewise used by early Native Americans to help keep the body well. This tea is unique in that it "rinses" body tissue of toxic chemicals and putrid matter. It is fair to say that "Mon Cheri Special Dieter's Tea" was prepared somewhat in keeping with the Native American philosophy towards natural health. The tea may be obtained by contacting: Spirit of Sausalito Marketing, 1001 Bridgeway Blvd. #888, Sausalito, CA 94965.

Lobelia inflata (Lobelia). Dried plant smoked to break nicotine habit; plant infusion taken to break smoking and whiskey drinking habits (Cherokee and Iroquois).

Marrubium vulgare (Horehound). Cough syrup made by simmering herb in double amount of water for an hour, then add sugar (Cherokee). Crushed leaves mixed with bear grease for salve (Costanoan). Plant decoction for stomachache and influenza (Navaho-Ramah). Root decoction used before and after childbirth (Navaho-Ramah). Leaf decoction for diarrhea (Round Valley Indians).

Melissa officinalis (Lemon balm). Used for old colds, typhus fevers, and chills (Cherokee). Decoction of the plant for intestinal flu (Costanoan). Infusion extracts of lemon balm have protected embryonated eggs when injected before lethal challenges with Newcastle disease, or mumps, and herpes simplex viruses. However, when gelatin was injected into the eggs after lemon balm extract, it totally destroy the antiviral activity of the herb. This is according to a report published in the *Annals of the New York Academy of Sciences* (130:474-82, 1965). What this scientific study suggests then are two things: (1) Native Americans understood what plants were good for infections; and (2) a tea made of this herb is better for you than the powdered material taken in gelatin capsules.

Mentha arvensis (Wild or field mint). During a brief season of doing some anthropological work among the Crow Indians in eastern Montana in the mid-1970s, I had the good fortune of meeting Joy Yellowtail Toineeta, who had compiled a paper for her graduate class on Crow Food and Medicine at Montana State University in Bozeman. She kindly provided me with an extra copy of her study with permission to use it as I wished. The Crow name for field mint is "Shu-shu-ah," meaning "spit, spit." This had reference to the strong biting taste of this particular herb. She said that some of the older women of her tribe had occasionally employed it as an abortifacent during the very early months of unwanted pregnancies. This is interesting in light of an article on this herb's postcoital antifertility effect which appeared in the November 1981 medical journal *Contraception*. It seems that when fractions of field mint were subcutaneously given to pregnant rats it caused definite interruptions in their pregnancies by increasing uterine activity to the point that some undeveloped fetuses were expelled.

Mentha piperita (Peppermint). The Cherokee Indians employed this herb to dispel flatulence and remove colic pains and for affections of stomach and bowels. This is interesting to consider in light of the fact that peppermint oil has been demonstrated to relieve the symptoms of irritable bowel syndrome in six males and 23 female patients according to the November-December 1984 issue of the *British Journal of Clinical Practice*. Apparently these Indians knew something about the hidden virtues of peppermint long before the white man ever discovered some of them. Both the Cherokee and Iroquois nations made infusions of the entire plant for colds and fevers, while the Menominee took the warm infusion and applied hot poultices upon the chest for pneumonia. Volume 124 (pp. 874-78) of the *Proceedings of the Society for Experimental Biology and Medicine* mentioned that peppermint extracts had been found to suppress the activity of influenza A, mumps, and herpes simplex viruses—which just goes to show again how smart the Native Americans have been with regard to their enormous understanding of the many marvelous medical virtues in plants.

Nepeta cataria (Catnip). Leaf infusions for hysterics, worms, stomachache, fever, tonic for infants (when combined with peach pits), coughs, colds, chills, sore throats, indigestion caused by eating rich foods, headaches, restlessness, insomnia, and diarrhea (Cherokee, Delaware-Oklahoma, Iroquois).

Nicotiana tabacum (Tobacco). The Lord told the Prophet Joseph Smith in a revelation found in the 89th Section of one of the Mormon scriptures called the *Doctrine and Covenants*, "Tobacco is not for the body, neither for the belly and is not good for man, but is an herb for bruises and all sick cattle, to be used with judgment and skill." Native Americans, while having smoked tobacco a lot for medicinal and ceremonial reasons, have also employed it for some of the same things suggested by the Lord. Leaf poultice and leaf juice to heal castration cuts on a young race horse (Navaho-Ramah). Poultice of crushed leaves applied to eczema or other skin afflictions (Paiute). Poultice of leaves applied to cuts (Shoshone). Poultice of leaves mixed with oil and soot applied to neck and chest for nagging cough

(Tewa). Poultice applied to insect bites to stop the pain and itching (Kawaiisu). Poultice of leaves applied to inflamed throat glands (Mahuna). An unusual application from the Iroquois nation: plant decoction taken to cure temporary insanity caused by excessive masturbation! Poultice of leaves used for boils (Cherokee). Juice from crushed leaves and plant applied to snake bite (Cherokee). Leaves used to stop bleeding (Micmac). A few Mormons have found tobacco to be very useful in allaying stress injuries to the nerves, despite their religion's strong prohibition against such a thing. Apostle Willard Richards frequently smoked a pipe for peace of mind. And church president John Taylor loved to smoke an expensive Cuban cigar after a good meal, according to an early Jewish friend of his in the book, *Reminiscense of Alexander Topanz*. The extraordinary case of Apostle James E. Talmage being commanded by the first president of the LDS church to take up moderate smoking of cigars for his health's sake has already been previously mentioned in this book. Following the examples of these good men, I too have resorted to cigars from time to time to help me relax more, even though I detest the smell of most tobacco products.

Phytolacca americana (Pokeroot). Root poultice for skin ulcers; root and leaf salve for cold sores (Cherokee). Stem decoction for chest colds; root poultice for bruises and raw berries rubbed on skin lumps (Iroquois). Root decoction as poultice to sprains, bruises, and swollen joints (Iroquois). Root poultice for neuralgia; leaf poultice for skin disease or to remove pimples and blackheads (Mahuna). Scientists have confirmed much of what early Native Americans have previously known about this wonderful plant. Extracts of pokeroot leaves "strongly inhibited" the growth of A2/Hong Kong/1/68 (H3N2) strain of virus (*Journal of General Virology* 22:225-32, 1974). A pokeroot antiviral protein (PAP) is effective against polio virus replication in the HeLa cells (*Annals of the New York Academy of Sciences* 284:431, 1977). PAP inhibited multiplication of herpes simplex virus by 50 percent in another study (*Antimicrobial Agents and Chemotherapy* 17:1032, June 1980). PAP efficiently killed acute lymphoblastic leukemia cells, reported *Science* for January 6, 1984.

Pinus glabra (Spruce pine). Scurvy is a disease with these characteristics: physical exhaustion, debility, anemia, edema of the dependent parts, a spongy condition with possible ulceration of the gums, and bleeding into the skin and from the mucous membranes such as the nose or lungs. The disease is due to a monotonous diet of salt meats and a lack of fruits, vegetables and herbs rich in Vitamin C. Virgil Vogel points out in his book on *American Indian Medicine* that Native Americans in both the U.S. and Canada understood very well how to prevent or cure scurvy. August C. Mahr, writing in the Winter 1955 issue of *Ethnohistory*, cited the 17th century explorer John Josselyn who wrote of the New England Indian tribes that "the tops of Spruce-boughs, boiled in bear (beer) and drunk, is assuredly one of the best remedies for the scurvy; restoring the infected party in a short time." Noteworthy also is the "spruce beer" used by Captain Cook on his 1776-1780 sea voyage and the spruce tea drunk by California gold miners in 1849 to prevent coming down with scurvy. From time to time when I have worked on my ranch in the wilderness of southern Utah, I have occasionally boiled up some spruce pine needles and taken sips of the bitter liquid for its rich Vitamin C content. Granted that it is not sweet orange juice by any means, but it is a good way to beat the cold or flu when no vitamin supplements or other Vitamin C-rich foods are readily available!

Plantago major (Plantain). Poultices of the leaves have been used for stings, burns, bruises, sprains, scalds, and snake bites; thorns and splinters to draw out the poisons therefrom (Mohegan, Ojibwa, Ponca). An infusion of the leaves has been used for bowel troubles (Fox).

Dr. Serge Duckett of the Jefferson Medical College in Philadelphia contributed a short piece about plantain's advantage in treating poison ivy rash in the September 4, 1980 *New England Journal of Medicine.* The folk remedy was first suggested to him by a Georgetown, Maryland resident, Mr. Peter Monk, who was well acquainted with Dr. Duckett's long history of recurring poison ivy dermatitis. Besides himself, some ten other family members, relatives, and close friends who were just as sensitive to poison ivy as he was, were all treated with plantain in the summer of 1980. Everyone rubbed the affected parts of their skin with freshly crushed plantain leaves; in some cases up to four times if necessary. As Dr. Duckett himself testified, the itching always stopped and the dermatitis did not spread to other parts of the body! This shows the Indian logic behind the use of plantain for rashes and itching.

Another medical report concerning powdered plantain seeds for treating stubborn constipation appeared in the Italian medical journal *Clinica Terapeutica* (86:433-39) in 1978. Some 40 geriatric patients (26 women and 14 men) with an average age of 72 1/2 years underwent a ten day treatment for constipation with a powder extracted from blond plantain seeds. This non-assimilable powder, capable of absorbing water and therefore increasing in volume, softened the feces, and stimulated peristalsis in all patients. This particular preparation was especially helpful in treating painful defecation, solid feces, abdominal swelling due to intestinal gas, flatulence, and disturbances of intestinal transit. Here again we find medical justification for an old Fox Indian remedy for bowel problems. These and other previously cited cases are just some of the many examples in which certain Native American remedies can be medically verified.

Populus balsamifera (Poplar). The Micmac Indians often employed the buds and other parts of the plant as a salve for sores, especially cankersores. The Ojibwa medicine men preferred to cook poplar buds in animal grease then rub some in the nostrils and around the corners of the mouth to treat cold sores. The Potawatomi nation, on the other hand, simmered young poplar buds in melted tallow to make an effective ointment for venereal sores and eczema.

Soviet doctors have clinically duplicated the healing success of these same Indian remedies in their own hospitals. An article entitled "The Effect of Birch Bud Tincture on Purulent Wounds" appeared in the November 1979 Soviet medical journal *Vestnik Khirurgii*. I hired a Russian translator for one day at a cost of several hundred dollars to translate this highly interesting article for me into English. This particular study was carried out at the I. P. Pavlov Medical Institute in Riazan, USSR. A 20 percent birch bud tincture was employed in treating 108 patients (70 women and 38 men) for a variety of either superficial, deep or cavitary wounds. Treatment consisted of soaking tampons in the birch bud tincture and then applying them directly to the surface of the skin. Some patients had bedsores on their buttocks and thighs; others had infections following appendectomies; a few had abscesses following surgeries for stomach cancer and so forth. Well over 60 percent of the patients had some type of monoinfection (i.e., pathogenic staphylococcus, *Bacillus pynocyaneus*, *E. coli*, etc.). The most stubborn viral strain to resist all known antibiotics was *B. pynocyaneus*. Before treatment began all patients had high leukocyte counts (from 10-28,000) and elevated temperatures. Once the application of tincture began, swelling and redness disappeared in less than a week, wounds generally cleared up in less than two weeks, and temperatures and leukocyte counts became normal and all wounds were cured in less than three weeks.

Prunus virginiana (Chokecherry). Joy Yellowtail Toineeta, a Crow Indian, gave me this recipe for chokecherry bark tea some years ago when I visited her on the Crow Reservation in Montana. Remove the top reddish brown bark from the chokecherry first of all. Next gather the green spongy layer underneath. Drop a handful of this into a quart of boiling water and continue boiling until the tea becomes a bright cherry red. This, she said, is what her people used for coughs, colds, chills, fevers, bloody diarrhea, phlegm in the lungs, hoarseness, sore throat, canker sores in the mouth, stomach cramps, internal bleeding, and as an external skin wash for measles, mumps, chicken pox, rash, eczema, and scalp dandruff.

Quercus species (Oak). The Neeshenams of Northeastern United States made poultices of powdered acorns and applied them to severe burns and scalds with remarkable success. Ishi, the last genuine Stone Age Yana Indian discovered near Oroville, California in the fall of 1911, told University of California anthropologist Thomas T. Waterman:

"White man puts good food in pot full of boiling water. Leaves a long time. Food cooks too fast, too long. Meat spoiled. Vegetables spoiled. The right way is to cook like acorn mush. Put cold water in basket. Place hot rocks in water till it bubbles, add acorn meal. It cooks *pukka-pukka*. Then it is done. Same way, make deer stew. Or rabbit stew. Cook *pukka-pukka*. Not too long. Meat firm, broth clear, vegetable good, not soft and coming apart."

People would be wiser and healthier if they followed Ishi's culinary advice. Ishi also informed Dr. Waterman that "if white man make tea of acorn (oak) tree bark, then soak feet, maybe not stink so bad!" I have recommended this to those with smelly feet and can say it really works great!

Rhamnus purshiana (Cascara sagrada). Used by the Green River, Karok, Klallam, Kwakiutl, Lummi, Makah, Quinault, Shuswap, Skagit, Squaxin, Swinomish, and Thompson Indians as a very effective laxative. In addition to this, the Squaxin made a poultice application of the chewed bark or else an infusion of the bark to put on or wash sores. Much information has appeared in the medical literature to support both remedies. As an example, the November-December 1982 issue of *Clinica Medica* (an Italian journal) reported on the success of cascara sagrada therapy in treating simple constipation in elderly patients. And the *Journal of Infectious Diseases* (119:593) in 1969 reported that cascara sagrada eliminates a lot of the harmful *E. coli* bacteria which frequently accumulate in the colon. An interesting sidelight to the Squaxin dermatological use for cascara appeared in the September 1980 issue of *Cosmetics and Toiletries*. It seems that Italian scientists have developed a nice sunscreen agent out of standard laxative herbs like aloe, senna, and cascara. The very components responsible for their bowel activations also just happen to shield the skin from harmful ultraviolet light rays as well.

Rubus allegheniensis (Blackberry). Infusion of root for diarrhea (Cherokee). Mashed berries with honey as a wash for sore throat and washed root chewed for coated tongue (both Cherokee). Decoction of roots and leaves taken to regulate urine flow (Cherokee). Infusion of roots taken by pregnant women threatened with miscarriage (Chippewa). Decoction of roots taken for coughs, colds, pneumonia and tuberculosis (Iroquois). Poultice of mashed roots applied to a newborn infant's sore navel immediately after birth (Iroquois).

Rubus idaeus (Raspberry). Strong infusion of leaves for pains right at childbirth; infusion for boils; root infusion for coughs; root decoction for bowel problems; root infusion during menstruation; smashed root poultice inside mouth to stop toothache with (all Cherokee). Infusion of root bark as a wash to get rid of cataracts in early stages; root and stem decoction for mumps and measles in young children (both Chippewa). Leaf decoction for painful, burning urination; leaf decoction for boils on necks; root decoction for regulating blood pressure; leaf decoction for sluggish liver; root decoction for gonorrhea (Iroquois).

Rumex crispus (Yellow dock). Root infusion for constipation; juice and root infusion as poultice and salve for a variety of skin problems; root infusion for dysentery; leaf infusion for sore throat; dried root infusion for bleeding in the lungs; poultice of pounded, dried roots for wounds and sores (Cherokee and Cheyenne). Poultice of moistened, dried, powdered root applied to cuts or for itching (Chippewa). Poultice of crushed green leaves applied to boils to draw out pus (Dakota). Root decoction for indigestion and inability to keep food down; root decoction for stomach flu; root and leaf poultice for reducing raging fevers and to relieve abdominal pains and cramps; plant decoction for hemorrhoids; leaf poultice or powdered root to stop bleeding; plant decoction for kidney problems; strong root decoction to induce pregnancy (all Iroquois). Cold leaf infusion for mouth sores (Navaho-Ramah). Poultice of pulped root for arthritis and rheumatism; poultice of pulped root for severe burns or bruises and swellings; root decoction for stomach disorders and venereal disease; boiled seed decoction to stop diarrhea (all Paiute).

Salvia species (Sage). Various tribes chewed the green leaf for relieving intestinal gas (Costanoan), heated the leaves and applied to the ear for relieving earaches (Costanoan), made an infusion of the green leaves for cardiac arrest (Costanoan), made an infusion of the entire plant for bronchitis (Mahuna), made a syrup of the leaves mixed with some honey for asthma (Cherokee), made a general infusion of the entire plant for coughs, colds, and nervousness (Cherokee), made a tea of the leaves for intestinal parasites and worms (Mohegan), or made an infusion of the leaves for children with measles (Rappahannock).

Sanguinaria canadensis (Bloodroot). Ordinarily such an herb would not be included here because of its virtual scarcity in many parts of the country. However, one strange Iroquois use is such a scream in the humor department that it warrants inclusion here. Quoting directly from Dan Moerman's book *Medicinal Plants of Native America*, the reader is made acquainted with the decoction of dried roots for ulcers or for women that are ugly. However, the majority of Indian remedies are very effective and warrant more serious consideration than this rare exception to the rule. For instance, the Iroquois, Ojibwa, and Potawatomi all employed infusions of bloodroot for oral problems such as canker sores and sore throats. Imagine then my surprise in finding in the March 1984 issue of the *Journal of the American Dental Association* an article on the role of bloodroot in treating dental plaque, of all things! There it was big as life in black, bold headlines: "Sanguinarine, a new antiplaque agent!" Dental patients who were given mouthwash extracts of sanguinarine (a component of bloodroot) had less dental plaque and retained levels of sanguinarine in the saliva longer than in other patients who used standard rinse solutions like erythrosine or fluoescein.

Taraxacum officinale (Dandelion). Poultice of steamed or wilted leaves for skin ulcers (Aleut); root decoction for stomach pain (Bella Coola); herb infusion for nervousness, believe it or not (Cherokee); root chewed for toothache relief (Cherokee); root infusion to induce breastmilk in nursing mothers (Chippewa); root infusion for pulmonary disorders (Fox); root infusion for back pain (Iroquois); plant and root infusion used as skin wash for liver spots (Iroquois); root infusion for dark circles under the eyes (Iroquois); plant and root decoction to wash and soak injured testicles (Iroquois); decoction of young leaves for women experiencing menstrual cramps (Kiowa); root infusion for heartburn (Ojibwa); blossom infusion for menstrual cramps (Papago); cold plant infusion to expedite childbirth (Navaho-Ramah); poultice of pulverized leaves mixed with dough and applied to bad bruises, and poultice of pulverized fresh leaves alone to dress bone fractures (both Tewa).

Ulmus rubra (Slippery elm). Inner bark decoction for dysentery; inner bark as a poultice for sores, burns, and wounds; powdered inner bark for upset stomach and irritable bowel syndrome; powdered slippery elm capsules for coughs and colds (all Cherokee). Inner bark decoction as a poultice for infected and swollen tubercular glands (Iroquois). Inner bark poultice to draw purulent matter from wounds (Menominee). Root infusion drunk and used as a wash for bleeding cuts on the feet (Ojibwa).

Urtica dioica (Stinging nettle). Root decoction to wash hair (Chehalis). Nettle infusion for upset stomach (Cherokee) and for women about to enter childbirth (Cowlitz). Infusion of stalks rubbed on stiff joints and sore muscles for relief (Klallam). I have tried this myself on occasion and can tell you that it really does work! Plant juice rubbed into the scalp to keep from going bald (Kwakiutl). I have also tried this in the past and can tell you that my hairline continues to recede in spite of the treatment!

Many times Indian remedies work just fine and sometimes they do not work well or at all. The previous two examples are offered as evidence of this.

Poultice of leaves soaked in cold water and applied to heat rash (Ojibwa). Root infusion for fevers (Potawatomi). Decoction of the root bark to stop nosebleeds (Quinault).

Here I would like to insert a bit of fascinating information gleaned from an old Confederate herbal written by Francis P. Porcher, M.D. and published in Charleston in 1863—*Resources of the Southern Fields and Forest or A Medical Botany of the Confederate States*. Having read about the success of some European doctors in inserting stinging nettle decoction into the vaginas of women with excessive menstruations to effectively staunch their bleeding, Dr. Porcher decided to conduct an experiment with some live sheep to determine for himself if such a thing really worked or not. He cut the right throat arteries of two sheep, then immediately applied sponges soaked with *cold* nettle infusion. In one sheep, as he noted, "The bleeding ceased entirely!" Furthermore, he wrote, "The juice of the plant seemed to have some effect in coagulating fresh blood poured out into the hand." Of all the dozens and dozens of herbals I have ever read, past and present, none save this one alone ever carried such valuable information. I consider Dr. Porcher's book to be a veritable gold mine so far as sound, practical knowledge of herbs is concerned. I paid a small fortune some years ago to Goodspeed's Bookstore in Boston for my own rare, first edition and often resort to it when writing on the subject of herbs.

Verbascum thapsus (Mullein). Leaf decoction for colds (Atsugewi). Root decoction for children suffering from croup (Catawba). Leaf decoction mixed with some dark honey as an effective cough syrup; poultice of crushed fresh leaves put on neck and throat for mumps; leaves scalded in hot water and applied to swollen glands (all Cherokee). Plant decoction for babies with diaper rash; poultice of scalded leaves for earaches; leaf decoction for fevers; poultices of warm leaves put on face for mumps; leaf poultice to side of face for toothaches (all Iroquois). Cold infusion of leaves rubbed on bodies of hunters and horses to give them added strength, and low-burning leaf smoke to revive an unconscious person (Navaho-Ramah and Potawatomi).

While I was attending the 28th Annual Meeting of the American Society of Pharmacognosy during the week of July 19-22, 1987 at the University of Rhode Island in Kingston, I attended a poster session given by Shawna MacKinnon of the College of Pharmacy at Dalhousie University in Halifax, Nova Scotia. Ms. MacKinnon presented scientific evidence to show that water extracts of mullein samples collected in and around the greater Halifax area, manifested strong activity against *Myocobacterium tuberculosis*. This remarkable antitubercular discovery in mullein supports some of the Indian uses for related viral diseases.

Zea mays (Corn). This is one of the finest foods that Native Americans ever bequeathed to the rest of the world. It is truly a plant item originating here in the Western Hemisphere. A tea made of roasted corn kernels is an ideal Cherokee remedy for kidney stones. A decoction of dried corn cobs was used by the Mohegan to treat poison ivy rash. Cornsilk tea is an old Southwestern Indian remedy to stop bedwetting in young children.

The following Indian corn dumpling recipe is a modification of one formerly used by Bessie Kewenvoyouma, a nice middle-aged Hopi lady who resided in the village of Moenkopi, located in northern Arizona.

Mix 1 1/2 tablespoonfuls of powdered juniper berries in 2/3 cup of boiling water; then strain the water into a wooden bowl containing 1 1/8 cups of fine yellow cornmeal and a touch of salt. Mix together, adding more cornmeal if necessary to form a rather stiff batter. Next, roll the batter out into balls the size of large marbles, such as those which boys use to play with at recess time in elementary school. Then put these small marbles of dough into a heavy skillet and pour some boiling water over them. Boil for about 20 minutes before eating with beef or mutton stew or plain boiled eggs. Quite a delicious pastime snack, I must say!

O great Red Man of the past,
May thy legacy last forever,
That thy wisdom thus endowed
In our culture be allowed.
And may we seek that great Unknown
Which to thy race has been shown.

"Mighty Spirit so divine,
Let thy light in us too shine.
Illuminate the way we pray,
Guiding our steps day by day,
In soft moccasins of peace
So that from war we can cease!"

John Heinerman

CHAPTER SIX

A LOVE AFFAIR WITH NATURE

Between Two Worlds

One of the finest explanations I have ever read concerning the Native American approach towards Nature in general may be found in the book *Silent Courage—An Indian Story*. It is the autobiography of the son of a Navajo medicine man, who later converted to the Mormon faith and eventually was called into the ruling hierarchy of The Church of Jesus Christ of Latter-Day Saints, where he now serves in the First Quorum of Seventy. He is the only member of his race ever to hold such a high ecclesiastical position in any Christian denomination in America!

Elder George P. Lee begins by noting that for most people religion is just a once-a-week habit to be practiced generally on Sunday. But not so for the typical Native American, with whom "religion is everything." But the average person cannot really comprehend what the Native American believes, unless the word "religion" itself is entirely discarded. In its place, he prefers to use the term "spiritual fulfillment," which is only achieved as an Indian's understanding of the "land, animals, and people broadens" more in scope and depth.

He discounts the interpretation which some anthropologists have placed upon Indian beliefs in the past as God being in everything and everything being God. The more correct version would be to say that the Native American senses or feels the Great Spirit's "primary influence" emanating into all things. In other words, it is "the combining oneness of total nature," he writes. One should think of it more as a special kind of background influence pervading all manner of life with which each Native American communes in his or her own silent way. His people, the Navajos, he says try to remain in tune with nature as much as is humanly possible to do. Any kind of illness indicates disharmony with nature, and the more immediate goal then to be realized is to try and somehow become well in order to get back in tune with things.

Staying in constant tune with nature is essentially the epicenter of all Navajo religious beliefs and practices. Developing one's own individual sensitivity to things in as well as on and above the earth is the primary goal for all devout Navajos (and for that matter, all other Native Americans too). Acquiring this unique intuition for the thoughts and feelings of nature herself came much easier to him, he feels, by growing up Navajo but being educated in the white man's Mormon world through the LDS Church's Indian Placement program.

Like so many others before and after him, George P. Lee was undoubtedly fascinated with high-level spirituality to be found within the pages of the *Book of Mormon*. But being a full-blooded Native American, some of the more precious parts of this sacred history of God's dealings with men in the Western Hemisphere, took on added meaning with him.

Such as the remarks made about the Great Spirit by an ancient Indian (called Lamanite) chief in Alma 18:4, wherein King Lamoni confessed before all of his people:

"Now I know that it is the Great Spirit; and he has come down at this time to preserve your lives. . . . This is the Great Spirit of whom our fathers have spoken."

Further along in the writings of Alma, this Great Spirit is identified as a divine being (a resurrected man who became a God, if you will) who worked by divine power (infinite and intelligent matter which fills a resurrected man from head to foot, thereby making him a God of sorts).

Other ancient records kept by *Book of Mormon* peoples (which were mentioned in the first chapter of this book) have been translated by the gift and power of God. Some of them reveal that this Great Spirit in ancient times was conceived to be two basic things by the ancestors of the American Indians: (A) Intelligent energy without emotions; and (B) life forms such as humans, animals, and plants possessed of emotions acquired in mortal states and obvious intelligence bequeathed to them by this immensity of power.

The records go on to show that these self-moving particles of the Universe are individually contained units of physical energy and functioning thought. Or they are pure energy and pure intelligence, if you will. But in order for this aspect of the Great Spirit to progress through eternity, it must of necessity acquire emotions or feelings, which in its present raw, somewhat chaotic state, it apparently lacks.

This is where the second part of the Great Spirit enters the scene in the form of created beings or things like spirit men and women, spirit animals, and spirit plants. These created life forms eventually move from their spiritual realm (called the Pre-Existence) into a mortal setting complete with flesh, bone, blood, fur, leaves, and chlorophyll (depending, of course, on which life form you are referring to at the moment). To this may be added feathers, fins, scales, antennae, and other such apparatuses that make up birds, fishes, insects, and the like.

The idea behind all of this, suggest the ancient records, is for each of these self-moving particles of intelligent matter and energy to acquire for itself emotions of some kind in order to progress. Some particles making up the tabernacles of mortal men and women will obviously acquire the highest possible emotions of love, tenderness, mercy, and so forth. In gradual descent to other kingdoms, animals, birds, fishes, insects, plants and so forth will likewise acquire for their own self-moving particles those emotions conducive to their respective environments.

For instance, a robin delighting in pulling up a big, fat juicy worm and gulping it down will not have these particular emotions transferred to those particles comprising a man and woman engaged in the most intimate of sexual relations. Nor would theirs be transmitted vice versa to the robin either. The ancient records say that each group of self-moving particles assigned to whatever life forms automatically inherit those emotions peculiar to that life and no other!

Conversely, the ancient ancestors of today's Native American races, also believed in a retrogression of sorts for some of these same self-moving particles, in that they could acquire negative emotions which would eventually make these particles bad energy and bad intelligence. George Lucas (producer of the *Star Wars* movie series), although not Native American by any means, understood pretty well this same ancient concept when he cast young Luke Skywalker as representing the "good" side of The Force and Luke's errant father, Darth Vader, as typical of the "dark" side of The Force.

To Native Americans through the centuries and millenniums, whether of *Book of Mormon* heritage or not, these things have always been rather consistent in their belief values. They have always held to the notion that the Great Spirit was essentially neutral intelligence energy void of feelings. And that this divine matter could be split into different life forms to acquire a wide variety of emotions in the various realms of creation to which each unit became assigned.

And just as there were good men and women, animals, birds, fishes, insects, and so forth, in a similarly corresponding sense there could be bad people, beasts, birds, plants, and what have you, each one rising or falling according to its separate nature and environment. In time, however, all of the bad life forms, be they men or mice or microbes would become dismantled and eventually cast back into those portions of space wherein such particles move chaotically until resummoned at a later period to begin the processes all over again somewhere else in the universe.

Carrying this unusual but highly advanced concept one step further, early and present-day Native Americans believe that even apparently inanimate life forms, such as rocks and stones, possess some of these self-moving particles of intelligent energy. But from where do they get their emotions? From the bosom of the earth itself and from whatever other life forms crawl over or handle them in any way.

This leads to several considerations. One is that a rock located by an anthill, for instance, will somehow sense and enjoy those tiny higher-evolved life forms crawling all over it. Just the same as a beautiful crystal might which has been excavated from within the bowels of the earth and eventually winds up around somebody's neck or on a finger or wrist or shelf for admiration and comfort. The more time its owner spends with this little gem, the more this priceless stone or natural crystal is apt to acquire whatever emotions have been radiating forth from the individual.

Sound far-fetched? Not at all, though for the uninitiated such practical, down-to-earth knowledge takes on more of a mystical, somewhat incomprehensible tone. Take the case of the famous Mitchell-Hedges crystal skull, found by Anna Mitchell-

Hedges and her adopted father, F. A. Mitchell-Hedges in the abandoned ruins of an enormous Maya citadel in the steamy jungles of British Honduras in 1927. In his fascinating account, *The Crystal Skull*, author Richard M. Garvin explores at great lengths the various characteristics which have been attributed to this ancient glass relic by dozens of people who have been in tune with it—namely, strange hypnotic trances, mysteriously glowing eye sockets, eerie cold light emanating from the skull, chanting human voices, clear-to-fading images of ancient temples adorned with severed skulls, material objects strewn about inside a home where the skull was once kept, a fleeting velvety smooth heavy earth-type musky odor given off, noticeable color changes within the clear crystal itself, and a general sense of imminent death whenever the powers of the skull have been ridiculed by skeptics.

Garvin concluded that the ancient Maya priests responsible for its construction, were undoubtedly men of great evil. And consequently, they somehow transferred to these once neutral particles of intelligent energy that comprised the crystal in the skull, their own negative emotions. So saturated then did the crystal particles become that they actually retrogressed by inheriting such murderous and wicked intents emanating from the hearts of the humans who built the skull in the first place. Garvin carefully pointed out that the skull would not always respond in any of the aforementioned ways with individuals who were basically upright and solidly committed to strong Christian or Jewish values. It required a certain type of individual whose life was somewhat morally bankrupt and spiritually in disarray to get in tune with these negative forces imbued deep within the crystal particles of the skull itself.

Along these same lines, I can recall a similar experience which I myself had some years ago with a father-son team of White Mountain Apache medicine men living in southern Arizona. Because members of the family are still somewhat prominent today within the tribe, I shall use pseudonyms for both so as not to bring further shame and embarrassment on any of their immediate relatives.

Now the father, Coyote-Sees-All (pseudonym), had been a tribal medicine man for approximately 27 years. One of the objects which he worked with in his healing ceremony was a smooth, white, somewhat translucent stone through which he would consult the Great Spirit for healing advice. Coyote-Sees-All was a humble, gentle man, living just above the poverty line, and seldom ever charging for his services. I never knew him to be an alcoholic, a thief, a liar, nor a whoremonger. In short, he was about the finest human being I believe I have ever met, outside of my own father, Jacob Heinerman.

During the several times that I spent with him, he taught me a little about the use of this stone and how he made it work for himself on behalf of others. But he never actually showed me the stone while he was alive. In time he died, and his son whom I will just call Coyote-Sees-All, Jr., contacted me with a desire to sell our Research Center his father's sacred medicine objects. It was then that I had my first long glance at the stone.

Coyote, Jr. allowed me to borrow his dad's rock for several hours. I retreated some distance into the nearby hills to a secluded spot, where I was able to meditate properly before actually trying to invoke the powers of the stone itself. I remember the old man telling me that it was very important for one to sanctify his or her heart completely before the Great Spirit in peace and humility, by sincerely repenting of all sins, before even attempting to use it. This I did as best as a white man could then do and soon settled myself down into a relaxed concentration on the stone. A while passed before I could begin feeling kind and pleasant sensations come over me. It was almost as if the old gent himself were there in person, but what I felt gradually build up inside me were actually his own emotions being released by the intelligent energy particles comprising the stone I then held in the palm of my right hand. I never saw anything in the stone, but can attest to feeling certain sweet and good emotions emanating from the rock I held into my own physical being. It is almost as if the spiritual essence of old Coyote-Sees-All was somehow radiating forth. The stone, I believe, had over a lengthy period of time, acquired much of the old man's wonderful emotional personality and was now imparting some of the same to me.

But the story does not end here. The more gruesome aspects of it are to follow. I returned the relic to the son, who demanded an exorbitant price for it far in excess of what our budget allowed. So I politely declined his offer and returned to Utah. This son was in the habit of frequently stealing things to support his drinking, gambling, and whoring habits. Believing the stone to be of some good luck in his ill-gotten fortunes, he drilled a hole in one end of it, ran a buckskin string through it and wore it around his neck.

This talisman remained with Coyote-Sees-All, Jr. for the next several years, up until he got into a fight with another man and fatally stabbed his opponent with a big hunting knife he usually carried inside his boot, strapped to his leg. While in jail awaiting trial for his foul deed, the son died of a ruptured aneurysm to the brain. His personal effects eventually were returned to members of his family. In time, they got in touch with me and asked if I was still interested in their father's medicine stone.

I replied back in the affirmative and soon paid them another visit in the hopes of acquiring this wonderful artifact. But this time I noticed that the translucent nature of the stone had become ever so slightly darkened. At first, I just assumed it was due to the body oil which must have somehow secreted from the skin of the son into the stone itself. But I could not have been more wrong. I then decided to apply the same meditative test to it as I had done before when the father passed away. Imagine my surprise and chagrin when I discovered a particularly bad feeling emanating from what had once been a stone yielding very good sensations. I therefore came to the inevitable conclusion that the father's positive emotions had been replaced by contrary ones radiating forth from his wicked son. Within just a matter of a few years, those self-moving particles of intelligent energy had moved from positive progression to a negative retrogression because of the stone's two very different mortal owners. I returned the object to the relatives without showing any further interest in buying it.

This true experience and Garvin's own remarks concerning the ancient Maya crystal skull underlie the most fundamental truth concerning the nature and character of the Great Spirit itself. It is for each one of us to line ourselves up with these self-moving particles of intelligent energy comprising all matter around us in order that we might perceive them and that they, in turn, may acquire from us our most noble emotions. Or, stated another way by Harvard anthropologist Clyde Kluckhohn writing on "The Philosophy of the Navaho Indians" in Volume Two of *Readings in Anthropology*, this particular tribe strives hard to eliminate social friction in human relations so that each one can enjoy greater harmony with the surrounding environment, of which man constitutes just a small part.

Of Buffalos and Snakes

In keeping then with such beliefs, it was not uncommon to find a tremendous respect accorded all animals found in nature by Native Americans everywhere. Often, such great reverence took on elaborate religious rituals, observes Ruth M. Underhill in her classic study of the *Red Man's Religion*. Using the buffalo as a typical example, she recounts the great lengths to which Plains Indians went to prepare themselves properly for great slaughters of thousands of these beasts at any one time. But their efforts had nothing whatsoever to do with personal marksmanship. Instead, they were concerned with their own attitudes and feelings prior to one of these great hunts.

In detail she describes how the Sioux or Omaha braves, who volunteered to lead the others against the buffalo, would pray at length for a quest vision on end before ever attempting such a venture. They did this in order to seek the approval of the Great Spirit and the individual spirits of the buffalos they would eventually be killing for food and clothing. Is this not, in a sense, attempting to communicate with those self-moving particles making up each animal? Is it not reflective of trying to get in touch with those individual units of intelligent energy comprising every shaggy beast roaming the Plains?

She takes proper note of various sacred objects utilized by such "buffalo callers," adding that if the group were in harmony and made little noise they could be assured of a great hunt. Is this not taking great care to be united with the forces of nature around them? Underhill pays particularly close attention to the different praying, singing, and dancing ceremonies preceding and following each hunt. One time, she writes, an eager hunter from some unnamed tribe attempted to persuade his group to omit the last three ceremonies so that the herd wouldn't escape them. It should come as no surprise that the very next day, he was the only hunter trampled to death by the stampeding buffalo!

Elsewhere in her chapter on hunting and gathering rituals, she mentions the permission often sought by some tribes from the very animals they intended to kill. Southwestern Indians apologized to the wounded deer before clubbing him to death. The bear was hunted with the greatest ceremony all over North America. Coming to the entrance of the bear's den, the brave would respectfully holler for the bear to come out. After the great beast had been smoked or prodded out, a group of hunters would then put it to death, while at the same time apologize to its departed spirit for the necessity of taking its life.

Nothing—repeat nothing—was ever wasted when any animal was hunted by early Native Americans. They felt it was most unkind to let something go to waste. The sole exception to this seems to have been the blood of some animals, but in several different cases tribes would even find a use for it somehow. Joy Yellowtail Toineeta, a full-blood Crow Indian, described just how thoroughly all parts of the buffalo were used by her people in her professional paper, *Absarog-Issawua* (submitted to Montana State University in Bozeman in August, 1970, and hereby used with her kind permission):

"Much has been written about the buffalo providing the backbone of the Plains Indian economy and tribal organization. This was quite true. From this shaggy animal of the Great Plains came food, clothing, and shelter. Nothing was wasted from the grunt to the hooves.

"The list of uses of the buffalo begins with the horns. These were shaped into drinking vessels, serving scoops, and spoons. The matted hair on the shoulders and sides was removed during the winter and early spring when the winter coat was shed. The hair was cleaned, stored, and used to line baby cradles. This became the first disposable diapers.

"The rawhide served many purposes, as soles for moccasins; parfleche bags, painted and decorated for packing all personal belongings and equipment; dried food for the winter and berry picking vessels; shields that the warriors carried in battle; and the covering of saddle trees. Also ropes and bridles were buffalo rawhide.

"Whole hides were used to cover a frame-work of willows to make a boat. Drum heads for tom-toms were rawhide. Clothing, robes, bedding, floor covering, covering for teepee, dew cloth, or interior curtains in the lodges, cradles and moccasins were made from tanned hides.

"Even the buffalo chips were useful as fuel and fertilizer in planting the sacred tobacco seeds in the spring of the year.

"Every bit of the meat was utilized. The flesh was boned to slice into big sheets to dry in the wind and sun. This was stored in the parfleche bags strapped with thongs and packed on horses as the tribe moved. The flesh of the buffalo is coarser and darker than beef, but the flavor is equal to the prime grass-fed Big Sky beef. The bones were cracked and boiled to extract the melted marrow fat. This was used in pemmican meat, with berry and vegetable stews.

"After the animal had been bled, skinned, and gutted, each part of the entrails was separated. This required knowledge, skill, and cleanliness. The marrow gut was carefully removed first. The casings used for weiners and bologna in present day meat packing houses were carefully removed and cleaned out in running water or streams in those days. The tripe was emptied and washed in running water or streams and peeled.

"The hooves were washed thoroughly and boiled with dried corn or hominy until the meat fell off the bones."

Compare this with the wholesale and wanton destruction of tens of thousands of buffalo by the white man for mere sport and pleasure. Buffalo Bill Cody, for instance, earned his first two nicknames by hiring himself out to Eastern businessmen as a guide and hunter. From the comfort of locomotive cars, he and his ilk would shoot with pleasure as many buffalo as could be found on the Plains or as many as the amount of ammunition in their possession would allow. None of the carcasses were ever butchered, but just left to decompose in the hot sun.

Author Frank B. Linderman eloquently captured the exquisite pain felt in the hearts of all Native Americans who witnessed such barbaric acts in the awful name of sportsmanship. Writing in his book *Red Mother* some sixty years ago, he stated:

"Plenty-coups, the aged Chief, had refused to speak of the days that immediately followed the passing of the buffalo, saying: 'When the buffalo went away the hearts of my people fell to the ground, and they could not lift them up again. After this nothing happened. There was little singing anywhere.'

"Now I asked Pretty-shield, 'How old were you when the buffalo disappeared?' She hesitated. 'Tst, tst, tst! I haven't seen a buffalo in more than forty years,' she said slowly, as though she believed herself to be dreaming.

"'Ahh, my heart fell down when I began to see dead buffalo scattered all over our beautiful country, killed and skinned, and left to rot by white men, many, many hundreds of buffalo. The first I saw of this was in the Judith basin. The whole country there smelled of rotting meat. Even the flowers could not put down the bad smell. Our hearts were like stones. And yet nobody believed, even then, that the white man could kill *all* the buffalo. Since the beginning of things there had always been so many! Even the Lacota, bad as their hearts were for us, would not do such a thing as this; nor the Cheyenne, nor the Arapahoe, nor the Pecunnie; and yet the white man did this, even when he did not want the meat. . . . If the Great White Chief in Washington had not given us food we should have been wiped out without even a chance to fight for ourselves.'"

Today, it is sad to say, the same wicked spirit of destroying animals for sport is still very much prevalent, even if some white men try to justify their cowardly and miserable hunting actions with the weak excuse of only doing it for food! Typical of such widespread evil and mental sickness is a recent incident which made headlines in several Utah newspapers during the month of March, 1989.

Located in south central Utah is the County of Sevier with Richfield as the county seat. The Sevier Wildlife Federation came up with the "bright" idea of sponsoring a "predator and pest control contest." The contest awarded points for the taking of coyotes, raccoons, skunks, pocket gophers, starlings, and magpies. Several Sevier County merchants even had the audacity and gall to donate prizes that would be awarded to those amassing the most points when the contest ended.

The Humane Society of Utah became especially upset because contestant organizers were encouraging youths to participate in the event, which began March 20th and ran through July 15th. The federation took out a full-page newspaper ad promoting the contest, which offered prizes for groups and individuals. Even sicker was the involvement of local Mormon ward Scout troops and area high schools. The Humane Society condemned such a contest as a "wholesale, community wide slaughter" of nature's innocent creatures, "not noticeably different from a scavenger hunt or a baseball game." Furthermore, the society warned, such flagrant disregard for the rights of animals would instill in young contest participants "a total lack of respect for nature, and everything good therein."

Since I frequently have to drive through Richfield on the way to my wilderness ranch in southern Utah near Bryce Canyon, I decided to investigate this matter further myself. It did not take me long to discover that nearly all of the principal participants in this abominable hunting scheme came from good homes and family backgrounds and belonged to the same predominant faith. From the Wildlife Federation officials who hatched such a bizarre idea to the local town merchants who offered TVs, stereos, tape decks, and trail bikes for the most animals killed, to the Boy Scout teenagers themselves who have been delightfully destroying such helpless creatures for the sake of fun and greed, practically everyone involved in such murderous mayhem are active and devout Mormons.

In and of itself, this would seem to some as being inconsequential. After all, who really cares whether these perpetrators are Mormons, Baptists, Catholics, or Jews? But when one considers what *early* Mormon Church leaders had to say about such deplorable behavior, then it becomes all the more curious and contradictory. Church founder and prophet, Joseph Smith, received a revelation from God sometime in March, 1831 strictly warning church members against unnecessary hunting. As found in current LDS scriptures, *Doctrine and Covenants* 49:21, it reads, "Woe be unto man that sheddeth blood or that wasteth flesh and hath no need." A few years later, while leading a company of several hundred men from Ohio to western Missouri, the Mormon leader had another opportunity to reinforce his strong beliefs in this regard. While pitching their tents for the night some of the elders discovered three large prairie rattlesnakes and were just about to kill them when Smith intervened.

Writing in his personal journal Monday evening, May 26th, 1834, the Mormon prophet observed:

". . . We found three massasaugas or prairie rattlesnakes, which the brethren were about to kill, but I said, 'Let them alone—don't hurt them! How will the serpent ever lose his venom, while the servants of God possess the same disposition, and continue to make war upon it? Men must become harmless, before the brute creation; and when men lose their vicious dispositions and cease to destroy the animal race, the lion and the lamb can dwell together, and the sucking child can play with the serpent in safety.' The brethren took the serpents carefully on sticks and carried them across the creek. I exhorted the brethren not to kill a serpent, bird, or an animal of any kind during our journey unless it became necessary in order to preserve ourselves from hunger."

His successor, Brigham Young, adopted even more stringent views regarding insects. Here are portions of two different sermons he gave at least a decade apart, showing incredible sympathy for the meanest, most repulsive, and destructive of all creatures—crickets! The first sermon was given on May 6th, 1855 before several thousand Saints in the old adobe brick tabernacle on Temple Square in Salt Lake City:

"Last season when the grasshoppers came on my crops, I said, 'Nibble away, I may as well feed you as to have my neighbors do it; I have sown plenty, and you have not raised any yourselves.' And when the harvest came you would not have known that there had been a grasshopper there. . . . Pay attention to what the Lord requires of you and let the balance go."

Similar sentiments were echoed a dozen years later on August 17th, 1867 in Tooele, Utah (located around the mountain to the west and just below the Great Salt Lake):

"According to present appearances, next year (1868) we may expect grasshoppers to eat up nearly all our crops. But if we have provisions enough to last another year, we can say to the grasshoppers—these creatures of God—you are welcome. I have never had a feeling to drive them from one plant in my garden. . . . "

Both sets of remarks appeared in a 26-volume work called the *Journal of Discourses*, published over a century ago by early Mormon leaders: the 1855 sermon is in 3:159 and the later speech is found in 12:121.

What has happened in the interim period since then? Why have modern church authorities encouraged the sport of hunting among their faithful members, when early leaders like Joseph Smith, Jr. and Brigham Young were adamantly opposed to such wicked conduct? For those well acquainted enough with the history of the Latter-Day Saints, the answer is quite simple to both questions: Smith and Young were *intimately* involved with the cultures of many different Native American tribes, whereas their later successors are not.

Mormon Church history is replete with numerous examples of frequent contacts which both men had with the Indians. Many are published and some are not. It is now a matter of record that some of the very first Mormon missionaries sent out by Joseph Smith while the infant church was still located in upper state New York, were directed to visit some of the tribes residing on the western Missouri frontier. Oliver Cowdery and Parley P. Pratt were the ones who led that 1830 delegation of elders and presented copies of the *Book of Mormon* to at least half a dozen different tribes.

Also in the public record is the historic visit of over one hundred chiefs and braves of the Sac and Fox tribes to Nauvoo in the summer of 1841 to visit Joseph Smith, who was then mayor of this city (at that time the largest in all of Illinois).

Led by Chiefs Keokuk (after whom Keokuk, Iowa has been named), Kikukosh, and Appenoose, this impressive body of Native Americans gathered in the Mormon leader's fruit orchard to hear a sermon and feast on corn, squash, plums, melons, and other natural goodies from his own garden. After Joseph's brief message, Keokuk arose and said with solemn dignity: "I have a *Book of Mormon* at my wigwam that you gave me a number of moons ago. I believe you are a great and good man. We are both sons of the Great Spirit. I have heard your advice. We intend to quit fighting, and follow the good talk you have given us." In essence, Smith preached to them the Gospel of Peace and they, in turn, acquainted him more with their own cultural values and novel beliefs.

Lesser known by very few Mormons, however, is the personal visitation which Joseph Smith received from an ancient Native American shaman known as Samuel the Lamanite (Lamanite is the Mormon word given to all Native Americans, based on the idea that they descended from Laman and Lemuel, rebellious sons of an ancient Jewish emigrant couple to the Americas, Lehi and Sariah). This visitation occurred while Smith was translating the *Book of Mormon* from precious gold plates by the gift and power of God. More complete background information concerning this Samuel the Lamanite may be found within the pages of the *Book of Mormon* itself (Chapters 13-15 of Helaman, inclusive). Briefly though, this individual had an unbringing which in some ways paralleled that of Elder George P. Lee, the Navajo Mormon Church authority cited in the beginning of this chapter. Samuel was born of Lamanite (Indian) parents, but became orphaned at an early age and was adopted by Nephite (white) parents and raised in that culture instead. Upon entering manhood, however, he returned to dwell among some of his own people who had converted to the Nephite religion and culture but lived separately from them. In time, though, the Lord sent him back to the Nephites, who had become extremely wicked by then, to warn them that unless they repented they would be utterly destroyed and only his people (the Lamanites or Indians) would be spared. He carried out this thankless task, but met with little success, as the majority of the whites to whom he spoke attempted to kill him instead. But protected by the power of God, he escaped their wrath and returned once more to his own people to "never be heard of more among the Nephites" as the *Book of Mormon* relates.

When this Lamanite fellow Samuel appeared to the young Prophet, he obviously did so in a very spectacular way, with consuming light and fiery glory surrounding his entire resurrected being. To say that young Smith was impressed by this grand entrance is quite an understatement. After quickly recovering his initial surprise from such a dramatic and unannounced appearance, he collected his thoughts together and began focusing all of his attention on the man's message. Samuel the Lamanite, of course, briefed young Joseph on his own life, providing just a thumbnail sketch in vision for the Prophet to understand who he was.

Then Samuel the Lamanite launched into a lengthy discourse about his own people (the Indians) and their special relationship with God or the Great Spirit. He explained to Smith that his people had been "guardians of the land," carefully preserving it in a way to please the Most High. Samuel told him that all of the natural resources about him—namely, the forests, the rivers and lakes and streams, the mountains, deserts, and prairies—had been given to his people, the Lamanites, for their sustenance and daily survival. But nothing was to be wasted, nor was greed ever to overtake any of them in attempting to exploit the earth for all she was worth.

Furthermore, Samuel explained, all manner of wildlife which roamed thereon or swam therein or flew above was to be used with prudence and thanksgiving—never wastefully nor maliciously. The Great Spirit or God had told them that they were accountable for every single creature they harmed or destroyed. It was apparently for this reason that most Native Americans began praying both to the Creator Himself and to the animals they wished to hunt, for permission to kill them for food and raiment. This explanation, however, was not given to Smith while Samuel the Lamanite spoke with him.

Smith's successor to the office of Church President, Brigham Young also maintained close contact with many Native Americans throughout his life. In an 1853 sermon published in Volume I of the *Journal of Discourses*, he remarked:

"I have studied the Indian character sufficiently to know what the Indians are. . . . I have been with them more or less from my youth upward. . . . "

His oft-quoted advice in those days was that "it is better to feed the Indians than to fight them." Had other non-Mormons followed his wise practice, many depredations and skirmishes between whites and Indians could have been avoided. Young even saw some positive benefits in several Indian uprisings which occurred among his own people; and, in fact, praised the red men for their troubles instead of condemning them as everyone else did. In that same sermon, he further observed:

". . . Amen to the present Indian trouble, for it is all right. I am just as willing the rebellious of this people should be kicked and cuffed, and mobbed, and hunted by the Indians, as not, for I have preached to them until I am tired."

Brigham Young became fast friends with one of the most powerful Indian chiefs, who ruled a great portion of southern Utah and western Nevada. His name was Chief Walker and he had a widespread reputation among many tribes for his unpredictable, sometimes surly and occasionally violent behavior. He could be friendly and treacherous at the same time. It is said that Brigham Young was probably the only white man who ever could stand up to Walker's fearsome and ever-changing nature, and yet command the respect and admiration of this emotionally-charged individual. And even, in spite of the infamous Walker War which raged in Utah from 1853-55 and put all Mormon settlers on the alert, this often ruthless and cunning Ute chief showed Brigham Young a secret gold mine, which only his people had known about for centuries. He permitted Young and several other trusted church members to take enough gold out with which to mint coins, and to use as ceiling and ornamental decoration in selected rooms of the Salt Lake Temple years later. Finally, when quite close to death himself, Walker asked not for his personal medicine man to attend, but rather that Brigham Young be sent for to give him a special Priesthood blessing. These few historical items are merely cited to show the special relationship which existed between Young and area tribal chieftains. Nor should it be especially surprising to learn that some of the Mormon leader's own views regarding the sacredness of things in nature originated from men like Chief Walker, his brother Aropean, Chief Pocatello of the northern Shoshone (after whom Pocatello, Idaho was named), and others.

This desire to learn all he could from the Indians is reflected in an 1857 sermon delivered by Young, as found in Volume 5 of the *Journal of Discourses*:

". . . There is not a tribe so enlightened, nor one that has so good a knowledge of its real position and standing before the Lord as have some of these Utah Indians. . . . Talk with them, and you will learn that they have a good deal of knowledge."

Young's constant admonitions to the Mormon people to always treat the Indians with kindness and to respect their environment, eventually won for him the trust and confidence of most western Indian tribes, which became obvious every so often from individual Indians. According to historian Leonard J. Arrington in his book, *From Quaker To Zion: Life of Edwin D. Wooley*, one such chief actually made an unannounced appearance in a Mormon church meeting. And when invited to the pulpit to speak, did so by informing the members that Mormons were good "tick-a-boos" or friends because they fed the Indians and were kind to them, but that other white men were "sons of bitches" because they only took advantage of or else desired to kill them.

Unfortunately, as the Mormon Church moved more towards the things of the world and became filled with rich, greedy and powerful people, it soon lost much of its 19th century innocence and spiritual values. Men like Joseph Smith and Brigham Young, who revered and loved the Indians, were in time replaced by businessmen, lawyers, bankers, and politicians. This probably helps to account for the embarrassing animal slaughter contest that was recently sponsored in Sevier County, Utah and mostly involved active Mormons. If LDS Church leaders themselves no longer set standards of respect for the environment and no longer preach Indian-type reverence for the things in nature, then how can they expect church laity to act any differently?

What is needed, of course, not only by Mormons but also for other denominations and ethnic groups outside of Indians, are some basic fundamental instructions with regard to the sacredness of nature and man's personal obligation to care for the environment as best he can. This, coupled with a change in attitude and heart, can lead us back again to the way Native Americans have always viewed such matters.

Worshipping Nature

Western writer George Wharton James had much good to say about Native Americans in his exceedingly rare book *What the White Race May Learn from the Indian*, which has been out of print now for well over three-quarters of a century. In speaking of their worshipful nature, he had this to say:

"I have seen Indians at their shrines, when they thought they were entirely alone, pray with the agony of seriousness and fervor that I have never seen equalled or at least suppressed. The priests of the (Hopi) Snake Dance . . . are as earnest and sincere and devout as the most consecrated Christian minister or priest I ever saw. And the dancers of the Acomas, Lagunas, Hopis, Navahos, and Zunis, enter into these, their religious ceremonies with an earnestness and reverence that put to shame the flippant, bustling, looking-around, whispering congregations of many of our so-called Christian churches."

In fact, so religious-minded is the Native American that "every act of his life may be said to have a religious thought attached to it, so powerfully is the religious instinct developed within him." As an illustration of this, James mentioned the common habit of smoking: "If you offer him a cigarette he will propitiate the Powers Above and Around and Below before he gives himself up to the full enjoyment of it."

Religion is not a matter of convenience for a true Native American. Neither is it something socially acceptable for just the Sabbath. As James and other scholars have pointed out in the past, religion permeates every fiber of the average Native American, who has not been corrupted by the white man's ways to any extent. Or as Mormon Church authority George P. Lee, the converted Navajo who was cited in the beginning of this chapter said, "With the Indian, religion is everything!"

In her book *Red Man's Religion*, Ruth Underhill gives several different examples of just how animate the world of the typical Indian was. During a ceremonial sweat bath, a Sioux warrior was apt to pray to the hot rocks on which water was poured to create more steam. While at a Zuni pueblo some shaman might be making offerings before his altar and referring to the spirits in cotton ("cotton woman") and clay ("clay woman") as being his "mothers."

Elsewhere in the *Handbook of South American Indians* (2:558-59) reference is made to the belief system of the Aymara Indians who inhabit a large portion of the Titicaca Basin in Peru and Bolivia. To these people, their surrounding world is very densely populated with innumerable supernatural beings of every conceivable description. And while most of these invisible beings are somewhat ambivalent in their attitudes toward people, depending of course on how they are treated or manipulated, some can be downright nasty and others extremely benevolent. Furthermore, the Aymara believe that all plants and animals found within their mountain domain are "owned" by various classes of supernatural beings. The most important group consists of several kinds of place spirits, which either guard the homes of people or inhabit the mountains, rivers, lakes, springs, and so forth. Each of these spirit beings lays claim to a variety of plants, animals, and minerals within his or her respective territory. In order to make use of any of these materials properly, an Aymara must appeal to that supernatural being to whom such things might belong, asking for permission to utilize some of them for his or her own personal needs. More often than not, however, the Aymara feel that a "prayerful" heart or attitude is more important for the procurement of these things, than actual uttered prayers to specific spirits. The Aymara seem to think that these spirits being able to read the thoughts and feelings of men, are satisfied if the person wanting some of their materials approaches the task of obtaining them with a thankful heart and a humble spirit. Thus, rather than frequent material sacrifices before some kind of an altar, these spirits, would prefer instead offerings of appreciation and gratitude from within the altar of the heart itself.

One reason man is so antagonistic towards nature and at seemingly constant odds with her is due to the conflict between the forces of good and evil within himself. The *Handbook of South American Indians* volume which deals with tropical forest tribes (3:90), explains a unique concept held by the Apapocuva-Guarani Indians of Paraguay and southern Brazil. According to them, two souls coexist in every man. The first one (ayvucue) emanates from the lofty mansion of some unidentified deity in either the east or west and takes possession of the body immediately after birth. This soul is identified with a peaceful, loving, and gentle disposition and an inclination for fruits and vegetables. The second animal soul (acyigua), however, resides in the nape of a person's neck and becomes his or her temperament. Patient and friendly people usually have butterfly souls, whereas jaguar souls tend to be ruthless and cold-blooded. Unrest, violence, malice, and an appetite for meat are often the traits ascribed to the acyigua.

Christian scriptures seem to bear this same belief out. The Apostle Paul often spoke about two different forces warring inside of him at the same time, admitting that when his spirit was inclined to do good, his fleshly disposition would try and prevent that from happening. In the *Book of Mormon* (Mosiah 16:3), one may find a statement to the effect that "all mankind became carnal, sensual, and devilish . . . subjecting themselves to the devil." The Apapocuva-Guarani teach (as do a number of other religions like Islam, Buddhism, Hinduism, Judaism, and Christianity) that all people must strive as much as possible to overcome the acyigua part of themselves, letting the better ayvucue predominate instead.

However, they go one step further than do most of these other organized religions, in that these tropical forest people advocate becoming one with nature and letting the spirit in nature become a part of your spirit too. Since much of early Mormon religious thought is identified with ancient Native American philosophy, it is not surprising to find similar ideas parallel to those of the Apapocuva-Guarani. Past Mormon Apostle and Church President Lorenzo Snow is a good example of this. At the time of his conversion to this "religion of nature," he admitted quite frankly that "it proved to be the fiercest struggle of heart and will I ever experienced before or since." His life before this incredible change took place, as briefly explained in *The Young Woman's Journal* (4:216) (an early Mormon publication), was one of "worldly aspirations, lofty material ambitions, 'liberal collegiate' ideals, aristocratic wealth and a blue-blood arrogance towards people or things of lesser note.

"It was a great trial, and required the strongest effort to form a resolution to abandon those prospects (and) disappoint (my own) expectations," he confessed.

"But through the help of the Lord . . ., I laid aside my pride, worldly ambition and aspirations upon the altar, and as humble as a child," he recalled, was willing to submit himself completely to this "religion of nature," which in its most comprehensive form means becoming totally saturated with the Holy Spirit through the simple ordinances of faith, repentance, baptism, and laying on of hands for the Holy Ghost.

What then followed soon thereafter, he recalled, was nothing short of miraculous "as the heavens were opened, the veil was rent from my mind, and then and there I received the most wonderful manifestations, grand and sublime, I believe as man was ever permitted to receive, and beyond the power of language fully to describe." In other words what Lorenzo Snow encountered was his own "vision quest" just as numerous Native Americans have in their own isolated spots somewhere in the great outdoors.

But Snow's experience is worth relating here because of the richness of the language he employed in order to detail his incredible transformation. Listen to his description of just how thoroughly imbued he became with the Great Spirit upon that historic occasion in his life:

"The first intimation of the approach of that marvelous vision was a sound just above my head like the rustling of silken robes, when immediately the Holy Spirit descended upon me, enveloping my whole person, filling me from the crown of my head to the soles of my feet, which was a complete baptism, as tangible an immersion in a heavenly principle or element—the Holy Ghost—infinitely more real, physical in its effects upon every part of my system than was the immersion when I was baptized in water. That night after retiring to rest the same wonderful manifestations were repeated, and continued to be for several successive nights. From that time till the present on numerous occasions miraculous manifestations of the divine power have followed me. . . . "

These wonderful words, written over a century ago, still carry powerful meaning to them and leave an indelible impact in those souls seeking after the truth.

The tropical forest Apapocuva-Guarani hold to the idea that absolute and constant goodness within an individual only becomes possible by an intermeshing of two very distinct kinds of noble souls. First, of course, is one's own personal ayvucue which each of us brings from the mansions of some supernatural deity. Second would be a portion of that particular ayvucue with which "Our Great Father" (Nanderuvucu) and his first wife, "Our Great Mother" (Nandecy) who dwell in the "Land-Without-Evil" are entirely composed. As each of their mortal children begins drawing nearer unto them through the mediums of faith, repentance, meditation, and prayer, they begin gradually imparting to each worthy soul some of this exalted ayvacue or "fluid soul" if you will. In other words, as a person brings his or her own evil and highly unpredictable acyigua under control, then the "Great Parents" above begin to endow that individual with their own soul personalities. In time then, one can become so filled with their ayvucue that his or her own ayvucue or inner goodness has become (quite literally) swallowed up in theirs.

This concept, while not new to fundamental Mormonism, is not to be found very much in the rest of orthodox Christianity or Judaism, where either being figuratively "washed in the saving blood of Jesus Christ" or else having faithfully kept all of the laws of the Old Testament prophets and rabbis are of paramount importance. You see, these inhabitants of the tropical regions of Paraguay and southern Brazil believe that one of the chief tasks of their two greatest personages, Nanderuvucu and Nandecy, is to effectively transform mortals into the same kind of exalted beings that they themselves have already become. And in order to achieve this, it is necessary for mortals to seek after them in the very environment in which so much of their soul personalities may be found, namely within the forces of nature herself.

Although he himself was never acquainted with the Apapocuva-Guarani Indian culture, Lorenzo Snow understood something about this same principle of truth in which both they and the Mormons share uncanny similarities. In his *Biography and Family Record of Lorenzo Snow*, written by his sister Eliza R. Snow some 100 years ago and now an exceedingly rare book to find, is an extract from his own journal showing us to what degree his own sinful nature was transformed by the Great or Holy Spirit:

"One day . . . I took my gun with the intention of indulging in a little amusement in hunting turkeys, with which that section of the country (northwestern Missouri) abounded. From boyhood I had been particularly, and I may say strangely attached to a gun. Hunting, in the forests of Ohio (where he grew up) was a pastime that to me possessed the most fascinating attractions. It never occurred to my mind that it was wrong—that indulging in 'what was sport to me was death to them'; that in shooting turkeys, and squirrels, I was taking life that I could not give; therefore I indulged in the murderous sport without the least compunction of conscience.

"But at this time a change came over me. While moving slowly forward in pursuit of something to kill, my mind was arrested with the reflection on the nature of my pursuit—that of amusing myself by giving pain and death to harmless, innocent creatures that perhaps had as much right to life and enjoyment as myself. I realized that such indulgence was without any justification, and feeling condemned, I laid my gun on my shoulder, returned home, and from that time to this have felt no inclination for that murderous amusement."

This illustrates the type of inner transformation which must take place before mortals can ever hope to ascend to a better dimension of life experience Hereafter. It is nothing less than the fusing together of one's own ayvucue with the ayvucues of Nanderuvucu and Nandecy, "Our Great Father" and "Our Great Mother." This "soul fusion" between mortal and immortal can then endow the worthy and fortunate recipient with a clearer and truer understanding of Nature herself; for it is only then that one can really worship Nature as she ought to be remembered.

But you do not have to be either an Apapocuva-Guarani Indian or convert to Mormonism to experience a similar transformation. Even an atheist, incredible as it might seem to some, can find the "God of Nature" through humility, faith, and much prayer. This I learned firsthand for myself during my 1979 trip to the Soviet

Union. It was while my group and I were in the City of Sukhumi, which sits directly on the coast of the Black Sea, that this came about.

While wandering around by myself for a while, taking in the sights that this resort city had to offer to tourists like me, I saw a woman in her early-to-mid-forties selling cut flowers on a street corner. As I drew nearer, she spoke to me at first in Russian, but upon learning that I was an American immediately switched to speaking near-perfect English.

She introduced herself as Ludmila Melnikova, who had formerly occupied a teaching position of considerable importance at Moscow University, where she instructed students in English literature. But in time she was dismissed for her extreme pro-American leanings and reassigned a lowly janitorial job in a department store in the city I was visiting. Her husband had divorced her, she had lost the benefits of a comfortable apartment in Moscow, and had been reduced to living in a cramped two-room flat with her two teenage daughters on Mir Avenue in Sukhumi. Furthermore, she had to endure the occasional embarrassments of having her mail opened, having her flat periodically searched by state security police, and being interrogated every so often by the KGB.

Yet in spite of it all, Ludmila had managed to retain her courage and spirit. I invited her to join me for lunch in a nearby restaurant where there were no menus, but only what the cook in the back kitchen decided was going to be served for that particular day. Here we became further acquainted with each other. I reassured her that she had nothing to worry about, even though she would nervously look about her every few minutes to see who may or may not have been watching us. Later, we strolled over to a small park and sat down to chat some more. I told her that the very best place for us to visit was "out in the open where everyone can see us," rather than in her apartment or some back alleyway where the police were more apt to be looking. "This way we're sure to be left alone," I joked.

Ludmila excused herself for a few minutes and soon returned, bringing both of her teenage daughters with her. Irina was then 17 and Alla had just turned 16. Both were as beautiful and delightful as their mother in spirit, personality, and physical looks. The girls had a myriad of questions for someone from America, which she translated for me into English and did the same thing in Russian with my responses to them.

At some point in our lengthy four-hour long conversation, I asked what her religious beliefs were. Imagine my pleasant, but curious surprise when she informed me that they worshipped "the God of Nature." Obviously intrigued by this, I pressed for more of an explanation. Referring back to my notes of that important trip a decade ago, here is what I wrote down regarding that portion of my visit with her and her daughters:

"Ludmila told me earlier this evening that she had been raised in an atheistic household—her father was a member of the Communist Party and her mother had been active in a Communist women's auxiliary league, the name of which has now escaped my memory.

"She said that during her years spent teaching at Moscow University, she fell in love with such classical American writers as James Fenimore Cooper, Nathaniel Hawthorne, and Edgar Allen Poe. She especially liked Cooper's *Last of the Mohicans* in which she found a deep admiration for everything the Red Man did. It was from this historical novel that the idea eventually sprang to become more identified with the things in nature.

"She admitted that her command of the English language, while adequate enough to carry on an intelligent conversation with me, wasn't enough to accurately describe the emotions within her soul regarding her feelings for nature in general. But she did manage to convey the idea with a combination of hand gestures and appropriate adjectives, the 'romantic rapture' (her words) she now felt with the outdoors.

"Waving her hand in the air first and then placing it over her heart, she solemnly declared, 'What sustains all of this you see, is what has entered here. The god forces about us I now feel inside of me here (pointing again to her bosom). My religion can be this grass (motioning to the lawn in front of us), those flowers over there (making a sweeping gesture with her hand), that tree behind us, or the squirrel running up it. I *feel* the life within them. Their souls touch my soul. And my spirit reaches out to their spirits. We are all one and the same.' Then after a moment's careful deliberation, she concluded, 'They (meaning those things in nature just referred to) are in me and I am in them. Their god force is my god force, and my god also their god.'"

This then is what Ludmila Melnikova meant by worshipping "the God of Nature." In other words, the Great Spirit sustaining the lives of grass, flowers, trees, and animals around us touched her as nothing else could. And that part of the Great Spirit in her was awakened or affected in a very positive way by those portions of the Great Spirit in each of these things. Their sacred worth reached out and touched her own sacred worth to the degree that neither wished to hurt or harm the other. This, according to her, was the ultimate religious experience—a real true "love affair with Nature," just as many Native Americans and a few from other ethnic groups have experienced for themselves in times past.

CHAPTER SEVEN

WHAT OTHER RACES MAY LEARN FROM THE INDIAN

An Informative Book

Extinction is a matter of survival. No matter how hard something tries, unless the odds are stacked in its favor, even just a little, it just is not going to last very long. Such is the unfortunate legacy of one of the best books I have ever had a chance to read about Native Americans. Its self-explanatory title described the internal contents quite well—*What the White Race May Learn from the Indian.* Authored by western naturalist writer, George Wharton James, it was published in 1908 in a limited edition by a since extinct Chicago publishing house (Forbes & Co.).

I keep my own copy, personally autographed by the author himself with many of my other priceless, rare books. The last available copy for sale in similar mint condition, but without Mr. James' embellished signature, went for some $300 in a rare book catalogue issued annually by an antiquarian bookseller in downtown Boston. Of all the countless books in my collection, it is only one of about half a dozen that I keep going back to for fresh insights into the culture and wisdom of an almost forgotten people.

It was this book, in fact, which provided the inspiration if not most of the title for this particular chapter. A lot of the material utilized herein has its indirect roots or outright quotation references from James' classic study. Since this long out-of-print book will probably never again be published, at least some of the main ideas connected with American Indian philosophy are presented here for the reader's benefit and to preserve for generations to come the timely wisdom of our nation's true, original settlers.

The Religion of Jogging

In the third chapter of this book on Indian deep-breathing techniques, author James mentioned the differences between the running exercises once encouraged by doctors at the Battle Creek health sanitarium in Battle Creek, Michigan with those employed by the Arizona Hopi Indians. Those exercises formulated by Dr. Kellogg were more precise and regimental, emphasizing just the physical benefits to be gained therefrom. But with the Hopi it was entirely different. Such routine running was without any formal order to it and practiced more along natural principles, he noted:

". . . To my amazement I saw fleeing through the early morning dusk a score (more or less) of naked youths, on each one of whom a cowbell was dangling from a rope or strap around his waist. Later I learned this *running* was done as a *matter of religion*. Every young man was required to run ten, fifteen, twenty miles, and even double this distance, upon *certain* allotted mornings, as a *matter of religion*."

This sight finally explained to him the mysterious sounds of cowbells which he had heard on previous mornings while sleeping in one of the Hopi villages. It was not a herd of cows heading off to graze in some nearby pasture as he fully expected, but merely a group of youths seeking to increase their spirituality through the medium of long-distance running.

Today several million Americans run or jog on a regular basis. Yet, as the Thursday, October 1st, 1987 issue of *The Wall Street Journal* reported, it has become more than just "a national love affair" with fitness; instead, it has turned into an "obsessive addiction" for many, as food or drugs have become for millions of others. This "exercise compulsion," the *Journal* noted, is one of the main growing health problems confronting upper and middle-class professionals. They tend to abuse otherwise socially acceptable exercise just as other people are inclined to abuse drugs, food, or alcohol. Many are seeking for the exhilarating "high" which prolonged exercise such as jogging can induce, but not without the same withdrawal symptoms when they cannot exercise as alcoholics and drug addicts do when they cease drinking and taking drugs: depression, nervousness, and insomnia.

This exercise "craze" has caused millions of otherwise fairly normal American men and women to become chemically "hooked" on their own bodies. Whether the fad involves fast aerobic dancing to jazz or rock music, strenuous weight lifting, or the ever popular jogging and running marathons, is beside the point. The fact is that under such great physical stresses the body kicks up its own production of particular hormones, which deliver temporary exhilirations to the mind in much the same way that acts of self-abuse to one's sexual organs might. In the end such grueling punishment to the body, wrote psychologist and addiction expert Dr. Stanton Peele in the October 1986 issue of *Sports Fitness*, tends to seriously disrupt the body and mind.

Dr. Peele then listed some important points on how to avoid these "exercise obsessions," while at the same time getting the most out of one's physical activity. Exercise should never be a way of escaping from the problems in reality. Exercise ought to have variation to it. Exercise should make other contributions to your life besides the more obvious physical ones. One's preconceived notions in regard to exercise should be revamped. Exercise should cease when pain sets in. Finally, he noted, "health is an overall balance in life," and no one thing should take precedent over that of another. As will be soon pointed out, the early Native American attitude towards exercise for spiritual growth and development ought to prevail in each and every one of us who chooses to exercise in some way. The habit cultivated last year

(1988) by a young friend of mine serves well to illustrate what I mean. Jason Fountaine, aged 13, began taking karate lessons over a year ago from a martial arts expert here in Salt Lake City. But unlike all of the other kids in his class, who were there merely for the "macho" stuff and to live out their Bruce Lee fantasies, he went there, believe it or not, to strengthen his budding spirituality.

Being very close friends with his mom and stepdad, I was invited on several occasions by him to attend special tests as he acquired his different belts. I noticed right away that he stood out from all the rest, not only in superb karate skills but in his character development as well. More peace, love, and gentleness seemed to radiate from his sweet countenance than from any of his teenage counterparts. This certainly was very strange to an art well known for its acute mental and physical intensities, warlike aggressiveness, and quick, sudden deathlike motions intended to inflict pain and injury.

When I posed the question to him later on after attending one of these sessions, he thought a moment and then casually remarked with his typical boyish innocence, "I guess it's because I pray to my Heavenly Father before I begin practicing and always say a prayer afterwards." When pressed more closely for details, he shyly admitted that he asked God to let the vigorous discipline demanded in karate make him a better person out of him so he could serve others as well as his God. He also prayed that he might never have to use the deadly skills he was learning, except in the defense of his friends and family or "anyone else whose life or property might be threatened by men of evil." I carefully noticed that he had not even included himself in this, but was more concerned about assisting others instead.

Additionally, he found that his own personal prayers to the Almighty took on more of a focus and became sharply defined as the months spent in karate training passed. Before this, he related, his prayers had sort of wandered all over the landscape, sometimes ambiguous in their meaning and occasionally uncertain of what he really wanted to pray about. The discipline which has come to him from karate, he said, helped better define who he was and enabled him to search out more on his own where he came from, why he was here, and just where he expected to go in the future. While not making him religious by any means, karate appears to have assisted this lad in developing a stronger determination to actively seek out God his Father, according to the dictates of his own heart and the beliefs he has acquired while growing up in the Mormon faith.

In similar ways have some Native American tribes utilized exercise for their own spiritual advancement. In his historic book, James mentioned how much oxygen the young Hopi runners he saw took into their lungs after a good 10 to 20 mile jog. Then they would return to their respective mesa dwellings or else gather in one of the ceremonial rooms to make special petitions to the Great Spirit. They believed that since the air was the breath of the Great Spirit, to take more of it into their systems would automatically attune their minds and hearts more towards that great creative force they worshipped so reverently.

While most Southwestern Indian tribes no longer run for spiritual reasons, much less exercise for healthy purposes, a modern day exception to the rule remains. These are the famous long distance runners inhabiting the Sierra Madre Occidental of northwestern Mexico. I have been there, and the entire regions strikes me as sort of a weird Alice in Wonderland. There you can find mountains rising so gently they seem almost flat and bottomlands appearing quite perpendicular; where canyons carved by creeks seem deeper than the Grand Canyon of the Colorado itself; where fruit trees have houses; where owls may be no bigger than sparrows, and where running Indians leave tire-tread imprints from their primitive footwear on lonely, dusty trails.

Somewhat southwest of Chihuahua, Mexico lies Tarahumara Country. Some of the many trails in this remote desert wilderness are rough but passable for burros or mules; others are scarcely more than goat paths that traverse harrowing ledges and thorny slopes. Over these the Tarahumara Indians stride quite easily in sandals with soles made from discarded pickup truck tires. As reported in Volume 81 of *Natural History* magazine, Tarahumara hunters can literally run the deer they are tracking into the ground. Once they discover an animal's tracks, several men will commence to jog after it for many hours, rarely ever losing sight of their intended prey. By the second day of steady, methodical chasing, the deer usually drops from sheer exhaustion, and the hunters immediately pounce on it with knives or rocks.

In this same article was reliably reported an incident which took place around 1930. A certain unnamed Tarahumara chief had been invited to send his very best runners to a well-publicized marathon somewhere in Kansas. Upon learning however that the intended course to be run was just a mere 26 miles, he instead decided to send three girls, who in spite of all the jeers received from a skeptical crowd, handily beat all of the male Caucasian participants. The ease with which even the women of this tribe can run has been documented elsewhere by an anthropologist, writing in the May 1979 *Arizona Highways*. Bernard L. Fontana mentioned a little wager he and others made with four local Tarahumara girls in either their late teens or early twenties. The trails selected were somewhat steep and rocky, moving up and down at various intervals. At a given signal, the girls dashed off barefooted, breathing heavily at an elevation of 7,000 feet above sea level. Within what seemed to be just minutes, the race was over. When Fontana and his pals arrived at the finishing point by jeep, they found all four young ladies patiently sitting on the hard ground and waiting to receive their reward monies. They were no longer breathing heavily, and they gave no indication that they had just run three miles.

In his *Natural History* article previously cited, writer Michael Jenkinson detailed the elaborate preparations made by participants for major *rarijiparis* or running kick-ball marathons. For almost a week prior to the actual contest, runners carefully avoid sexual contacts with women and do not eat any fat, eggs, potatoes, or sweets. They believe that to do so would not only disqualify them by losing, but also jeopardize their spiritual status as well, possibly having them end up in the Tarahumara version of Hell. When pressed for more specific physical details about this nasty place in the Hereafter, they only say it is a place where the devil lives with his bitchy wife, who continually gives birth to "their numerous offspring" which, they claim, are the Mexicans. To go to such an awful place, they insist, would mean an end to their peace of mind and tranquil lifestyle. Hence, the exceeding care taken to prepare themselves spiritually for the upcoming event.

Jenkinson also noted that magic is often used. A shaman is employed to cast spells on weaker opponents, especially to physically weaken them to the point that they will drop out of the race and let other stronger contestants win instead. The night before the grand occasion, numerous candles are lit on either side of small wooden crosses. Being of Catholic persuasion, most of the Tarahumara entrants will make simultaneous appeals both to the Virgin Mary/Jesus Christ and the Great Spirit. The runners also adorn themselves with the different fetishes they intend to wear to make them spiritually strong in this event: eagle feathers, hawk and vulture heads, glowworms, and rattles made of deer hooves. The shaman then chants and sings the "song of the gray fox." Participants make ceremonial turns around the crosses and candles, doing the exact number of laps they will be running during the *rarijipari*. Then they wrap themselves up snugly in their blankets and soon fall asleep on the hard ground next to the food and water they will be taking at various intervals throughout the race.

Such is a brief description of the serious ceremonial rituals preceding an event like this. How wonderful it would be if similar religious preparations were undertaken by those entering the Boston or New York marathons, much less by anyone simply jogging!

It would not be fair to close this section without relating one last memorable account about the incredible endurance of early Southwestern Indian tribes. This appeared in the February 1936 issue of the *Improvement Era*, a publication for the youth of The Church of Jesus Christ of Latter-Day Saints. It seems in the pioneer days that a famous bet was made between a Goshuite Indian and an arrogant Gentile. The white man wagered that the dirty-looking Indian could not keep up with a stage coach he happened to be riding in for a distance of some 25 miles.

Well, as the true story goes, the stage coach—called "Pitchin' Betsies" in those days—took off over the smooth road between Canyon and Willow stations in Snake Valley, with the driver whipping his team constantly into a running frenzy. Much to the white fellow's chagrin and dismay, he found the Indian brave loping alongside and just slightly behind the speeding coach. This went on for almost 20 miles and by then had generated quite a cloud of dust behind the stage coach. Anxiously looking out of the window to see if he could spot the Indian, the man let out a holler of glee, anticipating that he had already won his bet.

But imagine the sinking feeling which his heart must have experienced when one of the other passengers called his attention to the opposite side of the coach. There through the open window he noticed the running Goshiute, who momentarily turned to flash him a wide grin of white, even teeth, before dashing ahead in a sudden burst of speed. Some five miles later at the next way station, the driver reined in his exhausted team, which were by now frothing at the mouth and ready to drop in their tracks. But the Indian was sitting cross-legged in the dirt beneath the shade of an old willow tree, patiently waiting for his payment with an outstretched hand. As the discontented Gentile reluctantly forked over the promised amount, he was heard to mutter beneath his breath as we walked away grumbling to himself, "They oughta hitch up Indians to them stage coaches 'stead of horses; least ways we'd get there 'lot faster!"

Eating Habits Worth Considering

Several very important lessons may be learned from the dietary habits of Native Americans, both past and present. Some of them are good, with positive benefits to our health, while others are quite bad and very detrimental to our overall well-being. Careful consideration of both sides, however, should give us additional wisdom whereby we may be more prudent ourselves in what we select for meal consumption.

First, the good news. In his classic work, author James pointed out that many of the Southwestern Indian tribes with whom he became intimately acquainted at the turn of the century, often resorted to just one or two kinds of foods for days on end. Yet such limited fare proved more than ample for their energy needs. They also were in the habit of thoroughly chewing their food, something most of us do not do enough of today.

"The Indians, with their parched corn, had taught me years before the benefit of thorough and complete mastication. I had gone off with a band of Indians on a hard week's ride with no other food than parched corn and a few raisins. This was chewed and chewed and chewed by the hour, a handful of the grain making an excellent meal, and thoroughly nourishing the perfect bodies of these stalwart athletes, who never knew an ache or pain, and who could withstand fatigue and hardship without a thought.

"A marked and wonderful effect of thorough mastication is that it decreases appetite from 10-15%, and reduces the desire for flesh meat from 30-50%. The more we masticate the less we desire to eat, and the more normal our appetites become. This in itself is a thing to be desired, for it is far easier not to have an abnormal appetite than it is to control it when it has fastened itself upon us."

Fairly recent clinical studies have confirmed James' interesting analysis of some Southwestern Indian dietary habits made over three-quarters of a century ago. The November 1985 *American Journal of Clinical Nutrition* mentioned that more is eaten during a meal consisting of a variety of foods than during a meal with just one food, even if that food is the favorite. Then followed different examples of this. In one study, dieticians offered three different snack foods (pizza, sausage rolls, and pork/shrimp egg rolls) either together or separately to volunteers. It was observed that subjects ate significantly more of these bite-sized snacks when all three were available than when just one was available (19.4 versus 15.8 pieces).

In another study, slices of bread were offered either with just one choice of spread or else with five different spreads. Greater intake was naturally evident with the "mixed meal" spreads, than for any single food spread by itself. In the same journal issue, another article dealt with the preference for pleasure. A highly interesting experiment was cited to show that a variety of palatable food gave more eating pleasure, was chewed far less, and consumed more often by rodents than meals just limited to a single brand of ordinary lab chow. Some rats were placed in a warm, cozy environment and given plenty of standard lab chow to eat whenever they wanted. But just outside their warm home in a very cold environment (-15 degrees Celsius or 5 degrees above zero Fahrenheit) were placed different types of tasty but non-nutritious foods. Although they could easily feed within the comfort of their nice, warm den, every one of the rats ventured into the painful, below-freezing environment to eat the more palatable foods instead. And the more tasty such junk foods were, the longer were they inclined to stay outside in these bitter cold circumstances to feast, even to the point of nearly freezing to death.

What both reports suggest is that the common advice given by most nutritionists and dieticians today about eating so-called "balanced meals" that include a variety of things, is pretty much archaic if not downright stupid to say the least! I myself have proved the wisdom of eating just one kind of food per meal. On those many mornings that I am able to consume my usual large bowl of cooked oatmeal with milk and nothing else accompanying it, I stay full for a much longer period of time, than those few mornings when I opt for bacon, eggs, hash browns, buttered toast with jam, and juice. The latter fare demands that I snack more often in between to satisfy frequent hunger cravings which are not present when I stick with my plain oatmeal/milk regimen instead.

Now for the bad news. As Native Americans have gradually moved away from the traditional healthier foods of their forefathers and adopted the white man's eating habits, an assortment of physical problems have set in as a consequence of this. Obesity heads the list. Writing in the November 1986 *Journal of the American Dietetic Association*, a team of registered dieticians and nurses noted that prior to the 20th century most Indians were thin, whereas well into this century they have become increasingly overweight. Changing food consumption and a decline in exercise were two of the reasons given for this dramatic increase in obesity among some tribes. The same researchers also found that North Carolina Cherokee Indian teenagers, boys as well as girls, weighed considerably more than their black and white sex counterparts between the ages of 14-16.

Among the White Mountain Apache of Fort Apache Reservation just east of Phoenix, Arizona, a steady increase in obesity has been noted in many young people for the last quarter of a century. According to the *American Journal of Clinical Nutrition* for February 1981, since 1952 Apache boys and girls have been getting a lot heavier. Thoriac fatfold measurements were again taken in 1969 and in 1976, with definite increases in thickness being recorded each time.

The same article attributed this growing obesity problem to several things. One was the decline in hunting, fishing, and gathering wild plant foods, and a substantial increase in grocery shopping from either the local trading post or a non-chain supermarket. The second was the type of preparation for most foods favored by many Apache women who were surveyed—frying (74%) versus boiling and stewing (22%). There is an abundance of clinical literature available to show that greasy foods of this kind are not only hard to digest, but rapid promoters of obesity as well.

Unfortunately with obesity has come a great deal of diabetes. Among some tribes like the Pima Indians, for instance, the disease is rampant, affecting over 50% of all adults aged 35 years or older. Besides them, noted the *American Journal of Epidemiology* (113:144) for 1981, other nationalities like Israeli, Norwegian, and Japanese men who have emigrated to this country and adopted similar American junk food diets, have likewise experienced alarming increases in obesity and its accompanying diabetes. Right along with both of these problems has also come hypertension for many Native Americans.

Anthropologists like myself know that whenever a cultural group is introduced to refined foods high in fat, sugar, and salt, they are apt to abandon their traditional natural foods which are high in fiber, minerals, vitamins, and enzymes. The core of the problem, says an article in the March 29th, 1984 *New Scientist* is when people eat too much of what tastes nice but is nutritionally inadequate and not enough of those substances that taste neutral or unpleasant but are actually quite nutritious.

Three of the best research articles I have ever seen in this effect were published in the mid-to-late '70s and early part of the '80s. They all show just how dynamic a factor taste is in ultimate obesity! The October 1975 *Journal of the American Dietetic Association* cited a survey made in a cafeteria in the Student Union building on the Berkeley campus of the University of California, in which overweight individuals were more inclined to go for starchy, sugary, greasy foods as a rule, while leaner students went for fresh fruits, non-starchy vegetables, legumes, juices, and milk instead.

Ecology of Food and Nutrition (6:63-68) for 1977 published the results of lab animals fed two different kinds of American diets. Mice fed the standard "supermarket" diet so typical of most Americans these days, showed greater body weight and greater proportions of body fat than did another group of rodents subsisting on a carefully selected "natural" foods diet. The "supermarket" diet consisted of things like cornflakes, mashed potatoes and gravy, chocolate cake, french fries, apple pie with Cool Whip topping, frankfurters, cupcakes, bologna and cheese sandwiches, hamburgers with "the works," and ice cream. On the other hand, the "natural" foods diet contained granola, goat's milk, alfalfa tea, brown rice, rhubarb crips, chili con carne, cashew millet casserole, stuffed flounder, green beans, baked potato, vegetable soup, liver and onions, curried soybeans, and prune whip with custard sauce. While the researchers made a thorough attempt to match this type of diet with healthy foods that were tasty, when mice previously exposed to the "supermarket" diet were offered this as well, they invariably went back to their old foods simply because they tasted better! The final article which appeared in *Physiology and Behavior* (30:629) in 1983 again underscored what these and many other studies have confirmed: "supermarket" foods high in fat, sugar, and salt just taste a lot better in the minds of mice and men, leading both groups to "overeat to the point of obesity."

A Sioux doctor from the Rosebud Reservation in South Dakota informed me several years ago, during a visit I made there, that he had devised a relatively simple snack plan for his patients to help them cut down on their inclinations for "supermarket" foods. Instead of munching on fatty, salty potato chips and washing them down with sugary soft drinks, he prescribed red radishes and celery and carrot sticks chewed very fine and then washed down with either low-sodium tomato juice or else apple or orange juice. He also recommended figs and dates for those with an extra "sweet tooth." He discovered that those who followed his advice with reasonable consistency experienced small but noticeable declines in weight. Those who were on their way to becoming diabetics, in time showed measurably lower rates of insulin production. While not the ideal foods, perhaps, in terms of lower sugar intake (especially the dates and figs), they seemed to do the job well enough in getting some of his patients to turn away from many of their "supermarket" junk favorites in preference for healthier foods.

We now come to a mixture of good and bad news, but first the negatives. In 1908 Ales Hdrlicka of the Smithsonian Institute's Department of Ethnology reported a variety of diseases common to Indian tribes of the Southwestern U.S. and northern Mexico. Tuberculosis, pneumonia, gastroenteritis, smallpox, impetigo, whooping cough, rheumatism, ophthalmia, conjunctivitis, gonorrhea, dental caries, and dysentery were the most frequent problems encountered. The one main disease which he could not find however, was cancer—"Tumors occur infrequently," he reported. In spite of all these other problems, though, he concluded that "the health of the Southwestern and north Mexican *non*civilized Indians is superior to that of the whites living in larger communities." Also noticeably absent were coronary heart disease—out of 2,000 people examined he only found three cases of heart trouble (all valvular insufficiencies and no advanced arterial sclerosis in any of them)—appendicitis, peritonitis, stomach ulcers, or any serious liver disease to speak of.

Some 65 years later these diseases were prominent among Indian children and young people, as reported by *Clinical Pediatrics* for February, 1973: pneumonia, gastroenteritis, intestinal parasites, head lice, measles, mumps, chicken pox, diarrhea (due to more infant bottle-feeding), otitis media, meningitis, gonorrhea, syphilis, heart disease, and violent behavior leading to death (car accidents, suicides, and homicides), these last three being absent from Hrdlicka's 1908 report!

But the upbeat side to all of this is that most Native American tribes today record very little incidence of cancer as a rule! Not only did Hrdlicka hardly find any of it in Southwestern Indian tribes, but epidemiologists studying remote Indian populations in Northwestern Ontario in modern times have likewise observed considerably lower rates of cancer among them as compared to the rest of Anglo Canadian men and women elsewhere (*American Journal of Public Health* for May, 1983).

This peculiar health phenomenon has been detailed even more extensively by a retired Seventh-Day Adventist physician, Dr. De Lamar Gibbons, who worked among the Navajos of southern Utah for some 17 years. Writing an article entitled "Indians Hold Key to Cancer" for the Sunday, November 29th, 1987 edition of *The Salt Lake Tribune*, Dr. Gibbons noted that besides himself, now-retired Drs. C. D. Goon and J. C. Smith also practiced medicine in San Juan County 32 and 26 years, respectively. All three of them, he stated, had never seen a breast cancer or lung cancer in a Navajo during their entire combined 75 years of medical practice in that part of the state.

Furthermore, while still in practice in Blanding, Utah, Dr. Gibbons conducted an extensive five-year study of patient records of both the San Juan County and Monument Valley Hospitals in Utah, as well as hospital records in Shiprock, New Mexico and Cortez, Colorado. In tabulating the cancer cases just for the San Juan facility over this five-year period, he discovered that out of some 97 cancers treated, just three of them were in Indians (their patient breakdown was 40% Navajo and 60% white). The Monument Valley Hospital's statistics were even more striking. Between 1960 and 1973, the hospital had 13,000 admissions, he noted. Among these, the medical staff encountered only 13 cases of cancer.

Dr. Gibbons attributed Navajo freedom from cancer to several things. One is the manner in which they fix their food. Navajoes are in the habit of thoroughly cooking their meat—quite literally, boiling it to death! Many cattle and sheep these days appear to be infected with herpes, tuberculosis, venereal disease, wart viruses, and bovine leukemia viruses. These latter viruses especially provoke cancer in these animals. They are also closely related to the AIDS viruses as well. Veterinary science and animal husbandry journals report that half of the dairy cows and slightly less of the beef cattle and sheep in America are presently infected in some way with these potentially deadly viruses. The best way to avoid getting these same viruses into your body, Dr. Gibbons says, is to boil the meat well, just like the Navajoes do.

The second reason he gives for the virtual absence of cancer among the largest Indian tribe in North America is their near total abstinence from poultry consumption. In the last 30 years, just one of the 5,000 or so San Juan County Navajos has been found to have developed prostate cancer, an almost universal occurrence in a majority of non-Indian men, he explained. And the apparent reason that this lone Indian came down with prostate cancer is because he raised chickens and ate them and the eggs they laid. Devout Navajos never consume chickens or turkeys, believing them to be birds of evil omen. Chickens are carriers of several nasty viruses like Marek's and fowl leukosis viruses which produce cancer in chickens. These viruses are eventually passed into the eggs and millions of non-Navajos eat them without making sure they are thoroughly cooked first. Some of the chicken cancer viruses, says Dr. Gibbons, also belong to the same retrovirus family of which the AIDS culprit is part.

The Navajos as an ethnic group have certain food preferences that leave very much to be desired. They consume a tremendously high fat diet consisting of mutton stew, bread deep-fried in mutton tallow, potato chips, and fried, salted nuts. Additionally they love soda pop, coffee, beer, candy and are especially fond of Twinkies cupcakes. They hate fresh fruits and vegetables as a rule, and eat very little fiber. In a word, their nutritional habits are abominable! Besides this they have un-believably bad sanitation. Yet they do *not* get cancer, Dr. Gibbons observed. The bottom line to all of this, he concludes, is that Navajos consistently avoid animal-source foods which contain harmful cancer viruses or else cook the hell out of such meats before ever consuming them. That is why they do not get cancer! Clearly then, there are some food practices here which many Anglos, Blacks, and Hispanics would do well to emulate for their own good.

Fasting and the Quest for Vision

One of the best accounts I have ever read concerning the spiritual benefits to an Indian fast appeared in Henry R. Schoolcraft's *History of the Indian Tribes of the United States* (6:633), published in 1857. Schoolcraft noted that "when young men or women are approaching maturity, it is customary for them to prepare themselves for the duties of life by an ordeal of fasting, by which means they are enabled to determine their future career, and ascertain whether or not they are qualified to act as doctors." A young brave from an unidentified tribe located somewhere in the California-Oregon-Washington region shared the following sacred experience with Mr. Schoolcraft:

"When my father thought I was old enough to seek my *To-mah-na-was* (or guardian spirit), he told me his views, and wished me to prepare myself. I thought over the matter for three days (*klone sun nika wawa kopah nika tumtum;* or, three days I talked with my heart). At last, when I had concluded, I took with me my axe and my wooden bowl, and getting into my canoe, I paddled up the Whilapah River to the foot of that black-looking hill which you see (pointing to a bluff hill about six miles up the river), and, having hauled up my canoe, I filled my bowl with water and went up to the top of the hill where I built a fire. For three days and three nights I kept my fire blazing brightly, and did not sleep at all, nor did I eat. At sunrise, I washed myself all over with water from my bowl and dried myself by the fire. I kept awake by singing and calling to my *To-mah-na-was*, and by dancing and jumping over and through the fire. The third day I saw everything appear as if it was surrounded by the sea, and in that sea were the different kinds of *To-mah-na-was*. Those that we first see are not the medicine *To-mah-na-was*—it takes many more days before they appear; but I was faint, and I only saw an inferior spirit; but he has made me a canoe-builder and a hunter. If I could have remained longer, I should have been a doctor."

Such fasts are the most sacred act of an Indian's life, Schoolcraft wrote. The impressions they got during such ceremonies were forever fixed within their minds, not even to be obliterated in the Hereafter. The name of the *To-mah-na-was* or guardian spirit was never mentioned to anyone, not even your dearest friend or your wife. Only by hieroglyphic illustrations depicting whales, lizards, porpoises, or birds could a rough idea be formed of what the image of the spirit really was like or the shape in which it had been presented to the minds of individual seekers.

It is interesting to note here in passing some parallel beliefs found in the Mormon religion. Worthy church members are encouraged to fast and pray prior to entering a Mormon temple for the first time to receive their individual endowments. During the Endowment Ceremony each worthy initiate receives a "new name" by which he or she is known Hereafter; this name is never again to be repeated to anyone in mortality and only to be used in the Hereafter. Additionally, such participants learn more about the spiritual forces for good and evil surrounding them; and upon coming to that part of the ceremony having to do with "The Veil," receive additional instructions concerning the identity of a particular divine being standing behind the curtain, who is represented by various temple workers in the flesh. All of this knowledge, it is believed, is both sacred and essential, never to be repeated outside of the temple proper and vital for one's own advancement in the kingdoms of glory Hereafter. One also learns within the temple walls something about his or her own guardian angel and one's personal relationship with certain immortal beings. All of this contributes to a Mormon's own quest for visionary experiences.

The sacredness of Native American vision quests was underscored by anthropologist Wayne Suttles in the May 1978 *Natural History* magazine. With the Northwest Salish Indians, he observed, the search for supernatural vision was a unique experience involving considerable skill and bringing much tribal status to the individual seeker. But the exact nature of the event itself was always kept secret until just before a person died, at which time it might be vaguely referred to or hinted at but never fully disclosed in minute detail. The Salish believed that if you spoke about the experience, you could actually "spoil" it and even lay yourself open to sickness or death. A parallel to this feature can be found in the Mormon temple ceremony rituals, wherein every covenant made has a corresponding and like curse attached to it, to which each worthy initiate is most solemnly bound. If any single covenant is purposely broken or any aspect of the Endowment Ceremony deliberately made public, then such a one can expect to incur the wrath of an angry God who will in time mete out the particular punishment which went with that broken covenant.

Fasting was also employed by some of the ancient inhabitants of New Mexico for other spiritual reasons besides vision quests. Archaeological work done along the Pajarito Plateau on the eastern side of the watershed of the Jemez mountain range, revealed a number of stone shrines, which for many generations had been used for consecrating families before the Great Spirit. As mentioned in Edgar L. Hewett's

Pajarito Plateau and Its Ancient People, were usually located on or very near to mountain tops where the most secret and sacred type of rituals were customarily held. A young couple would ascend to one of these stone shrines with a newborn infant in the mother's arms for the purpose of consecrating such a one before the Great Spirit. A somewhat similar parallel within Mormonism has a husband and wife going through to the temple and having all of their children born or unborn "sealed" to them by the Priesthood of God for "time and all eternity." By doing so, they then believe that their family unit will be secure and solid for the rest of eternity. So whether it was an ancient Indian couple going to a mountaintop stone shrine with their child or a modern Mormon couple kneeling before a cushioned altar in a temple sealing room somewhere, is really beside the point; the important thing here is that fasting was and is often resorted to so that the experience itself might be made more spiritual.

We finally come to a last benefit for missing so many meals—increasing one's own consciousness to hear spiritual voices within. Unfortunately, more often than not, such "inner whisperings" are usually prompted by mischievous spirits of every sort, rather than by noble beings of a much higher caliber. Nevertheless, for those who think they have adequate discernment to tell the difference between devils or angels, fasting can surely accentuate your "spiritual listening" abilities to quite an extent.

This is what happened to Dr. Alfred Alschuler some years ago. Trained as a clinical psychologist and now a respected professor of education at the University of Massachusetts at Amherst, he soon became aware of internal chatter that was not of his own making. He realized that the tone of the voice, its style and content arrangement were not his handiwork. Interestingly enough, this first episode occurred about a decade ago (sometime in 1978), while he was methodically searching for an ancient Native American holy ground in southern California. Having temporarily fasted quite by accident and realizing he had become lost, Dr. Altschuler asked himself mentally (as many of us are in the habit of doing anyway), just where he might be. Imagine his pleasant surprise, when a voice within him responded back with specific directions to the holy site he was looking for. Repeated attempts by him to tune into this inner voice at will, soon taught him that the voice was a lot clearer whenever he engaged in brief fasting and just subsisted on mild, natural foods. He told a reporter in the July/August 1988 issue of *Hippocrates* health magazine that it was like having your own inner Ann Landers giving you constant advice and counsel. Experience had taught him that heavy foods could interfere with this friendly voice just like overhead power lines might cause brief radio static. Therefore, monitoring his diet became an important asset in improving the mental receptivity for his invisible friend.

Dr. Alschuler eventually shared this unique experience with his wife and children, who became very supportive (two of them even wanted to know just how he manages to do it). Even the students in his classes thought that his admission was gutsy and brave. Calling this experience a "transcendent education," the college professor thinks that his ancient Indian shaman friend has had as much positive effect upon him in the last ten years as a good psychoanalyst or spiritual guru might have had. He feels his unseen Indian pal has taught him Native American patience and love and to be less concerned with the material world around him.

So whatever the reasons may be, know that a mild food fast of reasonable length and duration (so as not to injure the body in any way) can prove of immense benefit towards your own spiritual development.

Education the Indian Way

George Wharton James was of the firm opinion that, if modern educators would just inject into their present system of teaching about three-fifths of the Native American methods for instructing the young, our entire educational system would be "immeasurably happier, healthier and more useful" than it is presently. To him, book learning was nothing less than storing "embalmed knowledge, canned inform-ation, and the dry bones of knowledge" into one's mind.

"I believe in books . . . education . . . schools . . . colleges . . . universities . . . teachers . . . professors and doctors of learning," he reassured his readers in *What the White Race May Learn from the Indian*. But they are only a means of limited use to a much greater end—namely, "the proper education of one child!" His antagonism against the public school system in this country as presently constituted approached near bitterness when he described the lives of children who had gone through the process as being totally "ruined, spoiled, and damned."

James argued that teachers in public schools work essentially with "plastic materials," trying to conform individual minds and different personalities to one easy pattern—molding diverse intellects and emotions into one mold, as he termed it. The end result he said is just like so many bricks "coming forth from a furnace, uniform, regular, alike, perhaps pretty to the unseeing eye," but thoroughly wasted and corrupted so far as original thinking and moral values went.

"The only human bricks that ever amount to anything when our educational mill has turned them out are those made of refractory clay—the incomplete ones, the broken ones, the twisted ones, those that would not or could not be moulded into the established pattern." Native Americans, he felt, fit this description to a tee. Regarded as apparent outcasts from the rest of American society, Indians have pro-ceeded along in their own, quiet methodical ways of gaining knowledge that to the rest of us may seem somewhat backward, if not downright silly. After all, how can learning to detect the signs in nature—animal tracks, the way the wind blows, or position of sun in the sky—have anything to do with earning a decent living?

But, said James, if you put any one of these primitive Indians alongside a bunch of Harvard graduates shipwrecked on an island in the sea somewhere, the former could easily survive whereas the latter group would perish. "The Indian can turn his hand to anything" when placed out doors, he noted. A Native American would know "how to build a fire in the rain, where to sleep in a storm, how to track animals, how to trap fish, flesh or fowl, where to look for nuts, seeds, berries or roots, how to hobble a horse when no rope is available, and so forth." Put an Indian with barely a grade school education in the desert beside a Ph.D. fellow and the college guy would perish. For an Indian "knows a thousand and one things that a white man never knows," James concluded.

Native Americans of the past and a few of the present who have not been completely spoiled by the white man's education, learn things the old fashioned way: careful observation, patient studying, quiet meditation, and an inner discerning with the soul. Time and time again I have noticed these qualities with tribes or cultures I have been associated with. Be they Montana Crow, Idaho Blackfoot, Arizona Hopi, New Mexico Pueblo or Yucatan Maya, these traits have always persisted, but mostly in those of little formal education. A few anecdotal experiences of mine will suffice to prove my point in this respect.

Now most of us are pretty familiar with the ethnobotanical knowledge of Native Americans. Countless stories have been told of this or that white person stricken with illness and an old Indian medicine man or woman going off somewhere, getting a particular herb(s), making it into a brew and having the sick one drink it to recover later on. But that is usually only half the story, since considerably more goes into the initial therapy process than meets the eye.

In July, 1981, in company with several other scientists I diligently labored among the Huastec Maya in the northeastern part of Mexico. The Teenek (as they prefer to be called) are a splinter group of Maya who have resided in the sweltering heat and stifling humidity of a tropical zone extending from the Sierra Madre Oriental mountains eastward to the Gulf of Mexico. Some 63,000 or so of these Maya are scattered among half a dozen small municipalities in the northeastern part of the Mexican state of Vera Cruz and in about eight similar townships in the bottom southeastern part of San Luis Potosi.

While there we became quite ill, either due to the food or water or mosquitoes or all three factors combined. A couple of the more seriously ill in our small party were taken to regional hospitals in either Tampico or across the mountains to San Luis Potosi. Intestinal parasites later turned out to be the culprits for our sicknesses. I elected to be treated instead by a local Teenek curer who resided in one of the small, neighboring villages located in the area we were then studying.

The first thing the healer did was to sweep me with a bundle of tsabalte shoots in the hopes of driving my illness away. *Cestrum dumetorum* yields a very disagreeable odor. I imagined in my slightly feverish state that he was holding a skunk up by its tail and waving this over me instead of a bunch of herbs. Unfortunately, the spirits responsible for my sickness he said, could not be persuaded to leave so easily; I surmised that they probably were addicted to the stuff.

The next thing attempted was to bathe my body with water. This had the good effect of cooling me down and lowering my elevated temperature a bit. Surprisingly enough, a strong concoction of rum and cayenne pepper was given to me, which hot though it was while being swallowed, had an initial refrigerant effect on me later. I have utilized this same procedure several times since (minus the rum, however) with amazingly good results. Much later after a full recovery from my awful ordeal, I asked my good Samaritan how he had made this interesting discovery. Simply by observation was the translated reply. He had witnessed several dogs in the village chewing on hot pepper pods in order to obtain some relief from the intense heat, and so he figured the same thing would work just as well for cases of fever. I could not help but to marvel at this simple ingenuity.

One other thing impressed me as well. My healer went off to a small cave one evening by himself in order to consult with his Miim and Pay'lom (personal god-powers) regarding my condition. He soon fell "asleep" and dreamed that I had an angry spirit lurking within my breast, which was aggravating my situation more. Upon returning to the hut I was staying in at the time, he began to move a curious-looking green crystal over my body, peering into it all the while. After a few minutes, he "located" something directly over my heart, and laying the crystal aside began to gently tap on my breastbone with his fingers. Through one of our party who had remained with me and knew the language better than I did, I asked what was going on. The healer replied that he had located the source of my angry spirit, and that now he needed my help in driving it away. I marveled at how he knew this, for indeed, I had been harboring resentment against myself for not taking extra precautions to avoid getting sick. I was anxious to be up and about my business of evaluating the native plant lore in that region, and was "mad as hell" inside for not being able to carry out these wishes.

He then energetically crushed some leaves from a woody vine I later learned was a species of *Centrosema* in a small wooden bowl of water. He then took an old rag and dipped it into this mixture. As he did so, he dribbled the water down my chest and stomach, and then across from shoulder to shoulder in the form of a cross. After which he quietly began mumbling some words to himself. I had enough sense to realize it was a prayer to either some Maya god or Catholic Saint, and so joined him with a silent invocation of my own. In just a few short minutes, my mental and emotional anxieties of confinement had left me and in its place, as crazy as it may sound, was a feeling of tranquility. Upon later closer questioning, the healer admitted to me in private that it was one of the Maya godpowers which had infused this peace within my being.

More surprising though was my discovery that his special crystal was nothing more than a broken shard from an old Coca-Cola bottle. My first reaction was, "What a ripoff!" This obvious letdown stemmed from the preconceived notion that in order for a crystal to work effectively, it had to be made of exotic materials, look nice, and cost a lot. How wrong I was in my early assumption. My healer friend patiently explained to me that is not what you look through that counts but the quality and condition of the looker that really matters. For beads and broken glass or real crystals to work, those using them must approach the godpowers (as he termed them) in supplication with a humble heart, contrite spirit, and reasonably moral decency. Anything short of this will not make such objects work or have the friendly godpowers respond through them.

Another example should suffice to illustrate George Wharton James' statement that an Indian "knows a thousand and one things that a white man never knows." While working on the Crow Reservation in eastern Montana some years ago, I happened to spend a little time with an old fellow by the name of Tim Two Bears. One day while we were out in the nearby foothills, he called my attention to an obviously azure blue sky with nary a cloud to be seen. "Pretty soon it rain," he snorted matter-of-factly. Naw, not a chance, I thought to myself, judging from what seemed to be an apparently fine day.

Well, I learned two lessons that afternoon. First is never to judge a sky by its color; and the second is never to doubt the word of an Indian, especially if he is deadly serious and downright sober! Before an hour had elapsed, we were in the midst of a steady shower that lasted for the space of 45 minutes or so. When the last drops had fallen and we found it was prudent to come out into the open again from beneath our covering, I asked him how he knew this inclement weather was coming when the skies showed no apparent signs of the same.

"By the wind," he replied. But there was not any wind, I reminded him. "Maybe not for you, but for me there was," he said. Two Bears then explained that the wind need not be very strong for him to detect it. "Can learn more from whispers of wind," he said, than from any evident breezes. "Lips of wind touch me here," he continued, pointing to his right and left cheeks. "Kissed by the breezes?" I queried. He managed a faint smile before resuming the dialogue again. "Wind whispered with moist lips," he said. "That is how I know it rains." I was left to ponder whatever messages remained hidden between these few lines of conversation. As I said before, Indians may be of few words, but they are certainly plentiful on the kind of knowledge we have lost through our civilized upbringings.

While many traditions have obviously disappeared from Indian life as tribes have become assimilated into the white man's culture (a process called "acculturation" by anthropologists), yet some of the old ways of learning continue to persist here and there. In 1941 the Bureau of Indian Affairs launched a massive research project into the personality, education, and administration of four different tribes residing in the American Southwest: Navaho, Sioux, Papago, and Hopi (the Zuni also were studied but the project was terminated before the final report could be prepared). The published results, however, of the other four tribes appeared in three different quarterly issues of *America Indigena* (Volume X, Nos. 1-3, January-July 1950). A large number of anthropologists and sociologists were put on the U.S. government payroll for a few years to assist with this herculean task.

Some very interesting things about the way Indians educate their kids emerged from these intensive studies. For one thing, Indian infants begin to acquire tribal attitudes and values at a much earlier age than white or black children. With the Navajo this is well under way by the time the child is only six months old. By then the Navajo "emotional and social climate" has already begun to permeate and mold the child in such a way as to "last forever."

The manner in which the Navajo child picks up certain habits is totally different from the way white, black or Mexican children learn the same basics. For instance, let us look at toilet training. In these other societies children usually learn the importance of elimination through the use of devices (toilet training seats or small "potty" chairs), verbal praise (in the form of constant parental encouragements) and small rewards (candy, pat on the head, kiss or hug). On the other hand, a Navajo toddler will accompany his mother or older sister to defecate or urinate outdoors (if the house or hogan lacks indoor plumbing facilities). He will notice that they exhibit a certain uneasiness while doing so, taking great care to conceal the waste matter they have just deposited. The child becomes intrigued by their unusual attention given to such necessary actions, and likewise impressed by the lengths they go to to assure privacy for themselves during such moments. More often than not, the mother or older sister will explain that she has just gotten rid of some very bad material which lay in part of her body; and that this must be done frequently or else she might get sick and die. The child then begins to feel that this kind of special hygiene is something worth doing for himself or herself as a means of self-protection. No other coaxing or rewards are necessary than the implanted idea that bladder and bowel duties keep you (the child) from getting sick or dying.

My father, Jacob Heinerman, reminded me some years ago when we were reminiscing a little about my early childhood that I began going to the toilet (that is, to my own little "potty" chair) when I was about 14 months old. This, he noted, was considerably earlier than other youngsters of surrounding families they knew. In fact, some had cause to marvel at just how well he had accomplished this. The "secret," of course, was that either dad or his mother (my grandmother Barbara) would take Joseph (my younger brother) or I into the bathroom when either of them had to defecate or urinate. Dad recalled how both of us were fascinated to watch him or his mom attending to their usual business, and that it was repeatedly explained to us in very simple language "evil inside" had to come out or else the body would become very "ill." Hence, "evil" wastes became readily associated with nasty "ills" in our precocious minds. Soon, dad said, we both were wanting to emulate what they had taught us by way of example. (My mother was not actively involved in raising us for a variety of reasons, which have no place here).

Among the Hopi, the child is permitted to absorb much from the adult world around him or her. He or she learns largely by imitating and experimenting and being treated as an important member of the group with his or her own individual rights and privileges as well as incipient duties and responsibilities. He or she is given a good deal of freedom in order to more fully explore the surrounding environment, while at the same time gentle but firm limitations of physical safety are set so as to prevent injury on the perilous mesa top. At the same time the child is allowed to experience some shock and fear due both to real and to imaginary dangers that he or she might better comprehend the actual and supernatural worlds around

them. But all of this serves to maintain balance and harmony in a child's matura-
tion.

With whites, blacks, and Mexicans there is usually the tendency to treat children
as a group separate and distinct from adults; but this has no place within the Hopi
culture at all. A child is regarded as an important member of the community with
real responsibilities and rights consistent with his or her stage of growth and development. Between the relatives there exists, not the type of inferior-superior relationship common among children and their parents in the U.S., but rather a recip-
rocal give-and-take in which the child's personality and role are definitely respected.
From the beginning the child is given meaningful work to do, work which the child
knows to be indispensable in the household. A minimum of pressure is put upon
him or her, but the child is keenly aware that this unique status depends upon
cooperation and personal accountability for actions taken. As long as the child is
able to show a willingness to work and some responsible behavior, then he or she
can enjoy the respect and admiration of adults.

This Bureau of Indian Affairs study on Native American personality education
and administration summarized some of its more interesting finds this way:

1. Development from childhood to adulthood is carefully conditioned and purposely structured regarding release and control of emotions, attitudes, values, and
behavior patterns.

2. This is largely accomplished in an extended-family situation where grandparents, aunts, uncles, nieces, nephews, in-laws, and so forth all participate in some
way in the upbringing of the typical Indian child. This face-to-face group approach
differs considerably from the one-or two-parent biological family unit that we see so
much of these days. In a sense, the community (here it would be tribal members)
raises the child instead of just one or two adults having to do it all alone.

3. In all tribes investigated, infants were treated with much affection, in relaxed
and gentle ways, and granted considerably greater freedoms than might come from
the normal two-parent family unit. In each tribe, infants were always kept close to
someone, who did not necessarily have to be an immediate family member. I have
witnessed only a couple of similar nurturing and training patterns among whites.
One of these with which I am intimately familiar and readily comes to mind is the
Bruce and Norma Armstrong family of Salt Lake City, Utah. Norma gave birth to
her fifth child, a boy named John, in the spring of 1987. The other four children are
teenagers, ranging in age from 19 (a boy, Mike), 17 (a girl, Teresa), 15 and 13 (two
boys, Matthew and Jason). Almost immediately everyone in the household became
involved in holding, hugging, kissing, caressing, bathing, diaper-changing, feeding,
and teaching this precious little baby. In fact, even very close friends to the family,
such as yours truly, contributed to a considerable extent in most of these things,
even to the point of bringing the little tyke over to my research center several times
for a few hours so that his mom could rest better. Of the family members themselves, probably the greatest attention given to this little one was from his older
brother Matthew. In fact, so close has the bonding become between them that now,

144 Spiritual Wisdom of the Native Americans

at the age of two and a half years old, John will bawl his head off if he cannot be with Matt nearly all the time. This creates some very interesting and highly noisy scenarios when Matt has to go to high school every morning and work in my office a couple of days a week. But out of this group bonding has come a most intelligent, highly active, and deeply affectionate little kid, more so I might add than is customary with many white, black, or Mexican children primarily raised by just one or sometimes two people.

4. Within each tribe studied, infants were never addressed in "baby talk," but rather the complete mother tongue; no cutesy slang here but fully enunciated words and proper grammar for everything spoken to the child from early on. Unfortunately such is not the case in other cultures, where "baby talk" is viewed with a certain sickening sentimentality by those who do not know better. In the case of the Armstrongs just cited, I attempted to establish a strong lead with normal words when John began his first clumsy attempts at speech. His brother Matt and his mom also tried to follow in the same path as well. However, other members of the family fell into the old habit of "baby talk" with him; hence, breastmilk became known as "diddy," and he acquired the odd nickname of "booper" for some strange reason. But wherever great care was taken to speak simple but normal everyday words to him, the result has been a wonderfully progressive vocabulary beyond what is usually expected of two-year-olds.

5. Indian babies are weaned away from the breasts of their mothers sometime after the third year as a rule, and then very gradually at that. This extra time spent in nursing gives the child a much stronger sense of security than may be among whites, blacks, or Mexicans. A deeper sense of commitment to the family and tribal community is engendered as well, not to mention the terrific bonding that exists between child and mother.

6. Also, the Native American child is permitted and encouraged to develop in accordance to his own natural rhythms and needs. Nothing is ever hurried or pushed—the child walks and talks when he or she wants to; and the child is not trained in personal hygiene until after evidence of walking and talking have become apparent. One major point stressed by this lengthy government study: Indians do not encourage or promote either a competitive spirit or a self-centered attitude among their children. The children compete with no one; rather, they participate within the culture that they are a part of, being taught to make valuable contributions of their own at an early age, be it chopping firewood or hauling water. And Indian children are taught that personal ambitions must yield to community needs. In other words, individuality is supposed to be swallowed up with group identity; what "I" may want to do, instead becomes what "we" ought to do. "Instead, they build up attitudes and habits of cooperation, self confidence, and security on the part of the individuals within the group, the report concluded in the July 1950 *America Indigena.*

7. Lastly, an Indian child is never disciplined by just one or two individuals (as is common with most traditional American families), but by a number of friends and relatives in the extended-family group. This is further supplemented by a variety

of supernatural agents. Physical punishment is hardly ever employed. In my own sojourns among different Western Indian tribes I never saw a child spanked, much less yelled at. Even with "impossible teenagers," discipline worked. No Dr. Joyce Brothers or other psychological enticements were necessary to elicit better behavior from older children. The key to this obviously lies with with how the child is disciplined while still quite young. "It's hard to shape clay when hardened, but very easy to mold when wet," goes an ancient Native American proverb. Anyone who has worked with preschoolers versus high schoolers knows only too well the truthfulness implied herein. From early on attempts are made to divert the child and to distract his attention away from misbehavior, to explain in supernatural terms why refraining from such is a better course to pursue. The child is often shamed into acceptable behavior and then accordingly rewarded for it. Strangely enough, the majority of these "knowing right from wrong" experiences come not so much from the child's close relatives as they do from "forces outside the immediate family." Such potent forces include: tribal (public) opinion; supernatural powers believed to inflict punishment for personal misbehavior; and Nature herself! The last is an especially intriguing one.

For instance, I was in a Navajo hogan (earth-covered lodge made of timber) some years back, where I witnessed a slightly heated debate taking place between a father and his 16 year-old-son. The son stomped off in anger, but not before telling his father in Navajo the equivalent of our "go to hell!" The father remarked before the boy left that the "skypowers" would punish him for his insolence. Well, wouldn't you know, a brief thunderstorm (minus the rain) soon rolled across the valley in somewhat ominous tones. It was not too long before the kid returned, and in more subdued fashion apologized for his rude outburst and asked the old man's forgiveness. A footnote to this, however: the boy had very little exposure to the white man's schooling, no exposure to television whatsoever, and infrequent exposure to the radio. Had he been fully acculturated with these abominable things, chances are he might just have snorted at such a suggestion and not come back later to apologize. As the government report summarized: The Indian child learns life by living and, at a far earlier age than is customary in most American culture, he becomes a responsible member of the community, participating in its work, ceremonies, and recreation.

The Benefits of Communalism

In the broadest sense possible, communalism is "a system or social organization in which material goods are held in common by many;" the opposite to this is capitalism, "a system that permits land, natural wealth, and goods to be accumulated in unspecified amounts by one or several individuals." Capitalism is the very antithesis to communalism (sounds less sinister than communism, which is what it really is) in that individual rights supplant group rights and a fiercely competitive spirit (read "free enterprise") is encouraged over group participation. In communal-ism everyone is a winner, because everyone shares in the goods and the success of a venture, whereas in capitalism many are losers and only a few emerge on top to become real winners in any sense of the word. Capitalism is probably best rep-resented by a pyramid with a wide margin at the base supporting a sliver thin top. On the other hand, communalism can be favorably compared to a perfect square, wherein all sides are equal! This, in its simplest form, is the paramount difference between the two.

Up until more recent times, most Native American cultures had always been communally oriented. For instance, when an entire Eskimo village in Point Barrow, Alaska goes out fishing and returns with their boats loaded, the catches of the day are generally divided evenly among all tribal members so that every person receives his or her fair share of things. However, with the recent inroads of capitalism the scenario has changed quite a bit—now it is every man for himself, hauling in as much as he can get and either selling it for a profit or else hoarding it away for himself and his own immediate family. This has caused dissension within the tribe, produced inward pain in elderly members who regret seeing the old traditions slip away, and brought considerable turmoil to a formerly stable society.

The foregoing is an example of what happens when the white man's ways interfere with the materialistic cooperation that may be already in force among a tribe. But what about the spiritual aspects? Are they not similarly affected in an adverse manner? In an old issue of the *American Anthropologist* (50:206-7, 1948) anthropologist Laura Thompson explored in depth what she called a common "power pool" jointly shared by all members of the same tribe or of several different tribes culturally interrelated with one another. This power pool enabled an individual to obtain power for himself, but for the benefit of the entire tribe and not just for his own self-centered purposes. More correctly, though, Thompson noted that the power source is conceived as a system of forces requiring communal ceremonies to keep it in order. Using the Hopi as an example, she noted that their rituals were the communal type in practice, intent and emphasis. The welfare of the group and its crops, rather than the welfare of the individual and personal illness, is the focus of ceremonies.

Imagine though what can happen when the white man's "capitalistic Christian-ity" enters upon the scene. Everything literally breaks down and instead of unity there is disharmony and fractionizing of the groups involved in such conversion attempts. Nowhere has this been more beautifully portrayed than in the July, 1947, issue of *The American Journal of Sociology* (53:18-21). Thompson, joined this time by Alice Joseph, looked at two different Hopi communities and how each of them separately approached the problems of acculturation.

First Mesa and Old Oraibi are two very ancient Hopi communities, dating back for many centuries of continuous, unbroken habitations. Both are located in northern Arizona. At First Mesa contacts with white men have always been more frequent and friendlier than those at Old Oraibi. And while some Protestant missionaries managed to convert a few outside the community, the Hopi religion itself, including the full communal ceremonial style, still flourishes. First Mesa people have worked hard to keep alive Hopi values, Hopi outlook on life, Hopi ritual, Hopi social structure, and most of the ancient technology. Yet the community has not been totally adverse to accepting some of the white man's more useful traits, methods, and inventions.

On the other hand, Old Oraibi residents challenged anything new from the outside world with almost fierce hostility. Strenuous attempts were made by village elders to remain completely insulated. However, with a great deal of persistence, the Mennonites managed to establish a foothold on the mesa top not too far from this ancient pueblo. Soon a feud, which had been developing for some time anyway at Old Oraibi, crystallized and split the ancient village into five different segments. This rift left Old Oraibi a mere ruin of its former self, with the shared political and religious administration and communal cycle of ceremonies incomplete.

Indian converts to the new religion were forced to leave Old Oraibi and soon thereafter joined with their new-found Mennonite friends in establishing New Oraibi. Today it is the only village on the entire Hopi reservation with a constitution guaranteeing individual liberties and a democratic administration. All remaining villages are essentially communal theocracies where the will of groups prevails through duly appointed committees. Interestingly enough, New Oraibi is also the most effected by internal struggles and factionalism, both Thompson and Joseph noted.

Other contrasts, however apparent or subtle, are evident between First Mesa and Old Oraibi. Children from First Mesa reveal a family setup in which both father, mother, the community, and supernatural agents all operate as powerful motivating forces for their development, not only utilizing fear and shame, but also abundant happiness as well. Old Oraibi kids are a lot different, though. More emphasis is now placed on the family instead of the community and the mother has emerged as the dominant figure for raising the children. Fathers at Old Oraibi have far less parental influence than do the dads at First Mesa. Likewise, elements of the supernatural are very inconspicuous in the Old Oraibi scheme of things, and the pueblo appears to have lost the firm, positive grip on its young people that First Mesa still retains. Also, boys of First Mesa are relatively spontaneous and quite outgoing, whereas those from Old Oraibi are very much constricted and troubled by a vague anxiety of not knowing exactly what's expected of them or precisely where they fit into things.

Boys at First Mesa seem to have a much more well-developed "all-around personality" than Old Oraibi fellows do. In fact, compared to other Hopi children in surrounding pueblos, Oraibi boys show a marked trend toward personality distur-bances of the type which, if discovered among white kids, would indicate compul-sive neurosis.

When both women had compiled all of their test results and properly interpreted them in the context of the total environment, it seems that at Old Oraibi the nicely adjusted, dynamic balance of the traditional Hopi communal social and religious organization had been completely thrown out of whack. Thompson and Joseph believed that the breakdown of the ceremonial cycle, which was the vital core of the traditional Hopi male world and the chief creative outlet of the men accounted for the upside down conditions at Old Oraibi. In spite of the Mennonite emphasis upon the family unit (instead of the group as a whole) and raising the prestige and importance of Old Oraibi women, and bringing them the message of Jesus, both female sociologists said, the teachings of the missionaries did not offer the Hopi a sufficient substitute for the old beliefs and way of life

By abandoning their former communal ways, wrote Thompson and Joseph, and by attempting to build themselves up through individualistic and competitive economic and political pursuits, the men of Old Oraibi have placed themselves in a rather dismal, somewhat hopeless situation. For this reason, there is more anxiety and less happiness at Old Oraibi than at First Mesa. Without the negativities associated with "capitalistic Christianity," First Mesa thrives economically, socially, and spiritually. At First Mesa the family, the community, and the supernatural world reinforce one another in a positive and negative role. With the communal ceremonial activities intact, First Mesa residents look after both the needs of "me and mine" as well as "thee and thine," while at Old Oraibi just "me and mine" attitudes of self-centeredness continue to prevail and divide.

Native American Manners

In his book, George Wharton James mentioned that "the Indians know how to be beautifully courteous" and then gave several examples of such. For instance, whenever he ate in an Indian's home as an invited guest, everyone else in the family would remain motionless until he had served himself before helping themselves. Then none of the family would eat until their guest had taken several mouthfuls himself. This prompted him to observe:

"Now, to me, the whole affair showed a kindly consideration for my feelings that is not always apparent in so-called well-bred strangers of my own race. . . . From the Indian we imagine that we ought not to expect much of what we call 'higher courtesy,' yet I find it constantly exercised; while from the civilized white race we expect much, and alas! often are very much disappointed instead."

Indians are far more thoughtful and considerate of others as a rule, he noted, than white people are. He illustrated this point with another anecdote:

"I was visiting the Hopi pueblo of Walpi for the purpose of studying the secret ceremonies of the underground kivas of the Antelope and Snake clans prior to the Snake Dance. For fifteen days and nights I never took off my clothes to go to bed, but went from kiva to kiva, witnessing the ceremonials, and when I was too tired to remain awake longer, I would stretch out on the bare, solid rock floor, my camera or my canteen for my pillow, and go to sleep. Occasionally, however, when something of minor importance was going on during the daytime, I would steal upstairs to a room which I had engaged in this woman's house. As soon as I stretched out and tried to sleep, she went around to the children and the neighbors and told them that the 'Black Bear'—my name with these people—was trying to sleep, and was very, very tired. That was all that was necessary to send the children far enough away so that the noise of their play could not disturb me, so that I could get a good nights sleep.

"This I take to be an extreme courtesy. I know people of both 'high and low degree' in our civilization who resent as an impertinent interference with their 'rights' any suggestions that they be kind or quiet to their neighbors,—much less strangers and aliens. But for my own sake I would rather that my children possessed the kindly sympathy shown by these Indian children than have the finest education (that) the greatest university of our civilization could grant without it."

Compare the thoughtfulness extended to him in his tired moments to that which I received in July, 1988 while visiting with some old friends in Scottsdale, Arizona. Bob is a chiropractor and a darned good one at that. Cheryl, his lovely wife, is a faithful spouse and devoted to a family of five children. Anyhow, I stayed several nights at their house in company with Matthew and Jason Fountaine, during our month-long trip around the United States. Many cordialities were extended to the three of us, with the exception of seeing that we rested well. Bob and Cheryl's oldest teenage daughter stayed up late long after both of them had retired to bed, chatting with another girl friend of hers who was sleeping overnight with her. Try as we might, nothing could persuade their daughter to keep the noise down and be more considerate of her parent's house guests. Finally, having run out of patience and through sheer exhaustion, I pounded on her bedroom door with my fist, nearly frightening her and her friend out of their wits. A few well-chosen profanities delivered in a most angry tone let them know that I meant business. The shock effect worked great for letting us get a good night's sleep, but upset both parents the next morning. They felt that no matter how misbehaved their girl and her friend may have been, my swearing was uncalled for. We parted on an obviously disconcerting note, but time eventually healed the wounds and kept the friendship going. This graphically illustrates the unfortunate differences between the well-mannered ways of most Indians and the utter rudeness of many whites.

Indians are forever grateful to the Great Spirit for everything around them and often express their gratitude in special food or tobacco offerings accompanied by prayers, in ceremonial dances and sacred chants, and particularly in reverent attitudes and emotions towards all life in general. I can truly say after having spent a number of years studying different Indian tribes throughout the Western Hemisphere that I have never met an ungrateful Indian. Oh, to be sure I have encountered drunken, deceitful, perverse, violent, filthy, and wicked Indians every now and again, but never an ungrateful one!

As I near the end of this last chapter, I cannot think of a better subject to close with than the simple words "please" and "thank you." While Indians may not always say them, yet they always seem to feel these words within themselves. You can often tell so by looking into their eyes—the words are there if they have asked you for something and received it. But with the rest of us, we pretty much have to vocalize these things if we are not to appear as being rude.

And speaking of rudeness, it calls to mind a strongly-worded article which appeared in the Thursday, March 12th, 1987 issue of *The Wall Street Journal*. Heavy bold, black type on the front page announced with ominous headlines: "RAMPANT RUDENESS!" The article then proceeded to paint a very dismal picture of manners across the entire United States: "small, everyday courtesies" are out and "me" oriented selfishness and rudeness are most definitely in. Some regions of the country—notably the South—cling more than other places to the prestiges of gracious behavior. And courteous ways seem to have hung on longer in the small towns of rural America than in her big, sprawling cities of corporate aggressiveness and pollution. A key to understanding how pervasive this alarming problem has become is just to notice how you are treated in stores and restaurants. For every "thank you" managed by some conscientious employees, there will be at least a dozen stares of silent ingratitude from those who take the money of others waiting in line behind you. It is so bad, says *The Journal*, that we are hopelessly becoming the rudest nation on earth.

It begins in the home and spreads its ugly tentacles out from there. Notes syndicated columnist Abigail Van Buren (and sister of rival columnist Ann Landers), young people are the worst offenders when it comes to discourteous behavior. Parents simply are "too busy" or unwilling to put forth all the hard work it takes to teach their kids polite behavior. Interestingly enough, as the family unit in America has consistently been breaking down with more divorces and moms in the working place, so there has been a corresponding curve upward in plain nastiness and boorish behavior. Impoliteness even spreads itself to inanimate objects. Overhead public signs in this country are downright discourteous. Here they say "No Smoking," whereas in Europe the same signs would read "No Smoking *Please*."

Jim Bouton did a short piece in the Friday, May 6th, 1988 issue of *USA Today* entitled, "Rudeness is Abroad in the Land" in which he said, we have less consideration for others. There is a constant rudeness in the land. This lack of concern for others' feelings allows littering in the streets, talking in the movies, smoking in a crowded room, or getting drunk at the ball park."

America was once more community-oriented (as in communally oriented). We took greater pride in our cities, showed more respect for the environment, and exhibited more concern for our fellow men than we do now. Between those days past and the immediate present something was lost—a sense of being an important part of a wonderful whole. More specifically, group motivation was replaced with undue emphasis on self. Self became glorified and started demanding its rights instead of thinking more of the group's rights. Whether reflected in something bad like the rights of kids to play their hellish rock music as loud as they damn well please or in something better like nonsmoker's rights to clean air, it is all the same—"to hell with you," and "what about me" instead.

More recently, writer Ann Kolson did an article entitled "The Age of Rudeness Intrudes on Us Every Day" for the Knight-Ridder Newspapers. In her May, 1989 piece she pointed out that rudeness is all around us in every conceivable form. President George Bush sarcastically barks to reporters, "Read my lips!" Popular TV talk show host Morton Downey, Jr. throws a Pulitzer Prize-winning biography to his noisy, mostly blue-collar, and male audience, then screams, "This book is a piece of garbage!" His audience roars right back with the same level of stupidity.

From the time the sun comes up until it sets at night, you are surrounded by unbelievable rudeness. Disc jockeys think it is cute to belch or pass intestinal gas on the airwaves. Angry drivers flash you the middle finger if you get in their way. Kids and adults wear t-shirts emblazoned with "I'm with stupid!" Bank tellers snarl at you; store clerks forget to say "thanks." Unofficial tell-all biographies of famous movie stars detail their most intimate bathroom habits before the world. Stage and film comedians turn the air a dark blue with their filthy jokes. And before midnight arrives, many Americans are treated to the sick and perverse ways of David Letterman. Where does it end?

Ms. Kolson pointed out that we are basically returning to an era of "becoming like Neanderthals" again. Says psychiatrist Aaron Beck of the Center for Cognitive Therapy at the University of Pennsylvania, "I think society has lost its closeness and cohesiveness because of self-assertion and self-realization." The "new honesty" dictates that you tell the other person exactly what is on your mind, regardless of his or her feelings.

For early Native Americans such things were practically unheard of. Even in times of war between neighboring tribes, a certain unspoken decorum or "etiquette of arms" prevailed. While the basic rules of battle always have remained the same, yet most Indian braves would show a certain respect and admiration for worthy opponents who fought well. Strange as it may seem, a certain perverse sense of respect was usually common between two enemies locked in mortal combat. Make no mistake, each was out to kill the other, but (and this is where Indians differed from today's racial groups) both manifested a certain consideration for the other's fighting skills and bravery. In other words, each one esteemed his enemy as an opponent worthy of meeting.

With the early Indians, you just did not fight your enemy in with recklessness and disrespect; to the contrary, you fought him with style and admiration even though you might have still hated his guts. An example of how well-mannered even warriors could be in ancient times comes to us from a short document signed by an early Mormon pioneer named Charles D. Evans sometime in April, 1897 and located in the Historical Department of the LDS Church of Salt Lake City. It concerns the final fate of the last white Nephite mentioned in the *Book of Mormon*. Moroni met his end sometime after 421 A.D. in a brief skirmish with several wandering Lamanites (ancestors of later American Indians). Joseph Smith inquired of the Lord how this man, after whose father the *Book of Mormon* and the nickname "Mormon" Church both derived their names, finally perished.

". . . In answer to prayer the Lord gave Joseph a vision, in which appeared a wild country. And on the scene was Moroni after whom were six Indians in pursuit. He stopped and one of the Indians stepped forward and measured swords with him. Moroni smote him and he fell dead; another Indian advanced and contended with him. This Indian also fell by his sword. A third Indian then stepped forth and met the same fate. A fourth afterwards contended with him, but in the struggle with the fourth, Moroni, being exhausted, was killed. Thus ended the life of Moroni."

It is interesting to see from the foregoing historical account that none of the Lamanites ganged up on him at once; instead, they chose to fight him one by one, thereby showing that certain rules of conduct prevailed even in times of war. The *Book of Mormon* itself is also quite specific in mentioning letters being exchanged between warring Nephites and Lamanites, each party firmly but respectfully insisting that the other surrender.

Furthermore, the ancient ancestors of today's Indians took the making of promises and pledges quite seriously. Despite all of their apparent savagery, they firmly believed in keeping their word even with their enemies. The entire 44th chapter of the book of Alma beautifully illustrates this. After some fierce confrontations with these people an earlier Nephite general also named Moroni commanded that the Lamanite king, Zerahemnah, after delivering up the weapons of his army, should covenant never to attack them again.

Ordinarily, vows less serious than this are hardly ever kept by many of us today. Teenagers promise their parents to do thus and so, and seldom ever end up doing what they said they would. Husbands and wives make pledges with each other, which are often either forgotten or broken. Nations make repeated treaties between each other, only to break them later on. A man's word today just is not as good as it was a hundred or a thousand years ago.

Now this Zerahemnah, besides possessing an exceedingly angry temper and violent streak, nevertheless, also had within him a certain sense of honor and dignity. These good qualities prevented him from trying to deceive General Moroni by making a promise with no intention of keeping it later on. Alma 44:8 records the wonderful manner of promise-keeping displayed by an otherwise blood-thirsty savage:

". . . Zerahemnah . . . came forth and delivered up his sword and his cimeter, and his bow into the hands of Moroni, and said unto him: Behold, here are our weapons of war; we will deliver them up unto you, but we will not suffer ourselves to take an oath unto you, which we know that we shall break, and also our children; but take our weapons of war, and suffer than we may depart into the wilderness; otherwise we will retain our swords, and we will perish or conquer."

The foregoing is pretty self-explanatory: Ancient Indians refused to make promises they could not keep, whereas today's whites, blacks, and Hispanics make promises promiscuously without seriously attempting to keep them!

Thus, we can see that while savage societies have always graced this continent, yet the more ancient ones at least were respectful with each other and not so blatantly rude as we are with each other at present. Those half a dozen or so middle-class blacks who recently attacked a young, white female jógger in Central Park, did so without any provocation or reason whatsoever. They were simply bored with their easy lives and were out looking for a little excitement or "wilding" as they called it. However, when ancient Lamanites attacked Nephites, they had some kind of purpose and logic to their mean ways. And they did so with a rough sense of honor and respect for the enemies they intended attacking.

Now on the other end of the spectrum we have relatively peaceful times and stable conditions still existing in our society. Except for mounting crimes of violence committed on an individual basis by many people, we do not have as yet entire cities or states going against one another as they did during the American Civil War. But sadly enough, our greatest irony is that we manifest greater rudeness towards each other than any Indians ever did against their adversaries of the past.

Probably the greatest lesson then we can learn from these early Native Americans is that they always seemed to hold a respect for life insofar as human accomplishments and skills went. And though they were guilty of murdering unmercifully at times, yet they did accord their helpless victims a certain respect which many of us do not even show to our closest friends or neighbors anymore. What can be said here is that Indians have always been more well-mannered and less rude than any other ethnic group of Americans as a whole.

CHAPTER EIGHT

RAISING CHILDREN THE AZTEC WAY

Contributions of a Catholic Friar

Bernardino de Sahagun (1499-1590) occupies a rather unique position in the chronicles of Mexican history. This Franciscan friar devoted his entire life to the study of the Aztecs, their language and their thought. His efforts are almost without parallel in his own or any other time. His *General History of the Things of New Spain* is a towering monument to the man and his times. It is altogether fitting that scholarly interest in his life and work continues to proliferate. In a way it is a measure of achievement that some scholars have been able to come as far as they have with his complex work.

Sahagun seems to have arrived in Mexico around 1529. From then to 1547 his missionary work appears to have been primarily linguistic in nature. His voluminous *General History* began taking shape it seems between 1547 and 1562. It was an enormous and highly complex enterprise. The composition of the Nahuatl text of what eventually became Book 6 on "Rhetoric and Moral Philosophy" dates to 1547. It is from this particular Book 6 that nearly all of the data in this chapter has been obtained and put into my own words. Sahagun's entire work was published by the School of American Research in cooperation with the University of Utah in 1969 as the *Florentine Codex—General History of the Things of New Spain.*

Had this man of the cloth not taken either the time or the interest to pursue diligent research into practically every aspect of Aztec culture including the raising of children, we today would be at a great loss without these many words of wisdom. Therefore, we owe him a debt of gratitude which cannot be measured in words alone.

Honoring Your Ancestors

One of Sahagun's observations about the way nobility raised their children, especially their sons, was to teach them reverence and respect for their departed ancestors. However, the approach taken was considerably different from the veneration shown to departed loved ones by the Chinese race.

An Aztec king or lord or prince would assemble his sons before him and pose this question: "To what purpose were ye born by one's grace?" The young men are given a few minutes upon which to ponder the answer to this question. If they failed to give the correct answer, their father would continue: "Ye were born by the grace of our lords . . . the rulers who have already gone beyond to reside." He would then amplify this into a much lengthier discourse.

The young men would hear from him how their grandparents (especially their grandfathers) ploughed the furrows of their family's long life and planted therein many good seeds (or efforts), which in time yielded abundant fruit (or deeds). Such food (or accomplishments) fed many (by enriching their lives one way or the other).

The father would next encourage his lads to "plant and sow" in the same field, but reminding them at the same time that whatever benefits might result from such efforts would not necessarily be of their own making. For the fertility of the soil (life) in which they were planting (accomplishing things) was already determined by "those by whose grace ye were born" (their ancestors before them). "They went caring for the ridges, for the ditches; they went planting in them," ascribing their own (meaning the ancestors) efforts of success to those who went before them (in this case, the ancestors of the grandparents).

In other words, the Aztec father would be trying to tell his boys that much of what they had and were, they owed to their grandparents and great-grandparents. These ancestral relatives had pioneered the way for their children and children's children after them. They were the ones to tame the wilderness first (began living life to its fullest) and learned the hard ways of planting (or the lessons of life by the things they experienced).

The sons were, therefore, enjoined by their father to also live their lives in such a manner as to continue improving the soil and planting better and better seeds than even their own ancestors did. But at the same time realizing that they (the sons) owed much of their own good lives and opportunities before them to their departed relatives and were strictly admonished never to take credit for themselves or glory in their own accomplishments; but rather to ascribe all the good done to these deceased ones instead.

The moral emphasized here was that young men were born by the grace of their fathers, who in turn were born by the grace of their fathers, and so forth. In a sense it was giving credit where real credit was due. Thus did young men in Aztec society develop a tremendous respect and reverence for their grandparents that has not been seen in too many societies before or since, with the possible exception of the Chinese and other Native American tribes.

In today's world, where even the parents are ignored, respect for grandparents is almost unheard of anymore. Yet the lessons taught by Aztec fathers to their sons centuries ago still hold firm even in our troubled, turbulent times and somehow offer hope for a better tomorrow if consistently applied by each of us with our children and grandchildren.

A Father's Wise Counsel

Friar Sahagun met and spoke with a number of parents as he studied Aztec life and thought in order to obtain for himself a much deeper understanding of their culture. Several Aztec fathers shared with him three pieces of advice, which they had given their sons and daughters upon arriving to young adulthood.

These fathers would gather their teenage sons and daughters about them to give them some sound words of advice. They would encourage their children to listen well and guard the things told them—"Place them in the chambers of your hearts," they specifically told their children. Their counsel, the fathers said, was "worthy of being guarded and remembered;" in some ways the same type of advice their own fathers before them gave when they were about the same age. Thus, it was special wisdom being perpetuated from generation to generation, and therefore, should be "inscribed in your hearts."

The first thing, they said, was that their children should always be sure to form a closeness with "the Lord of the Near" or "the Master who is nigh." He deserved one's complete devotions of the heart and one's entire physical energies. None of their children were ever to "let their feet go astray" or even, for one minute, assume that this Aztec god was not aware of what they were thinking or feeling or doing. "Our lord seeth, heareth within wood, within stone," and nothing can ever escape his all-searching glance and ever-penetrating eyes.

The second thing they admonished their children to do was "to live in peace with others." Do not be angry, do not be foolish, do not be hasty in your judgments, do not be quick in your actions. Think before you act, ponder before you, go slow not fast, and walk instead of run. Earn the respect of others, particularly your elders. Learn to resist peer pressures. Do no offend anyone deliberately. Do not become a law unto yourselves, but rather submit your own determined wills to the wishes of others older and wiser than you. Suppress inward rebellion; learn to listen before making assumptions of your own. "Do not blow as a violent wind against another." Simply learn to trust in your "Lord of the Near" for he "is (forever) watching thee" in all your actions, and "will avenge thee" and will support you in all of your worthy endeavors. So should you behave, because the "Lord of the Near" had "already arrayed thee" with many of his own good qualities.

Finally, the fathers would instruct their teenagers to make wise use of their mortal probations: "Do not waste time, and do not act uselessly on earth." Making good use of your allotted time here is just as important as taking care of your physical body through adequate exercise, sound nutrition, and proper hygiene. Show the "Lord of the Near" how grateful you are for what you have by making every single moment count!

Advice for Young Women

Aztec rulers believed in teaching their daughters those correct principles of truth which would better assist them in becoming well-behaved, responsible young women. Enough so, in fact, as to attract equally worthy Aztec young men and hopefully entice them into marriage by demonstrating what excellent wives and mothers they could become if just given the chance.

First of all the fathers would raise their daughters' own self-esteem by reminding them that they were as "precious necklaces" or "precious feathers" to them (the Aztecs adored birds and kept many of them in their homes, palaces, and temples). Furthermore, the fathers would tell their daughters that they were their own "offspring, blood, color" and even of their own "image." Then they would commence to inform their daughters why "our Lord of the Near, of the nigh, the maker, the creator" had sent each of them to earth.

The world, they began, is a lonely and dreary place; full of much corruption and evil, filled with considerable "torment, pain, fatigue, and want." Mortal life is very difficult. You should expect plenty of tears from the pain and sorrow you will eventually be receiving. "The cold wind passeth, glideth by," and so too is loneliness; for many will shun you in your moments of greatest despair, ignoring your own miserable plight in favor of giving attention to their own comfortable status instead. This world is also a place of hunger and thirst, not just for the food you eat, but also for the words of the "Lord of the Near."

The daughters were, therefore, told not to expect rosy lives filled with comparative ease. "It is not a place of contentment" by any means. Rather dual forces are always in operation: "joy with fatigue, joy with pain," and so forth. But so that "we may not go weeping forever, may not die of sorrow, it is our merit that our lord gave us laughter, sleep, and our sustenance, our strength, our force, and also carnal knowledge in order that there be peopling."

Wherefore, their daughters were admonished to make life as cheerful as possible for others "in order that no one go weeping." They should never think for one minute that life was only intended for weeping; instead it was meant for living, for experiencing every kind of thought and feeling imaginable. Seeking for good husbands, warm homes, strong marriages, and healthy children ought to be the goals of every worthy young lady, the Aztec fathers pointed out.

Oftentimes mothers would also be present while their husbands instructed these daughters. Pointing to various parts of their wives' anatomies, they would say: Look here at they mother, "thy noble one. . . . From her womb, from her breast thou were chipped, thou wert flaked." In other words, the fathers would tell their daughters that they were fashioned and molded from exceedingly fine materials of female clay (their mothers) just as men might chip a statue from stone or form heads for arrows and spears from flaked rocks. They were, in a sense, like "plants which hath propagated, sprouted, and blossomed" all at once; also as if they "had been asleep and just awakened."

Daughters were asked to think just how they intended to survive in such a dark and dreary place as this. "O my daughter, O dove; O little one," each father would gently call his daughter, and then ask them a series of short questions. Do you not know that you came from someone special; "that thou were born by someone's grace;" that you are literally the spine and backbone of a family unit; that you also are often the thorn of man's or child's life when you act in a contrary way?

After this brief recitation, the daughters would again be reminded of their high and noble stations in life. Being favorably compared to "precious green stone" like unto "precious turquoise;" to blood and the color of flesh (to signify their vital contributions to the processes of life itself); to the spine, "one's hair, fingernail, chip, or flake." With an additional reminder that they were also like unto the thorns, sometimes sharp and pointed and causing much unnecessary distress and grief. "Do not . . . bring dishonor . . .; do not in something cause embarrassment . . . do not lower thyself," the fathers would then instruct their daughters.

They were told to always conduct themselves as the noble women which they were born as. Their tasks were varied but simple: "be devout night and day;" pray frequently unto the "Lord of the Near;" do not sleep late in the morning, "awake and arise promptly, awake with a start at the parting of the night;" bow to your master "our Lord of the Night" and speak to him the first thing before you do anything else. And if you do these things, "then he will show compassion to thee, he will give thee thy just desserts, thy merits."

After arising promptly and "washing thy hands and thy mouth," young Aztec wives were expected to "seize the broom" and become diligent in the household chores of the day, making sure they were not "tepid or lukewarm" in their various duties and assignments. They were also told not to neglect offering some burnt incense unto the "Lord of the Near," since this was "the means by which his mercy is requested."

A list of "womanly labors" expected of every Aztec daughter was then recited: spinning, weaving, and especially fixing meals: "Look well to the drink, to the food, how it is prepared, how it is made, how it is improved." Much attention is required to "the art of good drink, the art of good food," since it is one's mortal "birthright" to be entitled to sound, nutritious meals, pleasing to the eye, tasty to the palate, and nourishing to the body. Through the medium of good food came good noblemen and rulers; inspiration is fed into the mind from the spirit of the "Lord of the Near," which itself only comes to those whose bodies have been properly nourished with inviting kinds of food.

Daughters were further commended for their chastity and virtues and encouraged to continue in their undefiled states until at such time that they married worthy young men. Their sexual organs were to remain "untouched, no where twisted, still virgin, pure, and undefiled" until they married. Premarital sex among the Aztecs was not only frowned upon, but considered punishable by death!

Limiting the number of offspring one could have was a definite no-no as well. Aztec daughters were told that the "Lord of the Near" determined that "the propagation, the multiplication of man on earth" was the single most important thing which a woman could ever hope to accomplish in this life. Consequently, she must never fail to deliver and bring forth as many children as her physical health will allow her to.

Young women in Aztec society were also reminded to revere their ancestors— "Cast not dust, filth upon their memory." They were told to avoid coveting material things. And if their husbands demanded something of them, they were clearly instructed: "Thou art not to refuse; thou art not to resist." At the same time, however, Aztec young men were plainly told to respect their wives and to always be kind and gentle with them, never to beat them, nor abuse them in any way.

The fathers reminded their daughters several times that chastity and fidelity to their husbands was paramount. "Give thyself not to the wanderer," they warned. In other words, women were warned against having so-called "bedroom eyes" in public when around other men, especially the good-looking, well-muscled ones. Adultery was just as serious as murder, and Aztec society would not stand for a woman making advances to another man.

Following this lengthy discourse from their fathers, young daughters next heard from their mothers, who would first of all encourage them "to guard well . . . the words of their fathers; to consider them as precious, as costly." Do not reject his words and counsel, but always strive to live by his wisdom. And be sure to "indoctrinate thy own children" with the same later on, when they come of age too.

Next, the mothers would enjoin their daughters to follow the examples they themselves have set with their fathers and husbands: "Look to me, for I am thy mother" and follow in my footsteps, they would say. Then speaking collectively for herself and her husband, every Aztec mom would say, "We are thy mothers, we are thy fathers who speak to thee, who cry out to thee; take our words, grasp them, guard them well."

And whenever Aztec maidens were to address their parents, husbands or children, they were to do so "in tranquility and with gentleness," not being "brutish, nor rushed, nor disquieting" in any way. Murmuring, grumbling, complaining, backbiting, and so forth were to have no place in the lives of noble Aztec women. They were never "to appear like a firefly," darting hither and yon in anger and without any reason or purpose; but to maintain solemn dignity and good deportment at all times—"Follow your road with utmost tranquility."

The old saying, "Hell hath no fury like a woman scorned," had no place in Aztec society or culture. Women were taught never "to put hatred in their face nor in thine eyes," but rather to "look joyously at everyone" they met. "Nor art thou to be a hypocrite," loving one moment and hating the next; such conduct was considered unbecoming and intolerable of Aztec women in general.

Especially strict were the rules governing personal adornment of the female body. Aztec daughters were forbidden to paint their faces with a lot of cosmetics or "darken the teeth" or "color the mouth" (probably with ancient lipstick), because such were the ways "of the restless ones, the dissolute ones, the evil women . . . called harlots."

Mothers encouraged their daughters to remember the instructions given them— "Place these words, my daughter, my dove, little one, well within the chambers of thy heart. Guard them well and do not forget; for they will become thy torch, thy light, all the time thou art to live on earth." We travel through life along a mountain peak, the mothers said. And on either side is an abyss, which if we are not careful, we can easily fall into. And difficult it is to get out thereafter, they said. Just the path "in the middle doth one go, doth one live."

Most especially though did the moms urge their daughters to always practice fidelity with their husbands—"Do not anywhere give thyself wantonly to another." For in the event they did so, they would never again obtain a moment's worth of peace—"For it will always be remembered of thee; it will always cause thy misery, thy eternal torment." Such adulterous conduct could only then lead to "the endless, the bottomless pit on earth" from which there was "no more a return." And although the "Lord of the Near, of the nigh" can be merciful if such guilty ones repent, yet he will definitely ignore those who feel no remorse or shame for their wicked deeds. "Pay heed" to these things, "my youngest one, my daughter, my little precious one," each Aztec mom would plead with her own daughter. By so doing, they could someday "enter with our Lord, the Lord of the Near, of the nigh" and dwell in perpetual peace and happiness with him forever and ever.

Advice for Young Men

Young men of late teenage years and into their early twenties would receive similar instructions from their fathers. Many words of wisdom were spoken in these "marvelous discourses and figures of great speech."

Fathers would begin by calling their sons their "precious necklaces" and "precious feather" in much the same manner as they did with their daughters. In counseling them as they would be doing, fathers felt a definite sense of urgency to see that their boys understood everything necessary to prepare them for married life and eventual fatherhood. They reminded them of just how fleeting this life is: count every moment "lest tomorrow, the next day, our lord, the Lord of the Near, of the nigh, will have hidden (taken) us." Nothing is guaranteed in this life, they would say—"certainly our living on earth is never assured" (the Aztec equivalent of "there's no free lunch in life").

No one really likes hard labor or heavy burdens, yet that is our lot to bear, the boys were told. Mortality "is a dangerous place, a revolting place, a boundless place, a place of no repose, a frightful place, and a painful and afflicting place." Wherefore young men needed to be strong, fortified with the words of the "Lord of the Near" so as to survive and "linger long." They must also realize that "the wind people" mock those of us on earth in our misfortunes and "laugh at others" in peril; for they are jealous of our mortal bodies and not having any of their own, exact vengeance by bitterly ridiculing us.

The key to really understanding the full purposes of life in general is to consider "the old men, the old women, those who go white-haired . . . those who go emaciated with ages, our forefathers." By studying their lives and observing their ways, can you too get along in life just as well as they did, explained the Aztec fathers. The sons can learn from the mistakes of their parents and grandparents, and hopefully avoid inheriting the same kinds of misery and sadness as they did. This is not to say, however, that they themselves will not be exposed to some deprivations in life; but at least they can lessen the degree of such hardships by learning from others how to live properly.

By their numerous afflictions did our forefathers acquire their innate humility and meekness, the young Aztec men were told by their dads. "Most certainly they came humbling themselves, came becoming meek, came becoming contrite." And "the more they were honored" for their obvious humility, "the more they wept," realizing how unworthy they were for the adorations of men. This then is the true mark of a real man: to understand his nothingness before the "Lord of the Near" and to know that greater ones than he have gone on before him into the realms of the just.

Fathers would remind their sons, "Thou art my eagle, thou art my ocelot, thou art my son!" and inform them that they were born in times "of pain" and "of great affliction." Their fathers and mothers had endured a lot and had suffered greatly in their behalfs, and had made many sacrifices so that they might come into existence and being. This they did so the lads would appreciate more what their folks had done for them.

Sons were also told that no duty was beneath their station. They should "bow low unto the Lord of the Near, of the nigh" and if necessary, go "crawling on elbows and knees" for truth. They were also expected to rise promptly in the morning, and if need be, "seize the broom" and become "diligent in the sweeping, the cleaning, the fanning" if their wives were unable to manage such things alone.

Boys were told of their noble lineages and favorably compared to some outward body parts just as their sisters had been—thou art one's hair, thou art one's fingernail." They were likewise told that they had in them the potential to become "a ruler's son . . . a palace nobleman . . . a precious one." And that achieving such in this life came by "humbling, bowing, inclining, weeping tears, sighing, and meekness;" that these same actions and qualities were what made men great and admirable.

Just the opposite of these virtues were the behaviors which were wholly unacceptable to the "Lord of the Near, of the nigh." Sons were warned against becoming too cocky or too smart for their own good—"Do not praise thyself . . . be not vain, be not proud, be not presumptuous. Vanity, presumption, pride truly provoke the annoyance, the anger of the Lord of the Near, of the nigh. . . . Just conduct thyself . . . (with) thy head bowed, thy arms folded, thy head lowered." Then in the midst of "thy weeping, thy sadness, thy sighing, thy humility, (and) thy meekness" can the "Lord of the Near, of the nigh" visit thee and help thee and assist thee, said the fathers to their sons.

And their humility was never to be phony, but always sincere. For their Lord knew them, and looked into hearts and could tell if they were being genuine or not. "Be not a hypocrite," fathers warned, but "offer (true) humility to our Lord."

Young men were encouraged to be chaste at all times. Fathers would often quote "the words of the old men" in this respect. " . . . The pure life is considered as a well-smoked, precious turquoise; as a round, reed-like, well-formed, precious green stone . . . no blotch, no blemish . . . (just like) the precious turquoise, which are (always) glistening, shining before the Lord of the Near, of the nigh."

Youths who have managed to retain their virginity command the special attention of the "Lord of the Near, of the nigh." For he pays great heed to "their sighs, their prayers, because, it is said, they are good of heart, undefiled, still clean, untouched, pure, still true precious green stones, still true precious turquoises." Aztec fathers told their sons approaching or already into manhood that "through them the earth yet endureth;" that such male virgins became "our intercessors" for good with the "Lord of the Near, of the nigh."

If these young men did not wish to become kings or princes or military officers, then they ought to seek to become temple priests on account of their extreme chastity and fidelity. They more than qualify to administer the ordinances and rituals of the temple because their "lives are undefiled, without ordure, without dust, without filth." They are perfectly acceptable and may "stand before the Lord of the Near, of the nigh," offering incense and prayers unto him continually.

"The old people, the wise ones, the keepers of the sacred books, go saying that the pure in heart are very precious;" that they see and make contact with the "Lord of the Near" when no one else can. Also those chaste young men "who die in war are well honored" too; "they are considered very precious on earth and they are also very much desired . . . much envied" by the people, more than those who have defiled themselves with premarital sex or masturbation.

"Children who die," said the fathers to their sons, "become as precious green stones, as precious turquoises, as precious bracelets." These innocent and undefiled ones "go not where it is fearful . . . the region of the dead;" but instead "they go to the home of Tonacatecutli (an Aztec god) (to) live in the garden of Tonacatecutli, suck the flowers of Tonacatecutli, live by the tree of Tonacatecutli." In other words, infant children who die "go to a good place" in order to be nurtured and loved and held because of their extreme preciousness.

Fathers warned their boys to forsake evil at every appearance; "thou art not to lust for vice, for filth; thou art not to take pleasure in that which defileth one, which corrupteth one, that which it is said, driveth one to excess, which harmeth, destroyeth one; that which is deadly." Enjoy your childhood while you can, for during those tender years "then is when our lord showeth compassion for one; then is when he disturbeth, giveth one his just desserts—the rulership, the governed, valiant warriorhood." Also in childhood is when "the Lord of the Near, of the nigh, giveth one his merit, joy and prosperity." To die "in the time of childhood, still in the time of purity" is much better than to die in manhood, full of sin and iniquity.

Young men were expected to be strong and courageous as they matured toward adulthood. Like the maguey (a succulent plant from which the alcoholic drink "pulque" is made), boys were taught to "form a straight stalk" in order "to fully ripen." Then they could be ready for marriage and would sire "children (who) will be rugged, agile . . . polished, beautiful (and) clean."

On the other hand, though, if young men ruined themselves by becoming seduced with pretty women, their entire life's progress would become drastically affected—"Thou wilt interrupt thy development, thou wilt be stunted . . . thou wilt be enfeebled, weakened, emaciated; thou wilt become a tuft of hair . . . thou wilt linger a short time on earth, very soon to be old, old and wrinkled." Especially so would these things happen to married young men, who were attracted to other women because of the lusts in their hearts. Inevitable ruin will always befall those young men who do not heed the words of the wise to remain chaste and pure, whether they be bachelors or husbands.

And when they were to have sexual contacts with their wives, they were expected to act with prudence and not be hasty: "it is as with food (which) thou art not to eat hastily; that is to say, thou art not to live lustfully; do not give thyself excessively to it" but behave "moderately (and) temperately" in the act of sex itself. Excessive sexual relations even with your wives, warned the Aztec fathers, can deplete your manhood strength if you are not careful. So practice moderation in all things, even in something as exciting and stimulating as this. Remember that it is like alcohol—a little bit goes a long way to make the brain feel quite invigorated. Fathers would usually conclude this portion of their remarks on sexual restraint by saying: "O my son, be very careful on earth; live very calmly, very peacefully (and do) not live in filth."

Next, fathers instructed their sons to retire early and "not to give thyself excessively to sleep, lest it will be said of thee . . . (thou art) a constant sleeper, a dreamer." Sometime in the night, sons were to "arise . . . to sigh, to cry out to, to make demands of our lord, the Lord of the Near, of the nigh. . . . "They were also admonished to be "prudent in thy travels," going about their business "peacefully, quietly, (and) tranquilly." And they were not to act foolishly by jumping up and down or hollering and shouting "lest thou be named a fool!" At the same time, however, they were not to drag their heels or be fat and lazy "lest it be said of thee that thou goest waddling, that thou goest like a mouse" or "travel like a pregnant woman" does. Nor were young men to go about strutting their stuff, walking with an air of contemptuous arrogance about them, "lest it be said of thee that thou art only an old thing" or hussy fretting about in the market place.

They were also told not to hang their heads nor incline them too much, so as not to appear stupid or be seen as "an imbecile (or) commoner" without much upbringing and manners. Instead, they were to conduct themselves with dignity, standing straight and tall but walking in humility and not pride. Likewise when they spoke, it should always be "very slowly, very deliberately" and never "hurriedly . . . lest it be said of thee thou art a groaner, a growler, a squeaker" by chance. Instead, they should speak in a soft tone of voice, so that the gentleness of their spirits might emanate forth in the words thus spoken.

Staring was also considered bad manners: "Thou art not to peer at one . . . not to stare at the esteemed one, especially a woman, much less at someone's wife; for it is said he who stareth at, who peereth into the face of another's wife; with his eyes committeth adultery, and that some (were) imprisoned (and) punished."

Young men were also advised to ignore gossip and idle chatter, and to take no part in the whisperings of others. If they were unable to totally ignore such back-biting, they should "only listen" and say nothing. They should only speak when things of merit and value ought to be said, and not talk of empty, idle, vain things. If they were not careful in this respect and permitted their tongues to get the best of them, then they would become just as foolish as the other idle gossipers around them. In essence then, young fellows were to be prudent in what they said, weighing every word for its value and benefit before it was spoken.

Another rule they were given was this: "When thou art summoned, be not summoned twice . . . (go) the very first time . . . arise quickly . . . (be) prompt . . . swift . . . (and) in no wise sluggish; like the wind are thou to go (and) to be diligent (lest thou) be considered as perverse, lazy, languid, negligent, or . . . regarded as one disdainful of orders, as a haughty one." Such are the times "when the club, the stone should be broken on thee."

And so far as men's fashions go, young Aztec males were expected to dress prudently and conservatively. "Thou art not to dress vainly, thou art not to array thyself fantastically . . . neither art thou to put on rags (or) tatters," declared the fathers to their sons. Young adult men were advised against imitating the silly fashions of others and rather to conform to the same decent modes of attire that their fathers set.

Finally, they were admonished to be "prudent in drink, in food, for many things pertain to it." Gluttony had no place in their lives, no matter how delicious the food or drink may seem at the time. They were eating for the purpose of nourishing their bodies, not to indulge in frivolous and wasteful appetites. Also, to eat slowly was a courtesy expected of them. "Thou art not to put a large amount in thy mouth; thou art not to swallow it unchewed; thou art not to gulp like a hungry dog, when thou art to eat food."

Proper hygiene went along with good nutrition. They were told to wash their hands, faces, and mouths before eating. And if they were to eat in the company of others, then they should be somewhat slow to sit down, letting others be seated first and only sitting down at the last. They were to extend every courtesy to others, making sure others had their plates full first before looking after their own portions. "And when thou hast eaten, once again art thou to wash thy hands, to wash thy mouth, (and) to cleanse thy teeth." Clearly, the Aztecs were a very clean people.

The sobering facts of elimination were also given. Sons were advised that the food which went into the body, somehow had to come out later on. They were reminded to examine their stools often to see if their bowel movements were normal (long and slightly soft) or small and hard like rock pebbles. Also, if they didn't experience any bowel movements for several days, then quick attention had to be given to this situation lest dire health consequences arise as a result of neglect.

All in all, it can be said that Aztec parents gave their kids a lot of good, sound advice, which if implemented with today's youth would make for a much better world altogether.

APPENDIX

Resource Guide

Further information on Native American food and medicine and general health topics frequently appear in *The Vitamin Supplement*.

The Vitamin Supplement
840 West 7th Avenue
Vancouver, B.C. V5Z 1C1

Some of the herbs and foods employed by Great Plains Indians are available in tablets and powders from Pines International.

Pines International, Inc..
1040 East 23rd, P.O. Box 1107
Lawrence, Ks. 66044
(913)-841-6016

Different herbal formulas used in the past by some Northwest and Canadian Indian tribes are available from Quest Vitamins (USA) and Quest Vitamin Supplies Ltd. (Canada). Quest also carries a choice selection of amino acids, enzymes, vitamins, and minerals derived from some of the natural foods once consumed by Native Americans in the past.

Quest Vitamins (USA)
1163 Chess Drive #F
Foster City, Ca. 94404
(415)-349-1233

Quest Vitamin Supplies Ltd.
1781 West 75th Ave.
Vancouver, B.C. V6P 6P2
(604)-261-0611

For further information on Native American life, please write to:
Dr. John Heinerman, Director
Anthropological Research Center
P.O. Box 11471
Salt Lake City, Utah 84147
(801)-521-8824